VALUES AT RISK

Maryland Studies in Public Philosophy

Series Editor: The Director of The Center for Philosophy and Public Policy
University of Maryland, College Park

Also in this Series

VALUES AT RISK

edited by
Douglas MacLean

ROWMAN & ALLANHELD
PUBLISHERS

ROWMAN & ALLANHELD

Published in the United States of America in 1986
by Rowman & Allanheld, Publishers
(a division of Littlefield, Adams & Company)
81 Adams Drive, Totowa, New Jersey 07512.

Library of Congress Cataloging-in-Publication Data
Main entry under title:

Values at risk.

  Includes index.
  1. Health risk assessment—Addresses, essays,
lectures. 2. Cost effectiveness—Addresses, essays,
lectures. 3. Social values—Addresses, essays,
lectures. I. MacLean, Douglas, 1947-   .

RA427.3.V35 1986   362.1'042   85-26064
ISBN 0-8476-7414-2
ISBN 0-8476-7415-0 (pbk.)

86 87 88 / 10 9 8 7 6 5 4 3 2 1

Printed in the United States of America

Contents

Figures

Preface

The Center for Philosophy and Public Policy was established in 1976 at the University of Maryland in College Park to conduct research into the values and concepts that underlie public policy. Most public policy research is empirical: it assesses costs, describes constituencies, and makes predictions. The Center's research is conceptual and normative. It investigates the structure of arguments and the nature of values relevant to the formation, justification, and criticism of public policy. The results of its research are disseminated through workshops, conferences, teaching materials, the Center's newsletter, and books like this one. General support for the Center comes from the University of Maryland and the Rockefeller Brothers Fund.

This is the tenth volume of the Maryland Studies in Public Philosophy. Previous volumes, listed across from the title page, dealt with the welfare system, the significance of national boundaries, immigration, energy policy, military manpower policies, lawyers' ethics, the theoretical and practical viability of liberalism, nuclear deterrence, and consent to airborne risks.

This book is one of a pair issuing from a research project funded by the National Science Foundation's program on Technology Assessment and Risk Analysis. The companion volume, *To Breathe Freely: Risk, Consent, and Air*, was edited by Mary Gibson. Each of these volumes grew out of a series of meetings of a working group comprising the contributors to the volume. The views expressed by the individual contributors are, of course, their own and not necessarily those of the Center or its sources of support, the National Science Foundation, or the institutions and agencies for which the contributors work. The first chapter was originally published in *Risk Analysis*, vol. 2, no. 2 (1982), and we gratefully acknowledge their permission to reprint it here.

The successful completion of this book owes much to the labor of many hands. Joshua Menkes, Vincent Covello, and Jeryl Mumpower, at the National Science Foundation, encouraged our attempts to bring philosophy to bear on the practice of risk analysis, and they continued to support us, even as our meetings wandered into some of the more abstract realms of philosophy. The work of administering the working group and of turning the products of its efforts into a book was shared by Louise Collins, Carroll Linkins, Lori Owen, Rachel Sailer, and Robin Sheets. I would also like to thank Mary Gibson, my collaborator in this project, Claudia Mills, the Center's editor, and Henry Shue, former director of the Center, for their active support throughout.

Douglas MacLean

VALUES AT RISK

Introduction

Douglas MacLean

Federal and state governments are responsible for many programs to protect public health, property, the environment, and historical and cultural treasures. These programs have different mandates, but even where the goals are similar, they often operate quite differently.

If we consider only federal programs aimed primarily at protecting life or health, we find some where an agency is instructed to balance safety or health against costs, and others where it must act to reduce risks in whatever ways are found to be technologically feasible. Thus, it seems, an agency must sometimes find an independent way to determine what we (as a society) are willing to pay to reduce risk, and then use that figure as a standard for setting policies; while in other instances, an agency is supposed to regulate on the basis of technological feasibility, with the result that the cost of complying with the regulations that are so enacted determines what we spend to reduce risk.

Regardless of what procedure is followed, the estimates about the risks and costs are usually going to be very rough. A recent National Academy of Sciences study, for instance, stated that estimates of the increase in bladder cancers caused by consuming normal amounts of saccharin over the next 70 years range from 0.22 to 1,144,000.[1] Uncertainties of this magnitude have been difficult to eliminate, and they have eroded the confidence inspired by analyses of risks and the costs of controlling them.

Even with such soft or imprecise numbers, however, risk analyses have uncovered some startling differences in standards among various policies with similar goals. A review of the cost effectiveness of some proposed lifesaving programs has shown that the median value of the estimated cost to save a life for alternative actions under consideration was $50,000 at the Consumer Product Safety Commission and $64,000 at the National Highway Traffic Safety Commission, while the same median value was $2.6 million at the Environmental Protection Agency and $12.1 million at the Occupational Safety and Health Administration.[2] Other values enter into the deliberations of different agencies, of course,

Note: Unless otherwise indicated, all quotations are from the chapters in this book.

1

and public opinion polls indicate that popular concerns for greater safety are very selective. But surely this comparison suggests that we are spending too much in some areas, too little in others, or both.

The estimated cost of saving a life should no doubt be brought more into line across different programs, not only for reasons of equity, but also for reasons of efficiency. We could save more lives for the same total regulatory budget if we allocated these funds differently. But which inequalities should we accept? How should other values weigh against the number of lives we could save? And what should the overall median value be anyway? How do we decide?

Policy analysts have been trying to answer these questions for some years now. One of their practical goals is to bring more order and coherence to the piecemeal approach to social regulation of the 1960s and early 1970s. The methods they have developed—different specific techniques for analyzing and comparing risks, costs, and benefits—are intended to help us think clearly and comprehensively about all these issues. Some critics of these methods have accused analysts of being cold and calculating about the economics of deciding who will live and die. But others have defended these methods, arguing that policy decisions to protect public health or the environment are essentially economic choices.

In a seminal essay, Thomas Schelling helped to formulate the rationale for risk analysis, by suggesting that it was not helpful to think of public programs aimed at saving human lives in moral terms. "Death is indeed different from most consumer events," he acknowledged,

> and its avoidance different from most commodities. There is no sense in being insensitive about something that entails grief, anxiety, frustration, and mystery, as well as economic privation. But people have been dying for as long as they have been living; and where life and death are concerned we are all consumers.[3]

Many of the most troubling and problematic public policies involve decisions that save or trade off lives only in a statistical sense. We need not get all worked up about the pricelessness of a human life, Schelling claimed, because "what the government buys if it buys health and safety, is a reduction in individual risks. The lives saved are usually a mathematical construct, a statistical equivalent to what, at the level of the individual, is expressible as a longevity estimate but not a finite extension of life."[4] It is different when we confront life and death decisions for a particular, identifiable individual. Those decisions involve, as Schelling puts it, "anxiety and sentiment, guilt and awe, responsibility and religion. . . . But most of this awesomeness disappears when we deal with statistical deaths, with small increments in a mortality rate in a large population."[5]

Statistical lives are the lives we expect to save or lose by actions that reduce or increase the risk of early death to the individuals in a large population. (Of course, these decisions also typically imply statistical changes in illnesses or injuries, as well as environmental and other impacts.) We can speak about the number of lives affected by such decisions when we refer to the entire population, but any individual is affected, *ex ante*, only by a change in the risk he or she faces. Schelling is suggesting, then, that the moral dimension of these decisions pales when we distribute expected lifesaving or death as increments of *ex ante* risk to each individual in a population, and that individuals can determine how they value these changes in the risk they face, just as they make other consumer choices.

It is not easy to discover how people value changes in the risks they face—how much they are willing to pay to reduce a risk or what other gains make an increased risk of death acceptable. In part, this is because the risk increments to any individual are often so small (for example, one in a million or less) that most of us find it hard to think about them clearly. We often misperceive risks and think the most publicized or most frightening dangers are actually most likely to occur, while underestimating the likeliness of others. Nor do we know whether the best way to discover a person's true values and beliefs is to ask her directly, to observe her behavior (which usually means economic behavior), or to find out in some other way.

Schelling was aware of these difficulties, and he briefly suggested several ways to get around them. A major focus of the new profession of risk analysis has been to develop methods that refine these suggestions and come closer to measuring people's true attitudes and beliefs. But the problems are enormous. Very few people would argue that the techniques of risk analysis can now succeed in measuring and comparing all the relevant factors with great accuracy. The question is whether these techniques give us better policies and decisions than we would get without them. The answer depends on how we understand their appropriate uses and their limitations.

One aspect of this problem involves the social values that enter into policy choices about the kinds, levels, and distribution of risks we find acceptable. These are the issues addressed by the essays in this book. Our goal is to explore both the nature of some of these values and some general features of risk analysis in order to see how well they fit together.

Beneath all the practical problems—the uncertainties, the difficulties in measuring and comparing very different things, the need for judgment, the potential for abuse, and so on—there lies a basic philosophical issue. As I see it, the issue is a dilemma about "subsumption": can risk analysis adequately subsume or encompass all our values, across the board, or are there certain values that escape its net, or, indeed, ground its justification?

Risk analysis is supposed to aid decision-makers by organizing large amounts of complicated information and by weighting different factors to indicate their relative importance. If we accept this picture of risk analysis as a neutral device that merely structures a decision problem, then we might be inclined to see it as incorporating all our values and giving them whatever weight we determine to be important. The picture suggests that a good analysis virtually justifies the decision it prescribes. Yet most people balk at the prospect that our normal and often grubby political way of making decisions should ideally give way entirely to technocratic analytic decision procedures.

Even proponents of risk analysis usually insist that it should only aid decision-makers and not dictate decisions (although it is difficult to see what many proponents would accept as a good reason to override the prescription of an ideal analytic technique). Many people are uncomfortable with the suggestion that risk analysis should be a decision procedure for making choices that seem important both for their consequences and for the real and symbolic value that attaches to how we make them. This backing off suggests that perhaps risk analysis promotes certain general, politically neutral values (like coherence, efficiency, and accountability) but not all values, so it stands in need of independent justification, thus allowing that some values might be prior to or independent of analytic techniques and might qualify their appropriate use.

We can pose this issue in the following way. One might argue that whatever metric is used to measure or compare values will introduce distortions and leave some values out of account. (This criticism is brought most frequently against techniques that monetize all values and identify how important something is to us with how much we are willing to pay for it.) The pragmatic response to this criticism goes like this: any metric may introduce some distortions, but we can make adjustments on an ad hoc basis, and using the metric gives us better results than we can expect from decisions that are not based on risk analysis at all or that use analysis as only one input into a basically intuitive process for making decisions of enormous complexity and scope. The strength of this reply is at least partly an empirical matter, of course, but it presupposes and appeals to another, more philosophical response. Even if we can't assign dollar equivalents to the importance of justice, basic rights, life and health, or other cultural, religious, and social matters, we must find some way of weighing their importance and comparing them. The alternative is to hold some values to be absolute. But if one of our values is absolute, then which one; and if more than one is absolute, what do we do when they conflict?

The problem is that most of us feel uncomfortable treating these values as consumer choices, as Schelling suggests we should, and yet that seems to be the way we are forced to treat them in the context of making decisions about allocating resources to government programs. It is the process of decision-making that is felt to be objectionable, not the need to make decisions and trade-offs. There can be little doubt, I think, that many of the objections to risk analysis are ultimately based on the sense that what is at issue is the values attached to different procedures for making decisions. It would not do, for example, to replace trial by jury or democratic elections with technocratic analytic decision-making techniques, even if these techniques weighed the losses to society of forgoing its cherished procedures and turned specific decisions back to the traditional methods when the analysis showed that we would achieve better results in the circumstance by doing so. Yet it is difficult to see how this reluctance can be rationally defended and how it can support an argument for limiting the role that risk analysis ought to play.

If a greater reliance on analytic techniques will save more lives, promote health, and so on, then surely the value of these gains must be weighed against the value of making social and political decisions in a more traditional way. Even if we attach great weight to these procedures, we are still being asked to think critically about the trade-offs and thus to subsume these values within the analysis.

This issue remains unresolved in this book. As the various chapters focus on different values or different aspects of risk analysis, however, it will be clear that the authors feel the force of this dilemma differently and would resolve it in different ways.

The first chapter in this collection is a survey of some philosophical issues involved in justifying the use of analytic methods for making centralized risk decisions. The point of this survey is to help focus the discussion in later chapters and to indicate why considering the question of justification will, in later chapters, take us into some deep and abstract matters of moral philosophy and moral psychology.

My basic concern in this chapter is to make three points. I argue, first, that the justification of risk-analytic methods has to appeal to consent, rather than to concepts such as efficiency or the protection of rights. I claim that appeals either to efficiency or rights will not succeed, or else they will ultimately reduce to appeals to consent, as a more basic notion. Second, I point out that different models of consent, some more direct than others, have been important in moral and political philosophy, and that different kinds of risk decisions will probably be justified by appeals to different kinds of consent. The crucial point here is to realize that consent alone has limited normative force: it must be combined with another concept, rationality (as in rational consent), to bear the burden of justification. As the kind of consent becomes more indirect, the role of rationality becomes correspondingly more important. My third point, then, is that once we connect consent to what it is reasonable to value, we should be prepared to look at a wide range of values and attitudes, which will include concerns for health and safety, but also much more.

The next six chapters take up the issues of consent, rational values, and justification directly. Herman B. Leonard and Richard J. Zeckhauser begin by defending cost-benefit analysis for making centralized risk decisions. Cost-benefit analysis pursues economic efficiency, and reasonable people, they argue, would consent to efficient decisions. Thus, cost-benefit analysis is supported by an argument based on hypothetical consent.

Leonard and Zeckhauser admit that cost-benefit analysis is unpopular, in part because it has been misused to serve political ends. They argue that it can be subjected to review and scrutiny, however, and opened up to wider public participation. Under these conditions, they believe it can help prevent abuses of power among decision-makers and will in general produce better decisions than alternative methods.

With Schelling, they assume that "risks are not different in principle from other commodities, such as park services, public transit, or housing." The market is the ideal place to decide appropriate levels of risk, because if market exchanges are fully voluntary, then the selected levels of risk are supposed to enjoy the actual consent of those affected. For many reasons, however, ideal market mechanisms will not always apply. First, risk decisions are often not fully voluntary, because we are not fully informed about risks and because we tend to have trouble interpreting the risk information we have; so we need analysis to correct our untutored judgments. Furthermore, transaction costs sometimes prevent us from joining together to make decisions we would collectively desire, and property rights needed to determine acceptable risk levels are often not well defined; so we have no choice but to rely on centralized decisions to "seek the outcomes that fully informed individuals would choose for themselves if voluntary exchange were feasible."

Leonard and Zeckhauser emphasize that their argument is a pragmatic one. Hypothetical consent for efficient outcomes is an imperfect solution, especially where individuals have widely divergent interests, but it is better than the alternatives of direct consent, which they claim is infeasible, and reliance on the political process, which, they argue, vacillates between an inertia that preserves the status quo and wild fluctuations that respond more to whims in public opinion than to considered judgments. To the charge that cost-benefit analysis will tend to overemphasize those costs and benefits that are easily quantified, Leonard and Zeckhauser plead guilty. After all, they say, it is designed as a method of quantification. But they reject the conclusion that the resulting decisions are systematically biased in any morally objectionable sense; no one group or set of interests is favored. "We take some comfort," they write, "in the fact that cost-benefit analysis is sometimes accused of being biased toward development projects and sometimes of being biased against them."

In the remainder of their chapter, Leonard and Zeckhauser reply to some other objections frequently raised against cost-benefit analysis, for example, that it does not insist that benefits be redistributed to compensate losers. They do not specifically address the complaint that the willingness-to-pay criterion distorts some values, but their implicit response is that willingness-to-pay is a better indicator of relative importance than any other measure. They also acknowledge that some values may simply have to be treated separately, and that we may on occasion decide to override the recommendations of a cost-benefit analysis. They insist, however, that the burden of justification rests with those who think some values are important and enduring enough to justify decisions that are deemed inefficient by the most refined methods of cost-benefit analysis.

The next two chapters, by Annette Baier and myself, offer a more skeptical view about the all-purpose virtues of analytic methods of public decision-making. I begin by describing two different issues that have been prominent in discussions of the justification of risk analysis: the distribution of risks, and the attempt to assign a value to saving lives or, more pejoratively, to put a price on human life. I draw different conclusions from these two issues, but they are meant to support a general claim about risk analysis and rational consent.

Our interest in the distribution of risk is complex, corresponding to the myriad ways risks can be distributed across the different dimensions of space and time. Most risk analyses, however, take up a single perspective from which some of these relevant differences can be obscured. Thus, if we report the expected consequences of a decision as the average risk per person, there are many ways in which importantly different consequences will look equivalent. A one in a million risk to an individual, for example, can mean that, on average, one person per million in a population will be killed each year; or it can mean that the entire population faces an annual one in a million risk of extinction. The risk to any individual is the same, but of course we may want to treat these cases very differently. Attempts to correct for such "blind spots," I suggest, are basically ad hoc and inadequate. Information about the specific context of the risk, moreover, may also introduce considerations relevant to our decision to control it.

My goal in discussing the value of human life is to explain what it might mean to claim that life is sacred, and to say what it certainly does not mean. Sacred values are marked by their connection to rituals and symbolic actions, and these, in turn, depend essentially on social context. I argue that the value of human life is also complex. Human life is sacred, and human life is also worth saving and prolonging. Not only are these two aspects of the value of human life not equivalent; they can actually conflict. This potential for conflict, I maintain, is the source of our uneasiness about assigning a value to human life.

A thoroughly analytic approach to risk will tend to emphasize one aspect of such complex values and deemphasize others. If this is true, and if it is rational to maintain and express these values in complex ways, then we have reasons to restrict the application of risk analyses. It is difficult to argue for general restrictions, because good risk analyses promote genuine values, even if they cannot promote all genuine values together, and because I suspect that our judgments about priorities are historically bound and context dependent.

Annette Baier also emphasizes certain complexities in our morality which, she argues, support restrictions on the use of analytic methods to determine our policies. Taking off from an idea that Michael Thompson also develops (to different ends) in his chapter, Baier views morality as "the culturally acquired art of selecting which harms to notice and worry about, where the worry takes the form of bad conscience or resentment." As she later explains, this is also a Rousseauian view of morality, that " 'the nature of things does not madden us, only illwill does,' and our laws reflect what maddens us rather than what merely distresses us."

If Baier is concerned to ward off the over-generalized application of risk analysis and other decision theories, it is because she rejects what she sees as the over-simplified view of morality that often supports them. One of the central purposes of morality, as she sees it, is to distinguish among killings between those we as a society can and cannot tolerate. She thinks the crucial question is not what will maximize life expectancy but "which policy-related deaths and impositions of risk we should have on our consciences." The conception of morality she wants to criticize endorses primarily "negative" rights (e.g., the right not to be murdered or assaulted), rather than "positive" rights (such as a right to life), because the corresponding duties of negative rights are seen to be refrainings from action, and hence not too onerous. Policies to reduce risks or promote health and safety, then, are seen as the optional pursuit of a common good.

Baier attacks this view of morality, first, because this distinction between negative and positive, or between refraining and acting, is flawed. So-called negative rights, she maintains, are worthless without programs for education and enforcement, which entail many positive actions and considerable cost. The distinction between negative and positive, moreover, is often a surface distinction, which results merely from the way we tend to formulate what it is we choose to be most concerned about. "Far from giving us some sort of minimal thin version of the right, . . . any popular version of a short set of moral *'don'ts,'* such as 'don't kill, don't steal, don't break promises, don't coerce (unless you are an official),' brings with it very rich cultural baggage, if it is to have any content at all."

The view of morality Baier favors is grounded historically in the writings of Hume and Mill. On this view, one of the essential purposes of morality is a positive one: to foster a certain climate of life. Quoting Mill, she says that our rights and duties are basically " 'the claim we have on our fellow creatures to join in making safe for us the very groundwork of our existence.' It is a claim to mutual succor, that they *join in making safe,* not merely a claim that they desist from assault."

If we traditionally have shown greater concern for preventing murder and assault than for preventing pollution, this is because the former actions were the ones that maddened us, the ones that showed illwill and malicious intent, and that most threatened the climate of life. It is far from clear, however, that acting to reduce murder and assault is more effective in saving lives today than cleaning up environmental degradation. Today, because of changes in knowledge and ability resulting largely from new technologies, the deaths we decide to allow from pollution or from hazardous technologies or from occupational risks take on a new moral significance, for these decisions can now threaten the climate of life that is central to this conception of morality and community.

To protect our moral culture, Baier thinks we must guard against "perverse" generalizations of efficiency and rationality. "Doubtless there are better ways to partition our public labor than we have yet devised," she writes, "but . . . 'rationalizing,' if that amounts to identifying some abstract common goal in several areas and then adopting an efficient total plan to reach it, aiming at consistency in all the areas affected, may be one of those rational strategies that it is even more rational to restrict." Apparently inconsistent policies might indicate important cultural differences which contribute to a desirable climate of life.

Like Leonard and Zeckhauser, Allan Gibbard gives priority to rational methods for measuring and comparing values in making policy choices. He differs from them, however, in two important respects. First, he is concerned primarily with giving a philosophical justification for ideal methods of risk analysis, and so he is less pragmatically oriented than they are. Because of this, perhaps, he also rejects cost-benefit analysis as the ideal method for analyzing risks.

Gibbard argues that rational social policies should aim to maximize something, but he rejects money or even the satisfaction of preferences as the proper object of maximization, preferring instead the vaguer concept of intrinsic reward. He claims that money can sometimes serve as a measure of intrinsic reward (which would be compatible with cost-benefit analysis) but not in most policy contexts, where "considerations of total wealth can . . . be offset by distributive considerations."

Gibbard then addresses the kinds of concerns raised by Baier and myself. He begins by noting that if analytic methods are to be distinguished from our intuitive moral beliefs at all, whether as better or worse, then they will make recommendations that strike us, initially, as morally dubious or shocking. In particular, even an ideal risk analysis, one that succeeds in factoring in everything that makes life more intrinsically rewarding, will sometimes determine that saving lives or promoting health is too expensive to justify, thus appearing to recommend that we sacrifice lives in order to save money or increase profits. But Gibbard insists that descriptions of policies as "killing to save money" are usually tendentious. "The phrase would allow us to dismiss a thousand man-years of sweat and toil as mere 'money' while underlining diffuse effects on health as 'killing.' " This is perhaps what Schelling had in mind in claiming that it is not helpful to think of policies involving statistical lives in moral terms.

Relying on risk analysis to correct our intuitive moral judgments, however, is to advocate what Gibbard calls technocratic moral reform. He acknowledges that technocratic tools like risk analysis might lead to abuse and that we might even come closest to realizing their goals by using other, more traditional methods of decision-making instead, but these practical issues are not at the heart of the philosophical debate. The central issue is that even if our actual feelings of urgency lead us to inefficient efforts to protect life and health, these feelings nevertheless matter because they are ours. "It is our actual feelings of urgency that determine much in the ways we experience our lives and the ways we experience each other."

What follows, according to Gibbard, is that "a risk-cost-benefit analysis that takes into account all contributions to expected total intrinsic reward must count things other than lives saved, injuries and illnesses avoided, and resources diverted to do these things." This response comes down squarely on one side of the dilemma of subsumption, and Gibbard realizes that the position needs to be justified. He thus focuses on what he calls the more profound charge, that the very process of making decisions by such calculation detracts from intrinsic reward and may be dehumanizing. Gibbard refers to this as the paradox of teleology:

> What values are achieved may depend on the very ways in which we make decisions, or on the very ways in which we stand ready to make decisions. That may be because certain aspects of ways of making decisions have intrinsic value, or it may be because these aspects have instrumental value. In either case, rationally pursuing maximum value may not maximize value.

Gibbard does not want to deny the importance of such ways of making decisions. Instead, he characterizes rationality as the ability to stand back from even our most cherished values and to reflect on them with detachment. This is the kind of detachment involved in relying on ideal risk-cost-benefit analysis, one that tries to remain sensitive to all the values and procedures that contribute to intrinsically rewarding lives.

Can sacred values, personal commitments, and the important but subtle conventions and practices that characterize a culture and educate its citizens be treated in this way? "It does seem to me," Gibbard responds, "that the kind of refined teleology I have been discussing is part of a worthy human ideal: the life that is engaged and committed, but also reflective." Others may think that the detachment Gibbard defends is not synonymous with respect, but merely a way of substituting one kind of moral disposition with another. Baier, for instance, says that "to resort to utility maximization is not to get *beyond* clashing sacred values, but merely to reveal one's own sacred value."

Michael Thompson's chapter, in effect, attempts to explain this and other debates without trying to resolve them. He too sees morality as the culturally acquired art of selecting which harms to notice and control, but he argues that culture also generates the norms of reason that rationalize different selections. Thus, differences in risk selection and different moral and rational convictions are together generated by different cultures or social contexts.

Thompson, an anthropologist, is naturally drawn to notice the particular perceptions and attitudes toward risk he sees in different groups and in different societies. He shows, with examples from some of his earlier research, how these differences appear among cultures in remote areas like the Himalayas; and he draws from his more recent research to illustrate differences in risk perception and risk selection among groups in the United States and the United Kingdom. Thompson sees different approaches to risk management in the two societies, which he explains as the result of cultural subgroups coming to exert governmental influence. The United States, for example, is generally an egalitarian society, while the United Kingdom is basically hierarchical. These differences manifest themselves in different regulatory styles and in different ideas of what risks a reasonable citizen would consent to bear.

Taking what he acknowledges is an intellectual risk, Thompson briefly describes a theory of social context, which is supposed to explain the differences revealed by his examples.[6] The theory posits two dimensions: the group dimension distinguishes between individualized and socialized contexts, indicating the boundary that people draw between themselves or their kind and the outside world; the grid dimension represents the distinctions and relationships that exist within a group. These dimensions form a matrix, with five possible kinds of social context located on it.

A central thesis of this theory is that institutions, values, conceptions of rationality, and perceptions—especially perceptions of risk and danger—come to be selected in ways that best preserve a particular social context. These social determinants, furthermore, will explain why people and groups argue over whether a risk is acceptable or not, and also why people perceive and estimate risks so differently.

The cultural relativism implied by Thompson's account will no doubt disturb many philosophers, not to mention risk analysts. If issues like consent and sacred values are central to the justification of risk analysis, however, it would seem that the perspective of cultural anthropology will have to be taken seriously, even if anthropologists treat philosophical dilemmas less as a real problem than as grist for their mill.

In assessing any given risk, we can separate two components: the consequences that may occur and the likelihood of their occurring. Most of the chapters in this book address the problem of how to measure and evaluate possible consequences and the procedures for making policy choices regarding risks. If little has been written on these philosophical issues in risk analysis, practically nothing has been written on the philosophical issues involved in the second component—measuring uncertain possibilities. Ian Hacking addresses this difficult subject here.

Hacking thinks probabilities, whether we interpret them objectively or subjectively, are seldom available for today's risk management problems. We often lack the experience necessary to have objective, statistical frequencies of the occurrence of bad effects, while the subjective interpretation of probabilities, as developed by F. P. Ramsey, applies clearly only to the "private" decision problems of a single actor. "Bayesians less sensitive than Ramsey assume without argument that their reasoning applies in public domains, but I do not accept that without argument."

Hacking is particularly concerned with uncertainty due to ignorance. In the first part of his chapter, he distinguishes between the kind of ignorance for which we can be held responsible, culpable ignorance, and ignorance of the things we could not be expected to know. The difference is between improbable events (even those with very low probabilities) which are "universals" because they are lawlike, and fortuitous events, which "under the description presented to us have no natural frequency at all." Hacking argues that we have a responsibility, especially in managing new technologies, to know general things that we can expect statistically to go wrong, but we have "no duty to determine every particular obscure possibility" that can lead to disastrous consequences, for "there is no end to such particulars."

Even if we can make this distinction reasonably precise, however, Hacking suggests that we confront the further problem of "fortuitous universals." Shortly after the discovery of X-rays, for example, nobody could have known that they cause cancer. "The good effects of the early and naive enthusiasm for X-ray machines almost certainly exceeded the harm that was done, but had one known of the harm, most of it could have been avoided." There is "an absolute lawlike regularity" linking X-ray exposure to cancer, which at the time could not have been known.

Hacking thinks that today we have enough experience with the nature of new technologies to support a meta-inference about effects produced by unforeseen universal facts, so the notion of culpable ignorance may apply to these after all. In the second part of his chapter, he explores an example of one kind of fortuitous universal, which he calls "interference effects."

Interference effects are different from side effects, which are produced when a new phenomenon interacts with a stable, pre-existing environment, often in unforeseen ways. Interference effects are produced when new phenomena interact with each other, and they occur when we move from the purified environment of the laboratory to the real world. As Hacking describes them, we almost surely must remain ignorant about interference effects until after they occur. They are increasingly common in new technologies, and they are nearly always harmful. "Interference effects are a new problem to worry about, different from side effects not just in degree, but, by now, in kind."

What policy implications follow from our ignorance of interference effects? Hacking rejects the prescriptions that follow from other forms of culpable ignorance, that our only morally acceptable recourse is inaction or severely curtailed technological endeavor; but he does think these phenomena justify the "mildly left-wing conservatism" of the environmental lobby. His main conclusion, however, is about risk analysis. Until the interference effects actually arise, Hacking insists, there are *no* probabilities there in nature to be discovered. He rejects the attempt to assign probabilities to such effects as "an imitation of reasoning," and he would "look with suspicion on others who would calculate on my behalf."

So, with regard to technological risk, Hacking joins some of the other authors in this book in dissenting from the claim that reasonable people would consent to safety decisions based on ideal cost-benefit analyses. Where the other criticisms in this book come from the side of measuring values, however, Hacking's comes from the probability side. Perhaps this difference leads him to warn, in closing, that the alternative to any "calculational" way out of the problems of risk management "cannot come from ethics alone, but requires harder thinking about the nature of phenomena, effects, and technology."

Amartya Sen defends the importance of the right to take personal risks. Contrary to my claims in the first chapter, Sen thinks that rights, properly understood, are important in the justification of risk decisions. He also seems to think that the value of rights can be appropriately weighed within the context of risk analysis.

Sen defends what he calls a "goal-rights" view, which can be distinguished from two more common philosophical conceptions of rights. In constraint-based deontological theories, rights are viewed primarily as protecting individual liberties against the pursuit of the general good. Respecting a right generally makes it impermissible to weigh the expected consequences of alternative actions in determining what to do. Rights "trump" consequences; they determine acceptable procedures for making decisions, rather than having any intrinsic value of their own. In utilitarian theories, rights also have no intrinsic value. The utilitarian moral justification for respecting rights is that such a practice tends to promote happiness or some other desired end.

Goal rights give people the capabilities to be or to do certain things, and we value these capabilities highly. Goal rights, then, are included among the things or states that are intrinsically valuable. Our duties, on a goal-rights view, are to bring about the most valued states of affairs, which will include valuing the protection of rights. It follows that we may have duties not only to refrain from violating the rights of others, but also to promote these rights. It also follows that a right-bearer is not automatically permitted to exercise his right. The state of affairs where he is allowed to exercise a right must be compared to the state of affairs where he is not. Thus, Sen defends a conception of rights that will not automatically give people veto powers over social programs that may impose risks on them.

Whether a person has a right, including the right to take a risk or to impose a risk on others, is determined solely by whether the action is important to that person's way of life. But other persons' rights and interests also enter into a determination of what it is acceptable to do, so we will often face trade-off situations. "Personal risks rarely come alone," Sen notes, "and that is undoubtedly one source of complication in dealing with the right to take personal risks."

Sen goes on to discuss the different typical kinds of effects on others of taking risks. He argues that, given the usual presence of such effects, it is a strength of the goal-rights view that establishing a right does not by itself settle the matter of what should be done. A further advantage is that both the existence of a right and its weight in moral arguments will depend on historical and social circumstances, which may vary over time.

Sen stresses the importance of balancing competing moral claims, even when a moral right has been established. He leaves completely open, however, the issue of how rights and other values are to be weighed. Whether his view is congenial to risk analysis, in the end, will depend on whether an acceptable metric for weighing values can be found. One might argue, for example, that a willingness-to-pay metric fails to give rights their intrinsic importance but treats them as instrumental to maximizing something else (wealth or whatever wealth is a surrogate for). Sen does make it clear that he rejects the metric of utilitarianism, and he insists that the importance of the right to take risks varies from person to person and with the nature of the activity involved.

This is a major issue in deciding how the dilemma of subsumption will be resolved. Consequentialist theories like Sen's goal-rights view, or like Gibbard's maximization of intrinsic reward, emphasize the need to make comparisons and trade-offs. To this extent, their views are compatible with the goal of finding all-encompassing analytic methods. Leonard and Zeckhauser, who share this goal, are willing to accept willingness-to-pay as a reasonable and practical measure of values, but Sen and Gibbard both seem to reject the kind of metrics usually associated with cost-benefit analysis. The challenge to them is to find some other metric, which would gain the consent of any reasonable person and be robust enough to supply data to an analysis that can correct our untutored intuitions. Otherwise, we might be better off giving up the search, consigning risk analysis to a more limited and less inclusive role, and focusing our attention, as Baier and I do, on directly examining our values and intuitions more closely, without presupposing that we can ever find a method that will make them orderly and systematic.

Notes

1. See William Ruckelshaus, "Risk in a Free Society," *Risk Analysis* 4 (1984): 157–62.

2. John Graham and James Vaupel, "The Value of a Life: What Difference Does It Make?" *Risk Analysis* 1 (1981): 89–95.

3. Thomas Schelling, "The Life You Save May Be Your Own," in *Problems in Public*

Expenditure Analysis, edited by Samuel Chase (Washington, D.C.: The Brookings Institute, 1968), p. 129.

4. Ibid., pp. 161–62.

5. Ibid., p. 142.

6. The theory is only sketched here. A fuller description can be found in Mary Douglas's essay "Cultural Bias," in Mary Douglas, *In the Active Voice* (London: Routledge & Kegan Paul, 1982), pp. 183–254. For another attempt to apply this theory to risk policies, see Mary Douglas and Aaron Wildavsky, *Risk and Culture* (Berkeley: University of California Press, 1982).

1

Risk and Consent: Philosophical Issues for Centralized Decisions

Douglas MacLean

At a typical conference on risk assessment or risk management, one session will be called something like "Social and Ethical Issues." It will usually be the last session on the program, and experts from the many professions who attend these conferences will then announce, with sincerity bordering on solemnity, that these issues are, after all, among the most important problems in the entire field. This session is as predictable as a litany. Members of the fraternity of risk experts, who may have quarreled for days, are now united in agreement. If no one dissents, it is probably because nothing very substantive is being said.

Their sentiment is genuine and justified. Activities that involve great risks and decisions that impose risks on others demand justification. This is an ethical or normative issue. If risk experts are not sure what to say about these issues, I believe the reason is that they involve philosophically difficult (or, as philosophers sometimes say, deep) problems. I shall not propose a method for solving ethical problems in risk management. In this chapter, I shall attempt, instead, to suggest a framework for thinking about some of them. This will involve identifying and relating certain philosophical concepts.

The concept that will focus this discussion is consent, which is a complex notion. First, there are different kinds of consent. This is a virtue, since the most obvious and intuitive notion of consent—explicit, actual consent—does not apply where decisions are centralized and large numbers of people are affected. We will need to appeal, therefore, to more indirect versions of consent. Second, for consent to have normative or justificatory force, it must be conceptually linked to other

*For many helpful discussions, and for comments on an earlier draft of this paper, I am grateful to Mary Gibson, David Luban, and Susan Wolf. Research has been supported by the National Science Foundation.

concepts, most important, to the concept of rationality. As our understanding of consent becomes more indirect or hypothetical, the concept of rationality becomes more important and plays a stronger normative role. This is what I shall argue. If I am correct, then we will see how the philosophical project might be linked to (and sometimes, perhaps, used to criticize) the work of economists and psychologists in this area, where rationality plays a central role.

In the next section I give a general and abstract description of some risk-management problems for which the issue of consent is important and problematical. Then, in the following section, I describe and relate three models of indirect consent. Finally, I offer some speculations about how some other philosophical issues—aesthetic issues—are related to consent and deserve to be examined.

Centralized Decisions and Consent

A primary practical concern of risk analysts today is to determine how safe is safe enough in situations where individuals, acting individually, are not able to reach a satisfactory solution. Some of these situations involve isolation or coordination problems, where individuals can reduce a risk by their actions (which involve accepting a cost or forgoing a benefit) only if everyone acts similarly, but where no mechanisms exist to ensure that others will cooperate. Or the situation may prohibit individual solutions because the transaction costs are too high, either because many different actors are each imposing slight risks that may be intolerable in their aggregate, or because one actor imposes significant risks that are distributed thinly over very many individuals. Still other situations involve large-scale projects to provide public goods, where a social consensus about safety may be difficult or impossible to obtain.

In all these circumstances, decisions must be made by central authorities, usually governments. The problems are disturbingly general. They are dramatic because they involve life-and-death decisions that arouse considerable public concern. They are also complex, because the risks may be poorly understood even by experts, thus raising further problems about determining and relying on public perceptions.

The work done in the area of risk analysis points explicitly to some deep philosophical problems. What special constraints are justified where risks are imposed on individuals (for example, members of future generations) for whom direct compensation may not be possible? And what is to count as compensation? Is compensation required only where the risks turn out badly—where they become actual costs—or should people be compensated for being subjected to risk? When do individuals have the right to reject a risk—or a risk-with-compensation package? When is it acceptable to impose a risk on others? Can we identify reasonable levels of risk with analytical techniques and use them to criticize individual perceptions? Or are individual perceptions the judge of reasonableness for the levels and kinds of risk that others may impose? And how do we accommodate fear? The fear surrounding many risks may be out of proportion to any reasonable measure of those risks (nuclear power and airplane safety, on the one hand; smoking and medical checkups, on the other). But fear is a cost, even where the risks do not turn out badly. We need to address problems such as these in a detailed and philosophically systematic way. My goal here is to lay some of the preliminary groundwork for discussing these more pressing issues.

The problems we are concerned with, where decision-making is centralized, will only occasionally yield noncontroversially to an "economic fix." An economic fix is a change in the structure of a situation that enables a satisfactory market solution. Where this is a desirable solution (and this point is often debated), it is because markets allow individuals to make their own choices, trading off values, as they see them, for their own advantage. Individuals may regret their choices, but they take responsibility for the decisions that affect them.

In order to find a market or a quasi-market solution to problems involving risk, we may seek to "internalize" costs. This may not always be a desirable solution, even where it is a possible one, but especially when we are dealing with large-scale projects, latent effects, irreversibilities, and the like, it may not even be a possible solution. Moreover, individual perceptions about many of these risks, as individuals will candidly admit, are not always trustworthy. Eventually, however, a governmental agency or other centralized authority will have to make a choice and impose a decision. Since these choices are between competing values, they require justification.

There are two very good reasons why we should think that consent, rather than some other concept, will play the crucial role in this justification. The first is that in less problematic cases involving risks, where the decisions do not have to be centralized and where fewer persons are involved, consent is necessary. A physician or medical researcher must obtain your explicit prior consent before she is allowed to impose risks by experimenting on your body. Detailed procedures are often required to certify that consent is obtained and to ensure that some act or empirical procedure, such as signing a form, truly counts as consent. A subject must, for example, be informed, uncoerced, and in a normal frame of mind. We should take these simpler cases as our paradigm and proceed from there to see how the nature or the role of consent changes as the contexts of the risk decisions vary and become more complicated.

The second reason for examining consent is that no other concepts look very promising. The requirements of justice or rights in this area demand a separate and fuller treatment, but these other moral notions will not take us to the heart of the matter. Suppose, for example, that we wonder about how to justify standards for toxic-waste disposal or standards for ambient air quality, and let us imagine that after compensations are made the risks and benefits are distributed more or less equitably. The problem of justice or equity would not arise in this unrealistically utopian setting, yet the problems of setting and justifying an acceptable level of risk remain.

Similar problems frustrate from the start any attempt to make progress on these issues by invoking a theory of rights. Consider what rights we would want to say individuals have in decisions that will affect their safety or in determining the right balance between increased risk or safety, added costs, and forgone benefits. Individuals have the rights over decisions that affect their property. Property, let us say, is either *real* or *personal*. Most currently popular theories of rights include the right of individuals to the use of their real property, and virtually all of them include the right of individuals to their personal property, especially their body and its parts.[1] A property right gives an individual veto power over decisions that promote social welfare if they involve boundary crossings onto property to which he has the right of use.

No theory, however, puts this forward as an absolute right. Over real property the state has power of eminent domain; but this is restricted, and in some ways defined, by the compensation clause of the Fifth Amendment. If a person loses his land, buildings, or some other investment, for example, in a major mishap, must he be paid? Must he be paid even to bear such risks? Or should property owners who gain windfalls from public policy (a highway near their store, for example) bear the costs of mishaps as well? These are familiar problems.

The situation is different in respect to rights over personal property. Here the right of the state to take what it needs for a public purpose is much more circumscribed; indeed, it usually requires some emergency, such as a war. The power of the state under eminent domain cannot be extended to the bodies of persons without raising severe political, legal, and philosophical problems. Hence the moral controversy over the military draft.

In some cases, an actor is not allowed to impose a cost, even with compensation, unless permission from the right-holder is obtained. In other cases, costs with compensation can be imposed. Under which of these principles should we include society's risk decisions? Does it make any difference whether an individual or a firm or the government imposes the risk? If we simply allow each individual the right to refuse, the results are intolerable. This analysis would imply, for example, that any individual has a veto power over any attempt to set standards for acceptable levels of air pollution. On the other hand, the right of eminent domain cannot be universal without posing too great a threat to the autonomy of individuals and communities. Someone's willingness to compensate, for instance, does not give him the right to play Russian roulette on an unwilling victim, even with a gun with thousands of chambers.[2] No analysis of rights that does not ultimately appeal to the notion of reasonable consent can sort out these cases.

Neither will efficiency be the central concept. In some risk contexts, it will not be clear what efficiency consists of or how it could be measured. But even where we know what efficiency is, we cannot use it alone to justify our choices.[3] Consent to centralized decisions is crucial in a society that is nonauthoritarian.

There are many public policy decisions we *could* make to promote efficiency, but that we do not make because they would be wrong. No doubt it would be more efficient to dispense with elections in picking public officials, to dispense with jury trials in criminal proceedings, and to implement on a broad scale technologically sophisticated surveillance equipment as a better means to law enforcement. Of course it would violate our rights to do any of these things, but we also refuse to consent to these ways of being more efficient. In the area of reducing risks, it is an outstanding problem when and how we want to be more efficient than we are. Other values might conflict with efficiency. In the end, therefore, efficiency is a reason for doing something only when efficiency is supported by an argument from consent.

Before describing some models of indirect consent, two further points should be kept in mind. The first is about risk analysis. One possibility for justifying a decision about risk is to make that decision on the basis of a method of risk analysis that measures and compares all the relevant factors. The argument, then, would have to show that ideally reasonable or rational people would consent to this decision because the method that generated it takes account of all the factors that matter. This argument would be based on conceptions of indirect consent. Notice, first, that the idea of rationality is immediately prominent in this way of arguing. Notice also what requirements this kind of argument would place on a method of risk assessment or evaluation that could be the basis of a decision. The risk-analytic technique must be abstract and general so that estimations of different health risks, and also of the expected costs and benefits associated with accepting, eliminating, or controlling these risks, are comparable. At the same time, this information must be presented in such a way that it is rational for a person to choose on this basis.

These are stiff requirements. The problem is not simply to come up with just any common measure of risk that will homogenize all differences and present all factors on a single scale. It is no more difficult here than anywhere to cook up an artificial technique that will churn out an answer in any situation. The literature on risk abounds with them.[4] What we need are *acceptable* techniques for measuring and evaluating risks, ones to which reasonable people would consent, even if this means in the end that no single metric is entirely adequate.

The second point is about the connection between rationality and consent. Even in the simpler cases I mentioned, rationality plays a role in determining whether the necessary condition of consent is also sufficient. Sometimes an act that normally counts as consent may strike us as so crazy or irrational that we discount it. Now, what we are likely to say in these cases is that the person has not "really" consented, but this way of speaking only demonstrates how some background of rationality is logically or conceptually connected to our understanding of consent. We may occasionally not even allow people to make certain choices because we are confident that no reasonable person could so choose. These are rare cases, no doubt, and consent is usually sufficient where people act individually with negligible effects on third parties, but the connection between consent and rationality is present even if it is not often noticed. I emphasize this because, as each successive model of indirect consent moves further from actual consent, the role of rationality becomes more important.

Three Models of Indirect Consent

It is useful, and not too distorting, to think of the different kinds of consent as situated along a continuum. At one end, consent is vivid, actual, and explicit, and the role of rationality in understanding the normative force of this kind of consent is present but minimal. As we move toward the other end of the continuum, consent becomes less explicit, more indirect, even entirely hypothetical, and the concept of rationality correspondingly becomes richer and takes on a more important normative role. The metaphor of a continuum perhaps should not be pressed too hard, for I doubt whether some conception of consent can be identified at every possible point or whether between any two conceptions of consent we might describe we can find another. Certainly there would be no interest simply in proliferating the number of such conceptions.

I will describe three conceptions or models of consent, but it is important to see how each successive model moves further away from the most explicit kind of consent, our paradigm. This is important because the last model is actually a suggestion for extending the "continuum" to the point where the concept of consent atrophies, playing a role in justifying risk decisions no more important than the role of the appendix in the functioning of the human body, while the concept of rationality bears the whole normative burden. I want to suggest at the end that the model that I will call "nonconsent" might help to justify some important risk decisions that today we find very difficult to justify.

Implicit Consent

Some of the techniques that have been devised recently to evaluate the acceptability of certain risks rely on implicit consent. Revealed-preference theory is one example.[5] The idea is that individual preferences for risk and safety trade-offs are revealed in certain areas, where markets function properly, so we can use data from these areas to justify decisions in other areas.

Market solutions to questions of risk are desirable, according to the defender of revealed-preference theory, not because market solutions are efficient, but because in a properly functioning market, people are supposed to consent to their transactions. Smoke detectors, for example, are sold to people who want to buy them. The costs of extra safety are known, and individuals make their own decisions about how to balance costs and benefits in determining the level of safety they shall have. Since they make these decisions explicitly, they can thereby be said to consent to the trade-offs they accept. Likewise, we find studies purporting to show that evidence from the labor market indicates what extra benefits people demand in exchange for accepting the greater risks of hazardous work. These data, too, are used as a basis for generalizations about preferences for risk and benefit trade-offs.[6]

Once these general preferences for risk are determined, they are applied in contexts where market solutions are unavailable. Thus safety standards can be set through centralized decisions that mimic the trade-offs that market data reveal. These decisions are said to be justified because the public implicitly consents to them. What this means is that the decision establishes a level of risk or safety, at a cost and in exchange for benefits, identical to the level that people explicitly consented to accept in other areas. The assumption is that they would have consented here had they been able to make a free and informed choice.

The development of a revealed-preference approach to risk analysis was motivated in large part by the desire to resolve debates about adequate safety in nuclear-power plants. Some people thought that criticisms of the risks of nuclear power were entirely irrational because the critics were advocating much more safety at much greater cost than they demanded in other areas, or so it was claimed. The particular version of implicit consent I have described was defended specifically in order to make this discussion more rational by advocating consistency in our treatment of risk.

Many controversial assumptions are needed to make a revealed-preference version of implicit consent into a normative standard of justification. Since choices in the market are voluntary, in some sense, while centralized decisions are strictly imposed, we must assume that we are able to infer choices for imposed risks from choices for voluntary risks. It is further assumed that market data, which indicate past decisions, reflect people's attitudes toward the risks from such new, enormous, mysterious, potentially catastrophic, and symbolically significant technologies as a nuclear reactor. Some of these criticisms have led to an alternative implicit-consent theory. This theory, called expressed-preference theory, uses psychometric techniques to uncover current attitudes and preferences about these relevant factors.[7]

Some important problems arise in using implicit consent to justify decisions, especially in revealed-preference theory. Can preferences revealed in markets be taken to reveal true and general preferences for balancing risks and benefits? In order for this to be true, consumers must choose on the basis of adequate information in a context of sufficient alternatives, and they must, furthermore, be satisfied with the choices they have made. Can we be certain that all of these conditions are met in the labor market when people choose to accept hazardous work? The answer clearly is no.

A related issue is this: People who might be willing to shop for safety in their homes and automobiles sometimes express a conviction that things like air and water should be treated differently. They do not regard these things as economic resources but tend to think that clean air and safe water are like social ideals or even rights. They want these things to be treated in different ways, even if the economic outcomes of this treatment will be different from the economic preferences they reveal for other things. We do not have to endorse this conviction in order to recognize that it is widely held. It is especially common where the costs of saving or of refusing to save extra lives are being considered. It is not so much that people believe we should spend more for lifesaving, but that we should consider these issues and make these decisions in other ways.[8] The belief is that the consent we reveal in a market as consumers is not implicitly consent to treating all allocation decisions as though they were market decisions. We might believe that some values require different procedures, not just consistent outcomes, and that it is not *reasonable* to treat all social decisions consistently *in this way*, as economic choices.

I am not defending this view simply by describing it. An argument or justification must be given for treating some values or goods differently. The problem with implicit-consent arguments, however (or at least the revealed-preference version of implicit consent), is that they simply beg the question about this socially important issue.

Revealed-preference theory and its problems illustrate a point about the role of rationality in a model of implicit consent. Consent in one area is taken to justify a choice in another area. The assumptions about rationality that are needed to make this argument basically follow the formal constraints of rationality, common in economics—for example, that rational preferences are consistent and transitive. These assumptions are beyond dispute, but what counts as consistency in behavior or in choice depends ultimately on how we interpret and judge certain background beliefs and values.

Are the critics of nuclear power who demand "excessive" safety really irrational, or are they only operating with some different assumptions and beliefs? Even the behavior of a schizophrenic can be seen as consistent, given the proper assumptions about his beliefs. At some point, clearly, we have to examine the background conditions that determine whether or not choices are consistent, and we must subject these beliefs and values to criticism and examine their rationality. This is a sense of rationality, of course, that is much richer and more substantial than the bare, formal (and noncontroversial) conception of rationality that is common in economics.

Hypothetical Consent

Hypothetical-consent models attempt to evade the problem of determining an individual's actual preferences and generalizing from them. They do this by asking instead what an individual would consent to under certain favorable conditions. Hypothetical consent differs from implicit consent in two ways. First, consent, which was indirect in the implicit-consent model, becomes even more shadowy. It is a complete idealization and never has to be based on any actual consent. Hypothetical consent is counterfactual, since it is based on an argument about what someone would consent to under certain specified conditions, and these may be and often are completely unrealized. What makes the model normative is the moral justification of these stipulated conditions. Thus we might specify certain ideal conditions that model what the world would be like if everyone were treated fairly and equally, and then we might ask about some particular decision what persons in that situation would choose to do.[9] Such an argument can be taken to support a conclusion about what we, in our current circumstances, ought to do.

The second difference is this: When we specify ideal conditions and ask what people in that situation would choose to do, we are not inviting ourselves to speculate about the effect of those stipulated conditions on human psychology. For all we know, humans are naturally perverse, so that in a morally ideal setting people would make bizarre choices that feed their neuroses in ways that the misery and injustice of our actual circumstances feed them now. I am not, of course, suggesting that our psychological makeup really is like this, but only that even if we had evidence that it was, this evidence would be irrelevant to the thought experiment that is supposed to generate hypothetical consent. What we want to ask in that thought experiment is not how idealized conditions would affect the choices of actual persons, but how ideal persons would choose in those circumstances. We idealize the persons, too, by making them ideally rational. What would a rational person do in those circumstances? That is our question. It is in this conception of rationality that we find the second major difference of the hypothetical-consent model.

In order to yield any answer at all to the question of what a rational person would choose under ideal conditions, we must assume much more about that person than formal conditions of rationality, such as consistency. These further conditions will include assumptions about the values of a rational person, such as preferring happiness to misery, or perhaps desiring to have more rather than less of what we think of as good. Even with these assumptions, there may be no answer to what an ideally rational person would choose in many circumstances, but without such assumptions no answer could even be attempted.

To illustrate the hypothetical-consent model, we can consider Pareto optimality, a principle basic to welfare economics, and examine how it is modified to apply to centralized decisions about health and safety risks. We define Pareto optimality in the following way. One allocation is (strong) Pareto-superior to another if, and only if, it makes no one worse off and at least one person better off. One allocation is (weak) Pareto-superior to another if, and only if, the gainers can compensate the losers and, after compensation, no one is worse off and at least one person is better off. A state of affairs is (strong or weak) Pareto-optimal if, and only if, it is technologically feasible and no Pareto-superior changes can be made. Pareto-superior moves produce only winners, no losers. Thus they avoid a defect of utilitarian moral theories, which allow choices that involve sacrificing some people as means for producing overall social benefits.

In fact, however, this improvement is of little importance, because in many of society's risky activities the losers cannot be compensated. What, after all, compensates for death or permanent injury? It will not do to point to procedures for determining appropriate damages in negligence cases, for this is not the kind of compensation required by a Pareto justification, because it will not leave a person as well off as she would have been had the risk not ended up harming her. If compensation is impossible, a weak Pareto principle will not apply, but a strong Pareto principle would prohibit undertaking any risky activities that will result in real losses.

In order to avoid this difficulty, the Pareto principle must be modified. It is recast as a counterfactual principle that takes us back to the time when a risk is imposed or, perhaps even earlier, to a point where we will determine the procedures for deciding how, when, and where risks will be imposed (for example, procedures for determining where toxic-waste sites or MX missiles will be located). From some *ex ante* position the losers will not yet be identified, and everyone will confront a situation in which there are only risks. Then, perhaps, compensation can be determined and an efficiency argument can be made to work. This is *ex ante* compensation, as determined by an *ex ante* Pareto principle.

Why, though, should someone who actually faces a loss, or who has already suffered it, be persuaded by any such arguments?[10] In the end it must be argued first that any reasonable person *would have consented* to the scheme that imposes these losses, and then that it is *fair* that these losses be suffered because of this hypothetical consent.

A virtue of the hypothetical-consent model is that it might justify decisions in areas where there is now controversy and where there will undoubtedly be winners and losers. It does this by dividing risk decisions into two stages. The first stage establishes procedures that are regarded as fair to all for making decisions; in the second stage the argument shows that a given decision would result from these procedures. It is therefore rational for a person to accept decisions made in this way. On the basis of this kind of argument some theorists claim that persons consent to their losses. This is quite misleading, for the word *consent* is being used metaphorically. It would be better to say that if a rational person, under conditions fair to all, would agree to procedures for making a decision, or to the decision itself, then the results of that decision are justified, even to the losers.

The problem with this model, of course, is in the argument that certain procedures are neutral and fair. If people know from the start how certain decisions are likely to affect them, they will not be easily convinced that procedures that will harm them are neutrally chosen. If we cannot find neutral procedures, then we must justify them on the basis of other principles we are willing to defend, principles that may have to endorse certain values. The issues will turn, then, on whether we can identify values that any reasonable person would accept, so that we are not unfair to some people by refusing to consider their legitimate interests.[11]

Nonconsent

A hypothetical-consent model provides a promising way to justify some risk decisions. If we try to develop this model and make it powerful enough to have any practical applications for policy decisions, we will find ourselves paying more attention explicitly to rational values and less to actual consent. As we proceed down this road, we will probably argue in ways that those who have advocated hypothetical consent would be reluctant to accept. Perhaps, then, we should identify another model on the continuum and call it ultrahypothetical consent or, more simply, nonconsent.

A nonconsent model recognizes that the justification of some decisions might require direct appeals to the values we seek to secure, even though this might entail endorsing and ranking social values through philosophical arguments.[12] Proponents of this model would argue that not all individual preferences should be given equal weight in the arrangement of social institutions. If we need to interfere with liberty to promote our interest in equality or security or posterity, we do this because one value is of greater weight—or, at any rate, more urgent—than another in the area in question. Consent need not always be the basis of this claim.

The arguments need to convince us, however, that the decisions they imply are not authoritarian. Moreover, we would need to establish the political mechanisms for making these decisions. Currently, in fact, such decisions are coming to rest increasingly with the courts, but even there the problem of justification remains.[13] If we restrict ourselves to hypothetical consent, our arguments sometimes appear desperately ad hoc. There may, in fact, be good social reasons to draft nineteen-year-olds and expose them to a disproportionately high risk of death in war, but it is highly artificial to resolve our doubts about whether this is a proper way to treat our youth by arguing that, despite their protests to the contrary, they have consented to the system or the process that selects them for this service.[14]

Qualitative Determinants of Consent

I cannot attempt to pursue an argument about rational values here, but I will mention one issue that a discussion of rational values would consider. Risks differ in their natures, and this raises some obvious problems for comparing risks and making decisions between them. Even where risks can be quantified, treating them merely as quantitative changes in a person's life prospects can obscure the qualitative aspects relevant to our social values. Extensive psychological research shows that risks are feared disproportionately to their dangers.[15]

The problem is this: We know that society demands greater safety at greater cost in some areas than in others. Airplanes must be safer than ground transportation; nuclear reactors must be safer than coal-fired plants. Sometime we might choose to save fewer lives rather than more lives at equal cost because to do otherwise seems to value human lives in an unacceptable manner. The question is: What makes these decisions acceptable?

Some risk analyses try to be sensitive to these important "intangibles" and to factor them into the equations as "psychic costs."[16] More often than not, however, the attempt to do so is ad hoc. Most such attempts fail to base their claims successfully in any established theory of psychology or on any moral or philosophical basis. They appear more to be attempts to save a method of analysis than to demonstrate its explanatory power.

A typology of risk may help us to guide our use of decision techniques and our application of such concepts as the social value of human life. It will enable us to explain when it is acceptable to generalize from individual decisions to social decisions. Thus a typology must explore the aesthetics of risk, the personal attitudes toward different risks that are relevant to formulating standards of social acceptability. No one wants a totally risk-free environment. In some activities we seek to concentrate risk, not to spread it, and this is essential to the value that those activities have for us.[17] They exercise human abilities and test human potentials. No one wants to spend more on mountain-climbing safety; many object to further safety measures on ski slopes or for motorcycles; and there is no shortage of test pilots or astronauts, although the compensation is often only standard military officers' pay. How far-reaching are the implications of such phenomena? Do they tell us something about spending money to reduce risk in private airplanes? In automobiles? The Hell's Angels may refuse to wear helmets for macho reasons we dimly comprehend, but we do not imagine that their thrills include descending on Three Mile Island to breathe possibly contaminated air. This suggests that many factors determine socially acceptable risk, in addition to the probability that one will be harmed or killed from some given cause.

In some cases, such as mountain climbing, the risks themselves are essential to the value of the activity. In other cases, even when we restrict ourselves to risks that are voluntarily accepted, risks that are not essential to the value of the activity are accepted or rejected for different reasons. Someone may buy a smoke detector because he plans to take up smoking and fears he might fall asleep with a lighted cigarette.

We should also consider examples of the different kinds of risk that individuals choose to accept. The few discussions of such cases invariably look at risks to life and limb. We naturally tend to think of activities that test one's physical limits and the values that people find in these activities. But we should also think about a different kind of risk altogether: those that individuals take when choosing a course of action—say, a career path or a decision to marry—that may turn out well or badly, or one that will change one's life in unpredictable way.[18] Some people enjoy such gambles; some think the necessity of confronting such contingencies strongly determines our outlook on and appreciation of life. It may turn out that understanding these kinds of risk will prove very valuable to understanding social divisions over risk and safety. Perhaps the fear and opposition to certain large-scale projects has been misperceived because our attention has focused exclusively on safety risks. Perhaps the source of the fear in some cases is about different kinds of risks to society, or the opposition may be to the way these decisions are being made. These issues may be highly relevant to questions about the use of risk-assessment techniques in social decision-making.

Notes

1. For a discussion of different theories of rights, see Ronald Dworkin, *Taking Rights Seriously* (Cambridge: Harvard University Press, 1977); Robert Nozick, *Anarchy, State, and Utopia* (New York: Basic Books, 1974); and Henry Shue, *Basic Rights* (Princeton: Princeton University Press, 1980).

2. For a sensitive discussion of these problems, see Nozick, *Anarchy, State, and Utopia*, chap. 4.

3. This is argued in detail in Ronald Dworkin, "Is Wealth a Value?" *Journal of Legal Studies* 9 (1980): 191–227; "Why Efficiency?" *Hofstra Law Review* 8 (1981): 576–78.

4. See Lawrence Tribe, "Policy Science: Analysis or Ideology?" *Philosophy & Public Policy* 2 (1972): 66–110.

5. See Chauncey Starr, "Social Benefit Versus Technological Risk," *Science* 165 (1969): 1232–38.

6. For a review of this literature, see Charles Brown, "Equalizing Differences in the Labor Market," *Quarterly Journal of Economics* 94 (1980): 113–34.

7. Baruch Fischhoff et al., "How Safe Is Safe Enough? A Psychometric Study of Attitudes Towards Technological Risks and Benefits," *Policy Studies* 8 (1978): 127–52.

8. I have discussed this issue in detail in other essays. See "Valuing Human Life," in *Uncertain Power*, Dorothy Zinberg, ed. (New York: Pergamon Press, 1983), pp. 93–11.

9. The most famous recent attempt to develop this model is John Rawls, *A Theory of Justice* (Cambridge: Harvard University Press, 1971). Some of the extensive discussion of Rawls's version of hypothetical consent as a method of justification can be found in *Reading Rawls*, Norman Daniels, ed. (New York: Basic Books, 1974).

10. See Dworkin, "Why Efficiency?"

11. In Rawls, *Theory of Justice*, the discussion of the values that justify the principles of choice is contained mainly in the sections on primary goods (pp. 62, 90–95) and on the sense of justice and social union (pp. 520–29, 567–77).

12. In a series of articles, Thomas Scanlon has developed a version of a nonconsent theory. See "Preference and Urgency," *Journal of Philosophy* 72 (1975): 655–70; and "Rights, Goals, and Fairness," in *Public & Private Morality*, Stuart Hampshire, ed. (Cambridge: Cambridge University Press, 1978), pp. 93–111. Classical utilitarian theories of course are another kind of nonconsent theory.

13. See Owen Fiss, "The Supreme Court: 1978 Term," *Harvard Law Review* 93 (1979): 1–58, for an enthusiastic view of the Supreme Court's role in making public policy. For a negative view, see John Ely, *Democracy and Distrust* (Cambridge: Harvard University Press, 1980), chap. 3.

14. See Thomas Nagel, "Ruthlessness in Public Life," in Hampshire, *Public & Private Morality*, pp. 75–92.

15. See Fischhoff et al., "How Safe Is Safe Enough?" Extensive work in this area has been done by Amos Tversky and Daniel Kahneman. See "Judgment under Uncertainty: Heuristics and Biases," *Science* 185 (1974): 1124–31; and "The Framing of Decisions and the Psychology of Choice," *Science* 211 (1981): 453–58.

16. For examples, see William Baumol and Wallace Oates, *The Theory of Environmental Policy* (Englewood Cliffs, N.J.; Prentice-Hall, 1975); Myrick Freeman et al., *The Benefits of Environmental Improvement* (Baltimore: The Johns Hopkins University Press, 1979); and Lawrence Tribe, "Ways Not to Think about Plastic Trees," *Yale Law Journal* 83 (1974): 1315–48.

17. The positive value of risk is explored and discussed in many adventure stories. For example, see Tom Wolfe, *The Right Stuff* (New York: Farrar, Straus & Giroux, 1979); Hunter Thompson, *Hell's Angels* (New York: Ballantine, 1966). For a particularly good philosophical discussion, see Woodrow Wilson Sayre, *Four Against Everest* (New York: Tower Books, 1964).

18. See Bernard Williams and Thomas Nagel, "A Symposium on Moral Luck," *Proceedings of the Aristotelian Society*, supp. vol. 50 (1976): 115–51.

2

Cost-Benefit Analysis Applied to Risks: Its Philosophy and Legitimacy

Herman B. Leonard
Richard J. Zeckhauser

Cost-benefit analysis, particularly as applied to public decisions involving risks to life and health, has not been notably popular. A number of setbacks—Three Mile Island is perhaps the most memorable—called into question the reliability of analytic approaches to risk issues, as well as the competence of public regulators and decision-makers. The public does not always believe that cost-benefit analyses employ its values, or that analysis is conducted dispassionately on its behalf.

In this chapter we examine the basis for this mistrust. Why does cost-benefit analysis not enjoy greater public acceptance and a better general reputation? We shall focus on the philosophical principles underlying cost-benefit analysis. On what bases can they be supported? We shall also examine problems of implementation. How can cost-benefit analysis be expected to perform in practice?

We shall not attempt a systematic review of the use of cost-benefit techniques. Any technique employed in the political process may be distorted to suit parochial ends and particular interest groups. Cost-benefit analysis can be an advocacy weapon, and it can be used by knaves. But it does not create knaves, and to some extent it may even police their behavior. The critical question is whether it is more or less subject to manipulation than alternative decision processes. Our claim is that its ultimate grounding in analytic disciplines affords some protection. It is widely (though not universally) agreed that cost-benefit analyses should be subjected to scrutiny and debate, and that the expressed preferences of the citizenry are the appropriate reference in making value judgments. Risks to lives or property, for example, should be assigned the same value by government decision-makers that the individuals at risk themselves would apply. We do not believe that cost-benefit analysis is inherently easier to abuse than any other system used to guide decisions.

The misuse charge is not, however, the primary objection to cost-benefit analysis. Most of those who claim that it is misused in practice would not be satisfied if, for example, a science court were made responsible for objective use of the discipline. Many observers contend that the fundamental moral and ethical underpinnings of cost-benefit analysis are at variance with our ordinary moral judgments. This is the argument we will address.

A second group of critics objects to cost-benefit analysis not for its methods, but for the outcomes it produces. These individuals reject cost-benefit analysis because they feel that, in the particular set of decisions society is likely to confront, their own interests are better served if benefits and costs are not systematically weighted. If the current political tug of war appears to overemphasize the values personally important to a certain faction, that group has little to gain from a change in the status quo. We have considerably less to say to these "ends-oriented" critics.

Risks to life, health, and property present a complex of troubling decision problems. Risks are especially difficult to deal with for three reasons. First, they are hard to measure; we do not generally know what "quantity" of risk is transferred or created in any given transaction. Even in private transactions like the purchase of an airline ticket, an individual will not generally know how much risk he is accepting. Second, people are generally unsophisticated in their treatment of risks. Even if fully informed about risk levels, they would have a difficult time interpreting them and making self-interested decisions about them. Third, people do not generally have property rights in risk levels to which they are exposed. Risks may be imposed or removed without compensation or charge. Quite frequently they are imposed by one individual on others: A drunk driver creates risks for others on the road; a nuclear-power plant may impose a risk on all individuals in its geographic area. In the language of economics, risks frequently involve public goods and externalities.

None of these problems would be particularly troubling if we could appropriately compensate injured parties after the fact. If we could costlessly identify the responsible party and measure the damage done, a system of *ex post* liability would lead to an economically efficient outcome. Only the creator of the risk would need to measure the risk level, and because compensation for damages would be guaranteed, no individual would care if risk(s) were imposed on him. Obviously, such a perfect system of *ex post* compensation is impossible. Many losses associated with risks—death is the most telling example—are not compensable after the fact. Even if they were, it is frequently difficult to identify the cause of an unfortunate outcome. Did the individual contract liver cancer from exposure to toxic chemicals or from his own voluntary use of alcohol? If there is joint causality, how should we divide the responsibility?

Since fully efficient *ex post* compensation cannot generally be arranged, society must devise institutionally feasible and morally defensible procedures for determining *ex ante* which risks should be imposed. This chapter concerns the use of cost-benefit analysis as a potentially defensible social mechanism for risk allocation. We consider the method both in principle (its philosophical foundations) and in practice (the features that have made risk analysis so controversial).

The central principle on which all of the following discussion rests is that if risks could be conveyed in voluntary exchanges as private goods, informed and competent individuals should be allowed to accept or decline them. We extrapolate from this basic principle to guidelines for decisions when voluntary exchange is not feasible. Since our analysis is complex, it is worth stating our basic argument briefly here.

> Since many important risks cannot be exchanged on a voluntary basis, it is essential to have a centralized decision process that will regulate or determine their levels. In choosing among alternative projects that create different levels of risk, the government (or other responsible decision-makers) should seek the outcomes that fully informed individuals would choose for themselves if voluntary exchange were feasible. Risks are not different in principle from other commodities, such as park services, public transit, or housing.

In many public decisions, it is not feasible to compensate those who would have preferred an alternative outcome. In such circumstances, assuming that the changes wrought by the decision are not extremely large relative to an individual's wealth position, we use "hypothetical consent" as a guideline for government action. Our test for a proposed public decision consists of two questions. First, are the net benefits of the action positive? Second, did those favored by the decision gain enough that they would have a net benefit even if they compensated those hurt by the decision? If so, our principle of hypothetical compensation calls for acceptance of the decision. It would of course be preferable to carry out the compensation, but that is often not possible. (We will discuss the distributional concerns raised by this proposal.)

Cost-benefit analysis, which begins by totaling the gains and losses of each party, is the appropriate way to determine which public decisions affecting risk levels would gain the hypothetical consent of the citizenry. We know of no other mechanism for making such choices that has an ethical underpinning.

Basically, we are taking what might be thought of as a constitutional approach to the morality issue. What mechanism for making decisions would individuals choose if they had to contract before they knew their identities in society or the kinds of problems they would confront? Our answer is that, on an expected-value basis, cost-benefit analysis would serve them best and hence would be chosen.

Two strong objections to this approach can be raised. First, one can argue that it is never morally acceptable to take property, which obviously includes imposing bodily risks, without compensation. Some would even reject the notion of compensation determined by a legislature or a court, for there can be no guarantee that such compensation would be sufficient to obtain voluntary assent. We cannot defeat this argument on moral grounds. Speaking pragmatically, however, we would observe that requiring voluntary assent for every government action would essentially paralyze the government. A second major objection to the cost-benefit approach is that, while acceptable in theory, in practice it leads to the usurpation of private decision-making power, the growth of government influence in society, and ultimately the loss of freedom.

The first of these arguments might be labeled the libertarian objection, and the second the slippery-slope objection. We believe that, interestingly enough, neither of these views would be espoused by the most vocal critics of cost-benefit analysis, who tend to believe that it hinders government action and the free flow of the political process.

Cost-benefit analysis is unpopular, particularly when used in applications involving the determination of risk levels. We will point out some problems that we believe explain the method's poor acceptance to date and argue that efforts should be made to win wider support for it. Cost-benefit analysis is *especially* important where risks are involved because less formal methods, which may be used for more routine decision problems, are not adequate for handling decision problems involving risk. Without cost-benefit analysis, we would be forced to rely on an unpredictable political process. That process frequently leads to stalemate and reliance on the status quo; at other times it careens in response to popular perceptions and whims of the moment. The government thus has an important role to play in regulating risks by finding, developing, and legitimating methods for making centralized decisions.

We are not arguing that cost-benefit analysis is a perfect representation of an idealized collective decision process. Rather, we feel that it is both the most practical of ethically defensible methods and the most ethical of practically usable methods for conducting public decision-making. It cannot substitute for—nor can it adequately encompass, analyze, or consider—the application of sensitive social values. Thus it cannot be made the sole or final arbiter of public decisions. But it does add a useful structure to public debate, and it does enable us to quantify some of the quantifiable aspects of public decisions. Our defense parallels Winston Churchill's argument for democracy: it is not perfect, but it is better than the alternatives.

Cost-Benefit Analysis and "Efficiency" as a Standard of "Hypothetical Consent"

We begin with the proposition that the outcomes generated by free and competitive markets set a standard of general welfare improvements through resource allocation that is difficult to equal through any other resource-allocating mechanism. Many societies—and especially their economists—hold a strong presumption that requiring the voluntary consent of both parties to an exchange is sufficient to ensure that the arrangement is productive for the parties involved and for the society. To function well, markets require the voluntary participation of many well-informed individual agents. The criterion of voluntarism is invoked to ensure that the outcome generated for each agent is, in his judgment, preferable to what he could obtain without participating. Voluntarism is an indication of "consent," and, using the assumption that agents are well informed and the basic tenet that people know what is good for them, consent justifies the belief that the outcomes achieved are difficult to improve upon.

We find these principles morally unobjectionable. The foundation of this logic is that if people were well informed we would be happy to rely upon their judgments. This does not mean, of course, that under all conceivable circumstances we would always accept individual judgment, nor that there is no room for a centralized decision process. Rather, it holds any proposed public decision process to a high standard of performance. A centralized decision process should try to achieve outcomes like those generated by full private consent in private markets. Such idealized markets are "efficient" in the technical sense that no agent can be made better off without making some other agent worse off. They also provide full and acceptable compensation to all parties; voluntary participation is compelling evidence that the parties believe they are fairly compensated.[1]

In decisions made by a central agent on behalf of large numbers of people, the standard of individual consent is not a realistic test of the social rectitude of the decision. While "consensus-building" is an important feature of any public decision process—and indeed is a partial test of whether the outcome conforms to widely held social norms—we cannot and do not require the consent of every affected individual in order to implement decisions that impose costs or risks. The "transactions costs" of assembling unanimous consent would be prohibitive, leading to paralysis in the status quo. Moreover, any system that required unanimous consent would create incentives for individuals to misrepresent their beliefs so as to secure compensation or to prevent the imposition of relatively small costs (on them) in return for large benefits (to others). This is sometimes called the "land assembly" problem. Each individual parcel-holder has the incentive to hold out so that his is the last piece acquired, the one that dramatically increases the value of the previously assembled package. This problem lies at the foundation of the nearly universal governmental power of eminent domain.

If individual consent is an impractically strong standard to require of centralized decisions, how should such decisions be made? We believe the chosen alternative should be the one for which benefits most exceed costs. This standard is often referred to as "efficiency." The underlying notion is that it is wasteful to choose alternatives that do not provide the maximum possible "net benefits" or "surplus." If benefits and costs are carefully defined, this criterion has a strong intuitive appeal. If, for example, benefits and costs were fully and appropriately measured and equally distributed over individuals, we would expect that the benefit-cost choice criterion would yield the same result as universal individual consent. In this polar case, consent and the benefit-cost criterion are equivalent, and in this sense cost-benefit analysis can be thought of as a form of "hypothetical" consent by the community.

The problem of collective decision-making arises, of course, only when the interests of individuals in the community are (or seem) divergent. It may be beside the point to observe that cost-benefit analysis coincides with universal individual consent when all individuals in the community are affected similarly under each alternative considered. It is much more difficult to determine whether the benefit-cost criterion is a useful means of defining "hypothetical consent" by the community when individuals have widely different interests.

Compensation

An immediate problem, both practical and philosophical, with the pure criterion of cost-benefit analysis is that it does not require compensation for those on whom a given decision imposes net costs. As articulated, our standard for public decision-making does not require that losers be compensated, but only that they could be if a perfect system of transfers existed. This is the issue of distribution as it affects losers. An attractive feature of the "efficiency" notion is that *if* decisions are made only when their total benefits exceed total costs, then, by making appropriate payments and imposing appropriate charges, it is theoretically possible to distribute the benefits (or other compensation) so that every individual gains on balance from the decision. If such a compensation system could be designed and implemented, then all individuals would presumably consent to the decision.

In practice, it is typically infeasible to design a compensation system that ensures that all individuals will be net winners. The transactions costs involved in such a system would often be so high as to make the project as a whole a net loss. But it may not even be desirable to try to construct perfect compensation systems. Any such systems would have to rely on the stated valuations of the losers in determining the compensation granted. This means that losers will generally have an incentive to overstate their anticipated losses in order to secure greater compensation. Complicated procedures exist for eliciting the views of all individuals and determining compensation in a way that does not provide incentives for dishonesty; such schemes are said to be "incentive compatible."[2] Unfortunately, they are difficult to apply in practice except in very simple problems.[3] Any attempt to build individual consensus for public decisions through schemes to compensate those on whom costs are imposed will create incentives for dishonest statements of valuations and thus build inefficiencies and inequities into the system.

A second reason for preferring a system based on hypothetical consent is that the compensation needed to secure individual consent may itself be inefficient. With regard to risk bearing, for example, the best form of compensation may predominantly involve *ex ante* payments.[4] In general, however, compensation for losses incurred will often be demanded (and awarded) *ex post* whether or not compensation was paid *ex ante*. The uncertainties of the political and legal system in meting out *ex post* compensation are an additional risk in the system viewed *ex ante* and impose a deadweight loss. Any system that relies on extensive compensation of losers as a means of building consensus seems likely to exacerbate this problem. *Ex post* compensation also creates inappropriate incentives to the risk bearer with respect to his own behavior.[5]

We have argued that it is typically infeasible and often undesirable to attempt to build a system of compensation that makes all individuals net winners. But unless those harmed by a decision are *actually* compensated, they will care little that the cost-benefit criterion of hypothetical consent has ensured that someone is reaping a surplus from which they could have been compensated. The theoretical availability of compensation will be of only intellectual interest to them if such compensation is not feasible in practice and, indeed, forthcoming.

This leads us to two questions. First, are there circumstances in which society (or, to take a more elemental view, individuals in forming their social contract) should choose alternatives that impose net costs on some individuals in order to gain net benefits for society overall, even though it is not possible to compensate the losers fairly? Many have recently argued that the apparent indecisiveness and inconsistency of the modern political process is largely a consequence of a social shift toward the view that losers should be compensated.[6] Whether or not society is becoming more sensitive to those who lose through centralized decisions, it has always tolerated some changes unaccompanied by full compensation and will clearly continue to do so. We are unaware of any philosophical tenet that fully resolves this issue, but the extreme position of always requiring full compensation—permitting, in the language of economists, only Pareto-superior readjustments—seems to us unduly impractical and ultimately untenable.

The problem of compensation is probably less important in practice than in principle. Society tends to compensate large losses where possible or to avoid imposing large costs when adequate compensation is not practical. It is only the ethical problem of relatively small uncompensated transfers that must be confronted in the practical setting. Moreover, compensation is sometimes overpaid; having made allowances *ex ante* for imposing risks, society still chooses sometimes to pay additional compensation *ex post* to those who actually suffer losses. Thus the practical ethical problems of compensation may be smaller than we sometimes suppose.

Assuming, then, that some central decisions will be taken that harm certain individuals without full compensation, will society's interests be best served by following the benefit-cost criterion, or should some other criterion serve as a proxy for "hypothetical consent"? Again, we do not know of any compelling elemental philosophical principle that readily settles debate on this question. The benefit-cost standard is surely not a complete guide for social decision-making. On the other hand, it would clearly not be desirable to adopt any criterion that regularly led to decisions whose costs were greater than their benefits. Thus the efficiency test seems to be a sensible basis for defining a standard of hypothetical consent.

Political conservatives raise one additional argument about the ethical basis of a system that does not require full compensation to losers. The argument can be based on either a theory of constitutional law, a theory of property rights, or a prediction about the performance of society in the absence of such rights—that is, when expropriation is possible. It alleges that a public decision process that imposes uncompensated losses constitutes an illegal taking of property by the state and should not be tolerated. This is a serious ethical dilemma for the cost-benefit criterion. If one takes a rigid view of either constitutional or property rights, this is a compelling proposition.

Our objection to this inflexible position is more pragmatic than philosophical. We believe it leads to an untenable position for society, one that would unduly constrain public decisions. But we are forced to agree that it is ethically more pure than the hypothetical and potentially uncompensated consent that we propose here. At least with full disclosure, we are willing to trade ethical purity for practicality.

Distribution

Distributional considerations are closely related to the issue of how and whether compensation should be paid or required of the decision criterion for public choices. Two distinct types of distributional issues are relevant in cost-benefit analysis. First, we can be concerned about the losers in a particular decision, whoever they may be. Second, we can be concerned with the transfers between income classes engendered by a given project. If costs are imposed differentially on groups that are generally disadvantaged, should the decision criterion include special consideration of their interests? Should the public decision process weight the interests of each individual in society equally, or should more weight be given to the interests of the disadvantaged or the losers? This question is closely intertwined with the issue of compensation, because it is often alleged that the uncompensated costs of projects evaluated by cost-benefit criteria frequently fall on those who are disadvantaged to start with.

The distributional issue is particularly prominent when risks to lives are concerned, as in the debate over the volunteer army. Despite the evident advantages of the volunteer military in terms of economic efficiency, many people are disturbed that the sons of the rich do not have to serve. Two of their objections appear to have logical support. (1) If the sons of the rich are not involved, we will enter more wars. Those who think that our nation is too bellicose may thus object on strategic grounds to having a volunteer army. (2) There may be an externality among members of a society that pertains to the social classes of its warriors. For example, if we as a society care more about the life risks members of the poorer classes take than about the financial compensation they receive, then we may judge that the poor may have suffered from the advent of the all-volunteer force.

This raises the natural question of whether lives or risks to lives are different from other goods in the way they affect our concerns about distribution. Would the same class of arguments apply if we were worried about excessively arduous jobs? Should this lead us to ban cigarettes, perhaps because the poor smoke them disproportionately and we care less about each other's smoking pleasure than about each other's health?

Accept for the moment that risks to lives are in some sense different from other risks. Is the critical factor the existence of different income groups within society? Or would we have the same attitudes if income were distributed equally? If we would feel differently with an equal income distribution, then we must recognize that we are hurting the poor if we deny them opportunities that they would take for themselves. Differences in medical care or health condition convey much stronger impressions of inequality and inequity than differences in income or wealth. Surely that is part of the reason that so much of society's aid to the poor is given through in-kind transfers, in particular of medical care.[7] It may even be efficient if the middle class likes to make transfers in this fashion. But if it tends to cloud perceptions of income inequality, such a pattern of transfers may be a bad strategic choice by the poor or their representatives.

The question of whether and how cost-benefit analysis should embody distributional concerns is difficult to resolve in principle. At the risk of appearing to take inconsistent positions on this issue, we would argue that (1) it is theoretically quite possible to build such concerns into cost-benefit analysis, but (2) there are good reasons for not doing so.

We see no reason why any widely agreed upon notion of equity, or weighting of different individuals' interests, cannot in principle be built into any cost-benefit-decision framework. This amounts merely to defining carefully what is meant by a benefit or a cost. If, in society's view, benefits (or costs) to some individuals are more valuable (or more costly) than those to others, this can be reflected in the construction of the decision criterion. It may be difficult in practice for the community to agree on what the weights should be, and it will nearly always be difficult to implement such schemes, but it is hardly fair to criticize the method because the problem is difficult—unless we can propose some more effective way of coping with it.[8]

Although distribution concerns could be systematically included in cost-benefit analyses, it is not always, or even generally, a good idea to do so. We should first make it clear that we regard decisions about the appropriate income distribution as one of the central legitimating functions of collective political organisms. It does not obviously follow, however, that questions about how the income distribution should be modified should be raised with each project a government undertakes. For several reasons, distributional issues should not be included in every public deliberation or indeed in any deliberations that do not significantly alter that distribution. Taxes and direct expenditures represent a far more efficient means of effecting redistribution than virtually any other public program. We would strongly prefer to rely on one consistent comprehensive tax and expenditure package for redistribution than on attempts to redistribute within every project.

The first reason for not considering distributional issues in every public decision is that they may be handled more consistently through a specialized function than if treated piecemeal. If distributional issues are considered everywhere, this is likely to mean that they will be adequately, carefully, and correctly treated nowhere. Assuming a given social propensity to redistribute, we suspect that the more diffused the redistribution process is, the less will be accomplished in total. Many critics of cost-benefit analysis believe that project-based distributional analysis would constitute a net *addition* to society's total redistributional effort; we suggest that it might instead be only an inefficient substitution. It therefore seems unwise, from the perspective of the very individuals whose welfare is at stake, to ask each separate public decision to carry part of the burden of income redistribution.

Second, treating distributional concerns within each project can only lead to transfers within the group affected by a project, often only a small subset of the community. Why should the larger society not share the burden of redistribution? It is unrealistic to expect project-based cost-benefit analysis to result in a fully equitable distribution of welfare across parties affected by the project. Cost-benefit analysis for a particular project should reflect distributional considerations only *within the confines of the project.* If we observe, for example, that those construction workers who bear the greatest risks in building public projects are also the poorest, some might want to weight costs imposed upon or benefits given to them more heavily. We should not, however, expect that doing so will correct basic underlying inequities in the distribution of income.

Third, the view that distributional considerations should be treated project by project appears to reflect a presumption that on average they do not balance out—that is, that some groups systematically lose more often than others and that transfers should be directed toward those groups rather than away from them. Minorities are a commonly cited example. If it were found that some groups were severely and systematically disadvantaged by the application of cost-benefit analyses that ignore distributional concerns, we would certainly favor redressing the imbalance. We do not believe this is generally the case, however. The systematically uncompensated impacts of public projects are typically fairly small. If it is clear that one group will be substantially affected by a project, some form of compensation is usually offered. This implies that the biases among the remaining, smaller, uncompensated costs imposed must be severe indeed to constitute a serious inequity on balance. If identified groups are systematically found to be uncompensated losers—or winners not required to pay for the benefits they receive—we would support general redistribution toward (or away) from them rather than piecemeal consideration of their interests in every decision, and we would propose to carry it out through the explicit tax and expenditure system.

In spite of our general view that distributional concerns should be handled separately, we can see one important practical reason for including them in the project decision process. The usefulness of cost-benefit analysis depends very much on whether the public regards it as a legitimate decision criterion. If the use of distributional weights contributes to legitimacy, it may well be a trade-off worth making.

In summary, we would characterize our views about project-based distributional considerations as follows.

1. It is generally undesirable to include them in project analysis
2. They can be included if it *is* desirable (or desired)
3. The uncompensated transfers engendered by public projects are generally small and largely random
4. When there are large and systematic transfers as a result of public projects, we should—and generally we do—arrange compensation for them
5. The principal argument in favor of including distributional considerations in project analysis is that it may improve public legitimacy, which is ultimately a crucial component of successful application of this approach

Consistency with Sensitive Social Values

The cost-benefit criterion for social choice can be reduced to a tautology by defining costs and benefits to include every possible consideration. The efficiency criterion could then be met by any decision merely as a matter of definition; by putting a high enough value on selected considerations, any outcome could be justified. Thus any serious attempt to use cost-benefit analysis must come to terms with the difficult problem of deciding which social concerns should be represented within it and how they should be treated—and how those that do not get explicit attention will be dealt with outside the pure analytic framework.

Cost-benefit analysis, it is frequently alleged, does a disservice to society because it does not and cannot treat important social values with appropriate sensitivity. We believe that this view does a disservice to society by unduly constraining the use of a reasonable and helpful method for organizing the debate about public decisions. This does not mean that every important social value can be represented effectively within the confines of cost-benefit analysis. Some social values will never fit in a cost-benefit framework and will have to be treated as "additional considerations" in coming to a final decision. Some, such as the nonsacrifice of human life, may be binding constraints. We cannot make a cost-benefit-analysis decision concerning which values should be included and which should be treated separately. This decision will always have to be handled in an ad hoc manner.

Obviously, we have to be extremely careful to give social values an appropriate role, neither too wide nor too narrow. Widely held and vitally important social values will act as a "trump" to cost-benefit analysis. Many of these values are "brittle": They cannot be bent without breaking. Suppose, for example, that a town would like to take several houses by eminent domain in order to complete a highway extension that is justified on a cost-benefit basis, but it does not have sufficient funds to offer owners the compensation required by law. The social value of following the law is likely to outweigh the cost-benefit analysis for that project. We cannot bend the standard of law easily, nor should we seek to, for if we do, we challenge the whole rule of law in society. We are willing to give up considerable short-run economic efficiency to retain this widely held value. Indeed, doing so will preserve efficiency in the long run, for it means that our basic operating rules are secure. Without this assurance, the economy will surely falter. We fully accept the role of "untouchable" values as overriding considerations in public decision-making. They do not invalidate cost-benefit analyses; they merely illustrate that more is at stake than just costs and benefits.

We would, however, make two observations. First, we must be very careful that only genuinely important and relevant social values be permitted to outweigh the findings of an analysis. Because of its associations with worldwide devastation, the question of whether to use nuclear power appears at this point, at least in many circles, to be beyond the realm of analysis of costs and benefits. But this does not mean that we should not use cost-benefit calculations in deciding what to do, for example, with existing radioactive wastes. Second, social values that frequently stand in the way of important efficiency gains have a way of breaking down and being replaced over time, so that in the long run society manages to accommodate itself to some form of cost-benefit criterion. If nuclear power were a thousand times more dangerous for its employees but ten times less expensive than it is, we might feel the national interest was well served by having rotating cadres of nuclear-power employees serving short terms in high-risk positions, much as members of the armed services do.[9] Such a policy would reflect an accommodation to the costs as a recognition of the benefits.

Few important social decisions cannot and should not be informed by cost-benefit analysis. But we would not promote cost-benefit analysis as the final arbiter of social decisions. Some issues are of such great social concern that no analysis can override them, but only relatively important values should be given such priority. The natural tendency is for lesser values to give way gradually when they clearly stand in the way of substantial efficiency gains. In a civilized society that values stability, it is well that such transitions take place gradually. Our informal accommodation and adjustment as a society seems to be the only feasible mechanism to resolve these problems.

Participation

It is often alleged that the decisions reached through a cost-benefit calculation are tainted by the process itself. While the efficiency criterion may result in better decisions from an objective social standpoint, the argument runs, the fact that the analysis must be carried out by a technically skilled elite makes the decisions less acceptable socially than decisions taken in a broader participatory framework.

We take this argument seriously for two reasons. First, however correct the mechanism may be in principle, in practice it cannot be effective unless it develops a political legitimacy that comes only with social understanding and acceptance. Second, it is not obvious that the mechanism is in fact better operated by "technocrats." We are not sure why centralized assessments, whether by technicians, bureaucrats, or consultants, should be presumed to be better than those of members of the community at large. The private marketplace is often a useful source of both information concerning the present and estimates about the future. There is much to be said for designing a more public process of cost-benefit analysis for social decisions that would incorporate as much information from the private market as possible.

This is not, however, an inherent problem either in principle or in practice with using cost-benefit analysis. If the community strongly believes, for example, that a minority group member should be in charge of the decision process for a project that impinges largely on that group, nothing in the principles of cost-benefit analysis suggests otherwise, and nothing concerning the implementation of cost-benefit analysis should stand in the way. We would hope that whatever group makes the decision will consider the findings of a cost-benefit analysis, but we would not expect it to be the only set of arguments considered.

Measurability

A final objection frequently raised about cost-benefit analysis is that some costs and benefits tend to be ignored because they are much more difficult to measure than others. The long-term environmental impacts of large projects are frequently cited as an example. Cost-benefit analysis is charged with being systematically biased toward consideration of the quantifiable aspects of decisions. This is unquestionably true: Cost-benefit analysis is *designed* as a method of quantification, so it surely is better able to deal with more quantifiable aspects of the issues it confronts. But this limitation is in itself ethically neutral unless it can be shown that the quantifiable considerations systematically push decisions in a particular direction. In other words, it is not sufficient to argue that cost-benefit analysis does not handle perfectly what is obviously a very hard task; rather, its detractors must show that its errors are systematically unjust or inefficient—for example, that it frequently helps the rich at the expense of the poor, or that the environment is systematically disadvantaged to the benefit of industry. We have not seen any carefully researched evidence to support such assertions.

We take some comfort in the fact that cost-benefit analysis is sometimes accused of being biased toward development projects and sometimes of being biased against them. Cost-benefit analyses have foiled conservation efforts in national forests. (Perhaps they systematically weight the future too little.) But they have also squelched clearly silly projects designed to bring "economic development" to Alaska—and the developers argued that the analysis gave insufficient weight to the "unquantifiable" value of future industrialization.

We do not claim that cost-benefit analysis can handle all problems equally well. We have already acknowledged, for example, that some social values will have to be considered outside the cost-benefit framework. But we know of no method that has a sound ethical basis for dealing with all issues equally well. An unfettered political process—one that does not embody and consider cost-benefit analysis in any form—is likely to make errors of judgment even in areas where most costs and benefits *are* quantifiable. This would seem to be a less ethical system than one that tries to come to terms with at least those aspects of a decision that are knowable, and permits socially legitimated political discussion about those aspects that are not knowable, before rendering a final decision.

Ethics and Risk Analysis

Even those who accept the ethical propriety of cost-benefit analysis of decisions involving transfers of money or other tangible economic costs and benefits sometimes feel that the same principles do not extend to analyzing decisions involving the imposition of risks. We believe that such applications constitute a *particularly* important area in which cost-benefit analysis can be of value. The very difficulties of reaching appropriate decisions where risks are involved make it all the more vital to employ the soundest methods available, both ethically and practically.

Historically, cost-benefit analysis has been applied widely to the imposition and regulation of risks, in particular to risks of health loss or bodily harm. There are good reasons for this. Few health risks can be exchanged on a voluntary basis. Their magnitude is difficult to measure. Even if they could be accurately measured, individuals have difficulty interpreting probabilities or gauging how they would feel should the harm eventuate. Complementing these problems of valuation are difficulties in contract. Risks are rarely conveyed singly between one individual and another. Commonly, risks are a public bad, as when a factory pollutes the air. If voluntary acceptance of risk were sought, it would be essential to deal with thousands of individuals. This would not be an insurmountable problem if the dollar magnitude of the risk imposed on each were substantial, but frequently it is not. A decision that potentially imposes a risk valued at five dollars on each of 100,000 people is a consequential decision, but it would hardly be worthwhile to spend ten dollars to draw up a contract with each "participant." Even if transactions costs were low, the "land assembly" problem would still remain. Given that the risk cannot be conveyed in a manner that excludes a few persons who do not wish to join, individuals will always have the incentive to demand far more than true valuations. Technologies rarely allow some individuals to be excluded from a risk at a relatively low cost.

The problem of risks conveyed in the absence of contractual approval is not a new one and has been addressed for centuries through the common law and specifically the law of torts, which is designed to provide compensation after a harm has been received. If only a low-probability risk is involved, it is often efficient to wait to see whether a harm occurs, for in the overwhelming majority of circumstances transactions costs can be avoided. This approach also limits debate over the magnitude of a potential harm that has not yet eventuated. The creator of the risk has the incentive to gauge accurately, for he is the one who must pay if harm does occur.

While in principle it provides efficient results, the torts approach encounters at least four difficulties when applied to many of the risks that are encountered in a modern technological society: (1) bankruptcy, (2) proof of causality, (3) the inability to make people whole, and (4) the inefficiency of *ex post* compensation. Bankruptcy is a problem because it allows the responsible party to avoid paying and so to impose risks that it should not impose. Suppose a company must decide whether to begin using a process that would yield $1 million in profit but would involve a 2 percent risk of incurring a $100 million loss. From a systemwide perspective, the new process is a bad bet. But bankruptcy protection limits the company's potential loss to the value of its assets—let us say $5 million. From the standpoint of the company, the decision has a 2 percent chance to lose $5 million and a 98 percent chance to make $1 million. Even a reasonably risk-averse firm might choose to accept this lottery, which is inefficient on a societal basis.

The paradigmatic torts problem involves a two-car automobile collision or the collapse of a retaining wall. Even in relatively simple cases such as these, it may be difficult to determine precisely which action caused the misfortune, assess whether appropriate caution was exercised, or find out exactly what happened. Nevertheless, the courts must make just such determinations, as well as assess the magnitude of the damages. With risks of these types, however, causality may be far more difficult to demonstrate than in the cases of the auto accident or the collapsing wall. When an individual contracts lung cancer, for example, there is no way to determine after the fact whether air pollution, his own smoking, fate, or some combination of these factors was the cause. Statistical analyses of excess risk are feasible, but the courts have always been uncomfortable dealing with probabilistic assessments. Virtually all court decisions involve probabilistic judgments, but the courts do not like to think of themselves as being in this business. The central problem is that most misfortunes have multiple causes. Moreover, these "multiple sources of risk" may interrelate in a synergistic fashion, which compounds the problem.

Even if we could accurately determine the source of the health loss or the bodily injury, the traditional torts requirement that individuals be made whole cannot be met in many instances. If a retaining wall collapses, we can make the builder rebuild, or we can require him to pay the cost of having it built correctly. A crumpled fender can be repaired. In the domain of health, however, the good that is lost cannot be purchased in the marketplace. An individual who loses his hand cannot go out and purchase another, nor will any payment cure the cancer victim.

In the strict sense, then, we cannot make the individual whole. But could we find a monetary amount that would compensate for his loss? Frequently, the answer is no. Consider the bachelor who is killed by someone's negligence. No amount of money given to his estate will make him as well off as he was before. The appropriate test of whether he is made whole is whether he would have accepted death in return for the amount that would be paid to his estate. In most instances, we imagine the answer would be negative.

Even setting these problems aside, paying compensation after the fact may well be inefficient. Workers who can be more or less careful around dangerous machinery, for example, are likely to be more careful if they will not be compensated for losing a limb. Looked at the other way, this implies that workers who *will* be compensated for losses *ex post* may be less careful. The inability to monitor "self-protection" perfectly thus also makes *ex post* compensation potentially inefficient.

We have argued that our normal market and legal system tends to break down when substantial health risks are imposed on a relatively large population. These are therefore precisely the situations in which the cost-benefit approach is and should be called into play. Cost-benefit analysis is typically used where our normal risk-decision processes run into difficulty. We should therefore not expect it to lead to outcomes that are as satisfactory as those that evolve when ordinary markets and private contractual trade are employed. It would even be unrealistic to expect the outcomes to be as satisfactory as many government procurement or transfer decisions, for in those decisions all the costs that are imposed on citizens come through the tax system. But we should be able to anticipate better outcomes than we would achieve by "muddling through." The ethical propriety of applying cost-benefit analysis to decisions involving risks should be no more—and no less—in question than in any other application.

Ethical Foundations of Cost-Benefit Analysis

The critical choice of a standard for public decisions is between actual consent and what we have defined as hypothetical consent—the cost-benefit criterion in the absence of required compensation. The ethical foundations of actual consent are unimpeachable, but it poses insuperable practical problems. Hypothetical consent provides an ethically acceptable and practically superior alternative. It is not perfect ethically—elemental theories of property rights would reject it outright—but it seems to be at least tenable ethically. It may sometimes engender uncompensated transfers among individuals, but we suspect that most individuals, in forming their social contracts, would accept a public decision process with this drawback in order to permit making any public decisions at all.

This accommodation—trading off ethical purity for practicality—is not a fully comfortable one, for we are left endorsing a system that is less than ideal ethically and yet not obviously highly practical. How practical the system is depends crucially on our definition of practicality. If we take it to mean the ability to make a decision that we do not know is wrong, then many decision methods are practical, and cost-benefit decisions are no more so than a variety of others. We take practicality to mean something more: that the process is *workable* but still has a strong tendency toward the appropriate decision. With this definition both actual consent and an unfettered political process are relatively impractical. We would rate the three decision processes on three criteria:

	Ethics	Practicality	Legitimacy
Actual Consent	A+	D	A
Hypothetical Consent	A−	B	Unclear
Pure Politics	B	B−	A−

While actual consent is fully ethical and therefore clearly legitimate politically, its impracticality rules it out: It is simply unworkable. Unfettered politics, on the other hand, although politically legitimated, has an unsound ethical basis: It provides no guarantee that it will seek efficiency or pay attention to general welfare. It is also impractical, not in the sense that it cannot get things done, but in the sense that it may not take advantage of the best available information. By contrast, hypothetical consent is only a bit less ethical than actual consent, but it is considerably more workable. Its practicality is a combination of being workable and of systematically considering at least some of the more important issues involved in any decision. It shows some promise of being able to get at least some decisions "right," as well as some ability to ensure that the decisions that are wrong will not be wrong by much.

We have left for future discussion the issue of the public legitimacy of the cost-benefit criterion. Obviously, we believe that it should be politically acceptable and legitimated on the basis of its claim to a reasonable ethical foundation and its relative practicality. It is apparent, however, that it has not yet attained that stature in the community at large.

Notes

1. Many critics of such free-exchange arrangements are motivated by a desire to secure greater resources for one party or another. (Frequently, for example, they seek more resources for those who accept risks to health in exchange for dollars or other material resources.) Assuming that they have sufficient power to create such a transfer, we would argue that all parties would be better off if the transfer process were divorced from the risk-valuation exchange.

2. See T. Groves, "Incentives in Teams," *Econometrica* 41 (July 1973), and E. H. Clarke, "Multipart Pricing of Public Goods," *Public Choice* (Fall 1971).

3. See Herman B. Leonard, "Elicitation of Honest Preferences for the Assignment of Individuals to Positions," *Journal of Political Economy* (June 1983).

4. If, as an illustration, the objective risk is small, but the variation of *ex post* compensation due to the random vagaries of the court system is not, the risk-minimizing compensation may be exclusively *ex ante*. See Christopher J. Zook, Francis D. Moore, and Richard J. Zeckhauser, "Catastrophic Health Insurance—A Misguided Prescription," *The Public Interest* (Winter 1981).

5. Ken Lehn, "Property Rights, Risk Sharing and Player Disability in Major League Baseball," *Journal of Law and Economics* 25, no. 2 (October 1982): 343–66.

6. See, for example, Lester Thurow, *The Zero Sum Society: Distribution and the Possibilities for Economic Change* (New York: Penguin Books, 1981).

7. See, for example, James Tobin, "On Limiting the Domain of Inequality," in *Economic Justice*, Edmund S. Phelps, ed. (Harmondsworth: Penguin Books, 1973).

8. We hope it is not merely contentious to observe that those who attack cost-benefit analysis for ignoring distributional issues rarely specify a fully articulated alternative that will obviously handle distributional considerations better.

9. Moreover, there would remain the question of whether some should be allowed to accept the high risk on a continuing voluntary basis in return for compensation. If this were not to be allowed, we would have to ask ourselves on what basis we were denying people this opportunity.

3

Poisoning the Wells

Annette Baier

Methodological Preliminaries

Morality is the culturally acquired art of selecting which harms to notice
and worry about, where the worry takes the form of bad conscience or
resentment. Were we to keep on our conscience all the harm we do, all
the risks we impose, and to resent all the harms and risks we are
subjected to, our moral energies would be, as Hume put it, "dissipated
and lost for want of a proper limited object."[1] When is a public policy
that entails death for some and risk of death for more a policy that
offends our moral standards? Which deaths, and impositions of risk of
death, are wrongful, and wrongs against those concerned? It is not
merely a question of whose lives we should save by what measures with
whose money, but whom, among those whose cooperation and whose
taxes we use, we will with good conscience kill, cause to die, or let die,
and by what measures or neglect.

Traditional moralities have evolved complex ways of selecting which
harms to focus on, which to turn into wrongs, and different moralities
turn attention on different humanly controllable dangers. But since,
until recently, our society has not embarked on many large-scale enterprises, other than war, that are known to affect security of life for large
numbers of persons in significant ways, our own inherited moral code
(or collection of codes, since ours is not a homogeneous culture) gives us
little direct guidance on the issues now facing us. Is accepting the higher
rate of disease and early death among nuclear-plant workers and among
the population living near such plants like accepting the deaths of
soldiers and some civilian war victims in wartime? Or is it more like
neglecting to do anything about the rising rate of death at the hands of
armed burglars and robbers? Or is it like not doing anything about a

If any progress has been made in the several versions this paper has gone through, it is
because of the help I received from my colleagues Robert Brandom, David Gauthier, Shelly
Kagan, Nicholas Rescher, and from Douglas MacLean.

plague, known to be spread by some human habits? We think we have a sort of rationale for exposing soldiers to death and danger in wartime. Our story is that young males are the ones who do best the vital job that carries the danger. But this can scarcely be said of the temporary workers who do the most dangerous cleanup work in nuclear plants. Their position is more like that of those who volunteer to fight in wars because no other job is open to them. It is not that they do a needed job better than others and so must be exposed to the dangers that go with a job that must be done; it is that this is the only job society offers them. The justification of the imposition of risk on them is not that that is an unavoidable occupational risk falling on those who do that vital but dangerous job better than others could. Is the fact that they "volunteer" for it sufficient justification? Is the risk they face, like the risk professional prizefighters face, justified, since in some sense it has been chosen by the victims? And can we say the same of persons who are endangered simply by living near such plants: Do they, too, *choose* to face the dangers they do?

The very fact that anyone wants philosophers to address these questions is a sign that our inherited stock of moral guides does not give us ready-made answers to them. Many of the problems are new problems; and moralities, although serving as all-purpose, fairly versatile guides, evolved for less rapid change in the human condition than we have had in the last century. What can a philosopher do to help answer the new, difficult questions? Some feel that the very recognition that different moralities focus on different harms is a reason for philosophers to attempt to step back and ask which harms any group should focus on, so that even if our own inherited moral guides did give us ready-made answers to the questions facing us, we should not trust those answers but should appeal to some first principles that justify that morality's dictates, to the extent that any of them can be justified. But the problem that arises is disagreement about those ultimate principles. Anyone who claims to know what the point of morality is—and so proposes to judge whether a particular inherited morality is a *good* selector of harms to focus on—must expect some others in the group whose policy is in question to reject that version of the point of morality.

Some utilitarian readers will have already rejected my fairly neutral Humean characterization of morality as a way of ignoring some dangers and of highlighting and coping with others, but even if one does accept that, it will still be a matter of controversy what the point is of such moral focusing devices, or blinkers, and what counts as their well or ill functioning. Rule utilitarians will see the point as the minimization of the total or of the average harm suffered, harm being equated with misery. Contractarians will have a different answer, and Kant believed that the point of morality was the progressive development of rational capacities in our species, even at the cost of war, conflict, misery, and incapacitation, suffered by the morally good as much as by the less good. Kant believed that each person should aim at his or her own perfection as a rational being, but so far as real possibility goes, he says in *Idea for a Universal History*, second thesis: "Those natural capacities which are directed to the use of reason are to be fully developed only in the race, not in the individual." Nonphilosophers, if they have any views at all about the point of morality, are as likely to disagree as are the philosophers. Many religious people take its point to be obeying or pleasing God, rather than promoting human well-being. So any assessment of a conventional morality's adequacy, and any attempt to appeal beyond it to its point, to get answers to hard questions, is bound to encounter opposition.

At this point—the realization that disagreement about meta-morals is at least as likely as disagreement about morals—some conclude that the proper reaction is to demote all these ultimate values, or opinions about what ultimately matters, to personal preferences and then at the level of social policy to maximize expected preference-satisfaction.[2] We are simply to throw the sacred values into the hopper along with every other preference, ignore differences of level among the "preferences" or "tastes" we are taking into account, and measure all of them by the amount of money the preferrer will pay to get her way, ignoring the different sort of *expression* values of different sorts typically get and simply trying to thwart as few people as possible as little as possible.[3] But such a reaction to disagreement about ultimate or sacred values is the reaction only of those whose own sacred value is utility-maximization. It would not be the reaction of the Kantian, who is quite willing to thwart mere empirical wills in the name of the progress of reason. So to resort to utility-maximization is not to get *beyond* clashing sacred values, but merely to reveal one's own sacred value.

We cannot step back from our inherited cultural blinkers, including our moral ones, to examine those blinkers with an unblinkered gaze. At most, we can turn our blinkered gaze on one another's blinkers and listen to others' version of our own blinkers and their judgment of the effect of those blinkers. Even our way of doing this, of studying other cultures or criticizing our own, will itself owe a lot to inherited traditions and practices and will not itself be free of cultural bias. So I do not see my role as philosopher to be to make any pretense of stepping outside the conventional morality in which I was reared to examine its "rational" credentials, to judge it by external standards, or to replace it by something better. I see my role rather to be to exploit that morality's own potential for self-consciousness and development, aware that it may have multiple potential so that others in the same tradition may go in different ways, and aware also that there are other traditions like mine with some techniques for recognizing, studying, learning from, communicating with, nondestructively disagreeing with, and sometimes coming into agreement with those inside and outside that tradition.

I began by agreeing with Hume that concern for human well-being needs a proper limited object and suggested that moralities typically provide their followers with just that. Hume also has a version of what goods are furthered by the part of our morality that imposes obligations and recognizes rights. He says that such a scheme of rights and obligations is a cooperative social venture: "By the conjunction of forces, our power is augmented: By the partition of employments our ability increases: By mutual succor we are less expos'd to fortune and accidents. . . . Tis by this additional *force, ability* and *security* that society becomes advantageous."[4] Now, this verdict on what goods socially enforced obligations and rights provide is one that might be disputed, and one that is a result of turning on a social scheme or morality a kind of reflection made possible by the social scheme itself: It is not the judgment of an impartial spectator, but of a reflective participant. Other reflective participants might not agree that power, ability, and security are what our morality promotes. I shall not defend this finding of the formal goods morality promotes; rather, I shall try to use it to do that stretching of the blinkers that seems needed to get an answer to the question of which policy-related deaths and impositions of risk we should have on our consciences. Hume's version of what goods morality promotes is promising for this purpose, since it is not a tendentious claim about the ultimate goal, but a possibly less tendentious analysis of the formal goods that are promoted. It leaves open what sort of power we want, what kind of abilities we wish to increase, what we want made secure. It is not an attempt to discern ultimate values, but it does look beyond the immediate judgment of right and wrong. That much stretching of our moral blinkers, widening our focus, may be enough for us to see when and why we may, in pursuit of our public policies, impose risk of death on our fellows and successors.

Hume applied his thesis that our moral constraints involve a cooperative conjunction of forces, partition of employments, and mutual succor, for the sake of increased power, ability, and security, largely to us as proprietors, concerned to have powers to appropriate, ability to get and own varied sorts of things, and to be secure in our ownership. I shall try to use these categories, as he scarcely did, to the morality of life and death dealing, to the protection morality gives to our concern to have power and ability to live a life of normal length and to do so with security of life.

Individual Rights and What Supplements Them

The social schemes Hume looks at—what he calls the "artifices" of property, gift, barter, promise, and government—all create (or enable the transfer of) rights and impose obligations. One of the commonest ways in which moralities select which humanly controllable harms to treat as wrongs is by the recognition of individual rights in some area, such as security of life, where danger lurks. Such rights are protection against danger from other persons through their assault or their neglect. The prohibition of murder is the most obvious way in which we cooperate to reduce insecurity of life. But lists of rights are fairly crude moral guides, since rights sometimes clash, and then we need some way of selecting which rights are the more important, or which of the interests those rights protect are the more vital. Nor is it only when one recognized right clashes with another that it may be overridden.[5] Sometimes it seems to be overridden by a vital interest that is protected not only by a recognition of individual rights, but also in other ways.

J. S. Mill discusses this possibility. After arguing that certain vital interests of persons (security of life, property, contractual agreement) ought to be given a special moral status—namely, that of recognized and protected individual *rights*—he goes on to say that although, as a class, these interests or "social utilities" are vastly more important and so more absolute and imperative than other parts of morality or of social efficiency, nevertheless in particular emergencies one justifiably puts aside these more "absolute" demands. "Thus, to save a life, it may not only be allowable, but a duty to steal or take by force the necessary food or medicine, or to kidnap and compel to officiate the only qualified medical practitioner."[6] The case Mill takes here is a controversial one, and his own position is interestingly complex. It is not, on the face of it, a case in which one recognized right clashes with others, since presumably the injured man whose life we try to save (by stealing and kidnapping what is needed to save it) does not have a recognized *right* to be rescued. He has a right not to be attacked, but in most communities no recognized right to rescue if attacked or to rescue if injured in an accident. We do not encourage persons to feel that their rights have been violated if they are not offered aid in such circumstances. (If they are paid-up members of the A.A.A., or some other such organization, they may of course have rights to aid from specific persons.) Presumably, Mill's version of "social utility" is to decide whether or not the interest each person has in assurance of receiving lifesaving assistance is sufficiently "vital" for this class of case to give rise to a recognized right to aid. Although formally this case does seem to satisfy Mill's criterion for a right and a correlative duty of justice—there is an "assignable individual" who is harmed if some moral duty is neglected—nothing that he says suggests that he believed that we should recognize an individual right to rescue. Any assistance a person gets in such emergencies will be, for Mill, given to satisfy those requirements of morality that are not duties of justice, that is, duties to respect recognized rights. Nevertheless, the moral requirement to rescue is to override the normal requirements of respect for rights of property and rights to liberty, presumably because it is part of that most vital interest, the interest in security of life, which the foremost of recognized rights partially protects.

Both the recognition of the right not to be assaulted and the expectation of rescue efforts contribute to what we can call a certain climate of life insofar as security of life is concerned. The victims of the nonrecognition of such a right or the disappointment of this expectation would not be merely those killed or injured by assault from others, or left to die unrescued, but all persons whose lives are at risk in these circumstances, whose security of life is thereby lessened. To quote Thomas Hobbes: "For as the nature of foule weather lyeth not in a showre or two of rain, but in an inclination thereto of many days together; so the nature of war consisteth not in the actuall fighting;. but in the known disposition thereto during all the time there is not assurance to the contrary."[7] We want, as Hobbes emphasized, not merely goods, but the assurance of getting and keeping them. Even in a Hobbesian state of nature, a lucky person who was not deprived of life by the absence of established rules, but who survived to old age, would have been deprived of security of life, and so of most enjoyments. He will have lacked what Hobbes calls "power" and have had no opportunity for "glorying," unless it be a limited case of glorying, say in his proven ability to live a precarious, powerless, and dangerous life.

Mill, who was no adventurer, judged that "security no human being can possibly do without; on it we depend for all our immunity from evil and for the whole value of all and every good, beyond the passing moment, since nothing but the gratification of the instant could be of any worth to us if we could be deprived of everything the next instant by whoever was momentarily stronger than ourselves."[8] Even if no individual *right* to rescue, or to safety in the workplace, in public transport, or in consumer goods is recognized, the reasonable expectation that such rescue measures will be taken and such safety standards observed contributes to the security climate of life in which we live. Nonviolence, general public safety, and the will to rescue are public goods. Individuals may die unrescued and die of accidents in the workplace although these goods *are* provided, but if they are not provided, the victims are not merely those who die through the absence of such services, but all those who live in fear of this happening to them.

Leaving aside for the moment the question of whose responsibility it is to see that they are provided, I want at this point to consider whether we should speak of *rights* to such public services. Are my rights violated if I live in a community without proper police protection, without ambulance services or rescue services, and am thereby deprived of a decent climate of life as regards security of life? Should we allow the concept of a right to cover rights to social climates of various sorts? If we were to, then we could construe Mill's case as a clash between rights— between the individual's property rights (and right to the maintenance of a social climate of respect for property) and the right of the injured man, and others, to a climate of life in which we have assurance that an attempt will be made to rescue us when we need to be rescued. If we say we have a *right* to these public services, then Mill's case becomes a clash of rights, although the injured man still has no right to be rescued—only a right to normal rescue attempts. Would it be wise to stretch the concept of a right to include the provision of such social-climate controllers as rescue services (and the special rights of rescuers) if we agree with Mill about the moral priority of providing them?

The pressure to say yes comes from a worry about the complexity—perhaps the incoherence—of Mill's unrevised position. Can we both recognize rights as "more absolute" protectors of vital interests that we all have and also allow the overriding of those right? And if we can override some of them for the sake of what another of them protects—namely, security of life—why not incorporate in the "right/(or rights?) to life" everything that a person is encouraged to expect to be done to protect her security of life, both the enforced prohibition of murder and the observation of safety standards and the provision of rescue services? I shall consider a good and a bad reason for rejecting this attempt to tidy up Mill's position by letting all the highest-priority moral requirements generate rights, some of them rights to a "share" in a public good and to the enjoyment of a certain climate of life.

The good reason to reject this tidying up is the impossibility of fixing the "assignable individuals" who are the main victims of any violation of a hypothetical right to a certain degree of security of life, and also of deciding who the violators are. The usefulness of the concept of a right, as Mill saw, lay in its being a quick way to determine both the wronged and the wrongdoers. But when we as a community have failed to provide ourselves with any ambulance system, it is not clear—unless some official or authority is charged with this duty—*who* has failed, nor is it clear which accident victims would have lived had there been an adequate service. All who live in fear of dying unaided are the victims of the bad social climate, but there is no way of saying who those are on whom it actually rains—those who would have been kept dry had we the proper climate control. Rights without clear victims or clear violators are as much pseudorights as are rights without remedies. So I think it better to leave Mill's views unrevised. Untidiness is better than misleading surface tidiness. What we must say is that we ought to have a certain climate of life, that this "ought" has high moral priority, but not that we have a right to this good. Only when there *are* assigned responsibilities for tasks concerned with ensuring the required climate of life will it make sense to speak of the public's right to the proper meeting of these responsibilities, and only when those responsibilities are fairly specific will there be any possibility of making good the claim that a given individual is a particular victim of the violation of the public's right so that some compensation is due.

The bad reason that one might give—that some do give—for rejecting the idea of a right to a climate of life is connected with this assignment of responsibilities. Some believe that the only genuine rights are those that impose on others negative duties of refraining from doing something or other, and that rights cannot impose unconsented-to positive duties to take some definite action on another's behalf.[9] If we are to have rescue services and safety standards, someone has to provide and administer them, and so a claimed right to such things may appear, like the United Nations "human right" to paid vacations, a pseudoright quite different from real rights like the right not to be robbed or assaulted. We can respect the latter rights simply by inhibiting our aggressive impulses, but to respect the hypothetical right to paid vacations or "good Samaritan" services, inhibition is not enough: Someone has to do something, to spend time and effort. Positive pseudorights are costly; negative real rights cost only the inhibition of evil, aggressive impulses.

That is perhaps a parody of the bad reason. There are places in Mill's writings where he might seem to give it some weight. After making room for recognition of rights as recognition of vital interests of persons, he says:

> Now it is these moralities which primarily compose the obligations of justice. The most marked cases of injustice, and those which give tone to the feeling of repugnance which characterizes the sentiment, are acts of wrongful aggression or wrongful exercise of power over someone; next are those which consist in wrongfully withholding from him something which is his due—in both cases inflicting on him a positive hurt either in the form of direct suffering or of the privation of some good which he had some ground, either of a physical or social kind, for counting on.[10]

Mill's attempt in this passage to distinguish active "aggressive" infliction of a hurt from a more passive infliction of a hurt by withholding something is problematic. "Withholding" is intentional nonsupplying, so Mill's distinction is not that between acting in some matter and failing to attend at all to that matter. I do not "withhold" care from those needy persons whom I have never bothered to notice or find out about, but I do withhold from the beggar I refuse. Mill is not succumbing to the liberal temptation to construe all genuine rights as "negative" rights and all of the core moral rules as prohibitions; but he does seem to want to make the *most important* rights "negative" ones, perhaps rights not to be harmed, and the *most serious* wrongs wrongings by "doings," while the less serious wrongs are wrongings by withholding, violations of lesser more "positive" rights, perhaps rights to be benefited. I shall give reasons for doubting that this distinction can be defended when it is thought to rest on the active/less active, positive/negative, or harm/no-benefit distinctions. As Mill himself says of his top-priority moral demand and correlative individual right—namely, that others not assault us—it is "the claim we have on our fellow creatures to join in making safe for us the very groundwork of our existence." It is a claim to mutual succor, that they *join in making safe*, not merely a claim that they desist from assault. To prevent all "inflictings of hurt," whether by doing or refraining, taking or withholding, persons must join in a cooperative scheme. To thus join is not merely to obey the main normative demand, whether it is phrased as a prohibition or a positive requirement, but also to obey related demands and to contribute to the enforcement costs that any such demand involves.

Obligations and What Supports Them

To think that some part of morality—the respect for rights—is both more stringent and more easily justified than the rest because it demands of each person no more than the "refraining" from certain "harmful" acts, such as murder, while other less easily justified moral demands impose on us "positive" duties or obligations, such as aid to the injured, is to make at least one of three mistakes. The first is the mistake of ignoring the positive cooperative contribution each person makes to the enforcement of *any* social or moral demand, whether it is the prohibition of assault or the requirement of parental care. The "cost" of a prohibition of murder is not merely the frustration of murderous impulses in those subject to them, but also the "training" costs on those educated so as to inhibit, repress, or sublimate aggression, the efforts of the educators, the social costs of getting them to provide such education, and all the enforcement costs (in taxation, effort, and inflicted pain) involved in having police, courts, and prisons, so that violators of the requirement be detected, tried, and punished.

This is parallel to the sorts of costs involved in a "positive" requirement such as parental care: The cost here is not merely in the efforts of parents, but in all the educational, propaganda, and enforcement machinery needed to get them to do their perceived duty. The first mistake, then, is to ignore the educational and enforcement costs that *any* moral requirement involves, costs that always demand active cooperation by large numbers of persons and "positive" contributions by all members of society. As both Hume and Mill emphasize, morality is a cooperative scheme: For Hume it is a "conjunction of forces," and for Mill it is a "joining to make safe the very groundwork of our existence." The joining and conjoining include bearing our share of enforcement and training costs.

The second mistake typically made by those who see our clearest and most stringent duties to be to *refrain* from certain active "harmings" is to let too much weight rest on the fact that some moral requirements typically get expressed in a negative way, such as "don't kill, don't steal," whereas others get expressed in a positive way, such as "obey legitimate authorities, keep contracts, care for your children." What is the significance of this surface difference between moral requirements? Is it merely surface?[11]

We can, it seems, force all moral requirements into a negative form (to get all in a positive form is harder): "Don't break promises, don't disobey governments, don't neglect your children." But perhaps these are all double negatives, so the contrast has not been lost. Is not breaking failing to keep, disobeying failing to obey, neglecting failing to take care of? Yes, and so is stealing failure to respect property rights. It seems that our effort at transformation succeeds in transforming some surface negatives into positives, but not yet in destroying the contrast unless we can construe "don't kill" as equivalent to something like "show respect for the right to life," as "don't steal" might become "show respect for property rights."

Can we do this? I think not. The "right to life" is much vaguer than the wrong of manslaughter. We have no clear conception of what "the right to life" is supposed to guarantee one, as we do have a clear idea of what are our property rights, contractual rights, duties as parents, duties as citizens. We have relatively clear ideas about all of these because all these rights and obligations are specified in determinate law-backed social artifices, as Hume called them. We need conventions to know what counts as stealing, contract breaking, treason, or failure to do one's parental duty, but we seem to have and need no social artifice to tell us what counts as killing.[12] This would give "don't kill" a special place among moral requirements, special in its independence of social artifice rather than in any pure negativity.

But of course it is not "don't kill" that is our rule. "Don't dispossess" would be an equally artifice-independent rule, were we to accept it, and so would be "don't change your expressed mind," or "obey the powerful." But our moral prohibitions are of murder, stealing, promise-breaking, disobedience to legitimate authorities, not of killing, dispossessing, disappointing aroused expectations, or disobedience. It is murder and manslaughter, not killing, that we prohibit, and to distinguish murder from execution or warfare we need to appeal to powers and duties that are as "artificial" and as culture-relative as property rights. Behind "don't steal" lie the complex property rules of a society; similarly behind "don't murder" lie complex rules telling one what counts as murder. The instructions we need to give and the laws and moral rules we need to recognize will be framed in the terms our way of life has forged.

Most human ways of life have given a fairly regular and prominent place to killing, whether in societies of hunters and fishers or of farmers and soldiers, or in industrial societies like ours in which the meat industry, the military, and the weapons industry are central parts of our economy. Restrictions on killing, and segregation of the contexts where killing is encouraged and where it is forbidden, have been essential in all human societies that depend, as most have done, on some sort of death dealing for the very possibility of their way of life. The crucial piece of moral knowledge in any human society, and one that war veterans may find very difficult to acquire, is knowing which times and places are the times and places to kill. Equally central in most societies is knowing when, where, and with whom to have sexual relations, and in both cases we have special words for the forbidden varieties: murder, assassination, manslaughter; rape, sodomy, fornication, adultery, incest. We also have some words for the allowed or encouraged kinds: self-defense, execution, combat, "wasting"; courtship, marital love. Precise norms that express our complex attitudes in these matters usually need to employ such special words. Our rule is not "do not kill," but rather "do not commit murder or manslaughter," where it takes an institutional and cultural context for us to know when killing, even of human beings, is and is not murder or manslaughter, just as it takes such culture-specific knowledge to tell adultery, incest, fornication, or even rape apart from allowed sexual relations.

If our moral requirements about killing are indeed intended to "make safe the very groundwork of our existence," then we must suppose that "we" are a somewhat exclusive set, and that "our" existence does not include the existence of members of enemy nations, or of human fetuses, or of animals, or of those found guilty of capital crimes. Our social and moral attitudes to the deliberate termination of a human life are as complex and baroque as are our attitudes to sex. Behind the short prohibition "thou shalt not kill" lie as many tacitly understood qualifications and cultural and legal discriminations as lie behind "thou shalt not love thy neighbor's wife." Just as the latter presupposes determinate institutions of marriage, determining individual marital rights, so "thou shalt not murder" presupposes a complex set of culturally specified rights, powers, and prerogatives.

Far from giving us some sort of minimal, thin version of the right, as liberals would have us believe, any popular version of a short set[13] of moral *"don'ts"*, such as "don't kill, don't steal, don't break promises, don't coerce (unless you are an official)," brings with it very rich cultural baggage, if it is to have any content at all.[14] Either it is a purely formal moral code, not yet prohibiting or enjoining anything, or else the form gets a determinate filling, in which case we are committed not merely to these "negative" rules, but to the rules of the background institutions and ways of life that supply the determinate content to these prohibitions. Their negative form, then, is simply an indication that the behavior they regulate is complexly organized, so that lines have to be drawn, limitations made clear, and the onus of proof laid. All of these apparently simple negatives can be rephrased in a less simple and less purely negative form this way: You may kill these, but not those; you may take and keep these, but not those; you may change your mind in these circumstances, but not in those; you may limit the options of others in these ways, but not in those. The simple negative formulation is merely the tip of the full normative iceberg.

The third error that pushes some to see negative rights to various sorts of "noninterference" as more basic than any rights whose respect requires some activity and effort is that of thinking that if we "leave people alone" we cannot harm them, so the basic rights are rights not to be harmed by others, while the more dubious rights are rights to be benefited by them; of thinking that the basic obligations are obligations not to harm, and the more dubious obligations—ones we need special devices like contract to take on—are obligations to confer benefits. On such a view, "don't murder" tells us not to harm another, whereas "rescue the perishing" seems to require that we do others a good turn, that we go out of our way to assist them. Such duties seem too strenuous, whereas refraining from murder takes no calories at all.

Now, it is a strenuous business to train persons so that they can and do inhibit violent impulses, no less strenuous a business than to bring them up to spontaneously offer aid to the injured. It just isn't true that helping another always costs more than not harming, especially if we include the costs of training. (And it *may* cost the Mafia real dollars to refrain from wiping out those who threaten their profits.) But what this third mistake primarily concerns is not cost to the agent so much as cost to the patient, what counts as harming and helping another. It is never easy to say where not harming ends and helping begins. Some, such as Robert Nozick and David Gauthier, want to make the benchmark relative to which one decides the matter the well-being of the "patient" without any interaction with the agent.[15] If his situation is improved by the interaction, we have benefited him by it; if it is worsened, we have harmed him. But this choice of benchmark prejudges moral issues. If it is used to support the claim that our basic moral obligation is not to harm, it presupposes that there is no obligation to join with others, that reclusiveness is morally unobjectionable, even if our nonjoining ruins the enterprise for those who join. For some pipings and some dances, "I have piped unto you and you have not danced" may be moral condemnation, but the Nozick-Gauthier position makes that impossible, unless one had contracted to dance if piped to.

It is easiest to see the unacceptability of a noninteraction benchmark if we consider its implications for duties of child care. Since without interaction, a newborn child would die, any interacting adult who does not simply maim or torture the child confers a benefit by the noninteraction benchmark. The child is not harmed by anyone (parents, let us say) who leaves it alone. Unless one has contracted with the child or someone else to care for it, there is no duty to do so if duties are duties not to harm.

One might try to see carrying to term and giving birth as a prior interaction, so that for the mother the question would become not "interaction or no interaction?" but "continuation or cessation of interaction?" However, this would at best generate maternal not paternal obligations (which may be what the "no interaction without contract" theorists hope to show). It would generate these obligations only if prior unconsented-to interaction could be construed as implicit promise of continued interaction, which seems absurd. Whatever pregnancy is, it is not a promise. So the outcome is that no one is obligated to care for the child, and it must hope that someone will do it a good turn. This methodological solipsism in ethics, espoused by Gauthier and by Nozick, seems to be both question-begging and ultimately self-destructive. If there is no harm done to a newborn child by simply leaving it alone, and there is no duty to benefit it, then by adopting the benchmark of no interaction to determine wrongful harming, we are opting for a morality that cannot ensure its own continuation, since it condones the letting die of new members of the moral community.

Defenders of this version of morality typically want to ward off the sort of objection I have raised by claiming that they have described a "core" morality that deals with relationships between human adults, and that this would need supplementation to cover relationships with children, the infirm, the aged, animals, and any others who might get into the moral picture. Although I do think that there is a "core" morality that concerns relations between those who have, will have, or had obligations, as well as being ones to whom obligations are owed, I see no good reason within that core to single out adult-adult relations as especially central. Our relations to those who are becoming moral agents and to those who have been such agents are as important as any others. In any case, no sharp line divides the adolescent from the adult, the competent adult from the infirm aged person, so we need a morality that does not force us first to classify persons as competent adult or not before we know how to deal with them.

It is hard to avoid the suspicion that this liberal version of morality is a morality for males, parasitic upon an unacknowledged, quite different morality for females.[16] Both the hidden costs of training persons to be good capitalists who sublimate violence, respect property, and keep contracts and the implicit exceptions from the "no duty to benefit" principle fall upon the women. As Nancy Chodorow has acutely pointed out, the women's duty includes the training of daughters willing to continue with this version of mothering, so that the double standard, if that is indeed what it is, becomes self-perpetuating: Women make one another accomplices in the system.[17]

I have thus far argued against bad reasons for rejecting a right to public goods, such as a climate of life that gives security of life against the dangers of child neglect, assault, dying in accidents without any rescue attempts, dying from unsafe conditions on roads and in the workplace. These bad reasons would, if accepted, be reasons not merely for rejecting the right, but for demoting the obligation to help supply such goods. I have allowed that there may be good enough reasons not to speak of a right to many of the services that protect security of life, but, with Mill, I argued that we can still give high moral priority to the duties to support and help supply such services. Rights require not merely the complementary obligations not to violate them, but the supplementary obligations to support the institutions that train persons to be responsible moral agents who respect rights and seriously recognize duties; and all prohibitions need the support of the possibly strenuous doing of related duties. Such security of life as we enjoy has been provided not merely by those who obey the criminal law prohibiting murder, but by all those who do their duty as law enforcers, as moral educators, by those who protect the young, the injured, and the aged from neglect, and prepare others to do the same, and by those who observe or enforce safety standards and train others to do the same. A complex network of some rights and many more obligations has given us such security of life as we have enjoyed until now. How can this scheme be adapted to cope with new sources of danger? Is there in the existing scheme some implicit principle of selection of which harms to give attention to, which can help us get such conservative guidance? I turn now to that question.

Fortune, Accidents, and Illwill

Hume's cited version of the point of our rights and obligations emphasizes their role in giving us, through mutual succor, security against
fortune and accidents, but the details of his account make quite clear that
some of the relevant misfortunes and accidents are at the hands of our
fellows. It is indeed because the goods we would like to keep can be
"ravish'd from us" by others that Hume's first artifice—that of property—is seen to be necessary. Although later artifices, such as contract
and government, make it possible for people to undertake such cooperative protections against nature, fate, and accident as draining meadows
and improving harbors, the first artifice protects people against dangers
from one another. This seems to apply to our social and legal reaction to
danger to life as well as danger to possessions. We first prohibit assault
and pay for the supportive institutions that requires, then think about
public hygiene, health service, ambulance services. Is this our choice
because this is the most efficient use of our social resources, because we
save more lives more cheaply by a prohibition on assault than by other
possible measures? Or is it salience that selects this measure? Is assault
simply a more obvious danger to life than are other dangers? Although it
will be a salient danger in groups who live by assaulting other living
things, neither salience nor perceived efficiency is enough to explain the
near universality and complete uncontroversiality of socially enforced
prohibitions of civilian assault.

   If, starting from a blank tablet, legislators asked themselves, "What
can we do and how best can we allocate resources to reduce risk to life
across the board?" would the prohibition of, or even the required
compensation for, assault be the obvious first move?[18] That would
depend perhaps on the psychology of the population and their access to
means to satisfy their perceived needs. If they were not quarrelsome by
nature, and if they did not need physically to worst a human competitor
to get what they needed or wanted, a law forbidding what is known to
be the poisoning of the wells (by careless personal habits perhaps) might
have a much higher life-preserving effect than a law against murder,
even in a society of hunters accustomed to deliberately killing animals
and of warriors accustomed to killing human enemies. Yet it seems to
have been clear, not merely to Hobbes and Mill, but to most human
societies, that the most vital of our interests in the area of security of life
is security against malicious attack. Why? If I am to die because of what
others do, should I prefer to die of infection because my fellows
defecated thoughtlessly in the wells, than because one of them knifed
me with malicious intent? Why, as legislators, have we first prohibited
murder and only later worried about the knowing or unknowing poisoning of our wells? Is it merely because we were first hunters and only
later deliberate poisoners of animals, so that restrictions on assault
preceded restrictions on poisoning?

Rousseau pointed out that "the nature of things does not madden us, only illwill does," and our laws reflect what maddens us rather than what merely distresses us. Perhaps Rousseau should have allowed that negligence as well as obvious illwill can madden us, and that all the range of degrees of illwill, from thoughtlessness to malice, need not madden the victims, but can produce the suppressed rage that is resentment. The criminal law prohibits the sort of harming of others that, whether or not it is prohibited, the victims resent, and resent because it displays illwill. Once prohibited, we call such harming with intent "injuring," or "violating a right," thereby implicitly assimilating *all* the prohibited harmings to violent assault, to intent to inflict bodily injury. Security of life is partially protected by the prohibition of assault—itself part of what is correlative to "the right of life"—and other duties protect other equally complex rights, such as security or possession (property rights), security of contract, and security of liberty (noncoercion) in some areas of life.

In all these cases, as with security of life, the recognition of the right amounts only to partial protection—protection only from threats from certain sources. A person can have security of property lessened by inflation and depression as well as by likelihood of theft, can have security of contract threatened by acts of God as well as by breach of contract, and can have security of liberty threatened by need and by obligations as well as by any coercion by private or public agents. The threats we are protected against by these rights and recognized obligations are threats stemming from what can be seen as the absence of good will in others. Thus illwill includes not merely aiming at harming another (the evil eye), but also ignoring the interests of others, or knowingly sacrificing vital interests of theirs to lesser interests of one's own (turning a blind eye).

Intentionally killing another who has not asked to be so killed, with any motive other than self-defense, clearly exhibits illwill. Defecating in the wells need not. It could be an ignorant endangering of lives, and the ignorance need not be culpable if attention had not been drawn to the effects of such action. Only children need to have attention drawn to the effects of stabbing and battering. Even before such actions are explicitly prohibited, an adult knows what their effects normally are. It does not take social emphasis for these ill effects to be known, whereas, for poisoning, some "labeling" by society is needed. Before that labeling occurs there can be ignorant poisoning, and the ignorance need not be culpable. Even when the poison label has been attached—that is, when there is common knowledge of the lethal effects—and when a person shares in that knowledge, he may ignore or forget or not attend to that knowledge. There is culpable ignoring as well as culpable ignorance. There can be nonculpable ignoring, but it is harder to excuse one's action by the claim, "I forgot that the effects could be so bad," than by the claim, "I didn't know they were so bad," even when the claim is true. Whether ignoring what one knows is or is not culpable will depend on whether what one ignored was highlighted common knowledge, and whether, when it is special, esoteric knowledge, one is an expert in that field of knowledge.

What a society invests in making criminal, then, depends not merely on what knowledge of dangerous effects of actions exists somewhere in that society, but on how widely that knowledge is disseminated, on how much that danger has been highlighted, and so on what can reasonably be construed as harming with illwill, with knowledge that one is neglecting the interests of others affected by one's action. Not merely the criminal law's selection of harmings to focus on, but the selection made by other agencies—regulatory, educational, and service—depends on available knowledge, on its commonness, and on what consequently appears as illwill if done or left undone. It is now common knowledge that people are poisoned by what steel mills and automobile exhaust put into the atmosphere and by what many factories and farms put into rivers, seas, and soil. Despite vigorous disagreements, there is a large body of common knowledge about radiation dangers, both from medical diagnostic procedures and from nuclear plants, military and nonmilitary. We cannot, then, as officials and as private agents ignore such dangers without being guilty of illwill. If our morality is to adapt itself to our new common knowledge, we must update our registry of poisons and records of poisoners. We must recognize the new instrumentalities of poisoning as such.

I see no reason why those who use these lethal methods of going about their business, who knowingly impose on others significant risk of death by radiation-related cancers—by poisoning from slow-seeping chemical wastes, from poisons emitted into air and water—should not be dealt with in the same way and in the same place as we deal with those who, for gain, send poisoned chocolates to their elderly relatives. Once there, their defenders may try to invoke the doctrine of double effect to get them off the hook, but it will take that dubious doctrine to show any relevant difference. And even that doctrine may not succeed in distinguishing the two cases. Just as the steel-mill owner can claim that she deplores the deaths her mills cause, that she wishes her profit-making did not require such lethal means, and that she is not relying on the deaths, as such, to get her profits, so the chocolate-sender can claim that he regrets the need to adopt this means to come into his inheritance and relies for his success not on the death as such, but simply on the property transfer. Were the laws of inheritance changed so that the mere age of his aunt sufficed for that wanted transfer, he would gladly have spared his aunt. The honors for illwill seem equal.

Consent to Risk

Some risks that avoidably or unavoidably are imposed by those with power to do so are not escapable by those on whom they are imposed, although those affected may have some control over their relative magnitude. Declaring war imposes risk of death on members of the armed forces and risk of death by bombing or invasion on civilians. Democratic processes are supposed to amount to some sort of consent to such risk impositions on the part of legitimate authorities acting constitutionally, and also to empower them to decide which escapable risks they will impose on people and which imposition of such risks by private agents they will tolerate. I shall discuss these escapable risks, where, by not "escaping," a person may be thought to have consented to bear the risk.

Some people choose to play Russian roulette, some enjoy watching, and yet others make a living by catering to such tastes. Some choose dangerous sports—choose to ski, box, play football—some enjoy watching, and yet others profit from catering to these tastes for first- or second-hand thrills. Some choose work in coal mines, accepting the risk in return for a coal miner's wage, although few want to watch. Most of us incur significant risk of death on the roads in return for convenient travel. Since some choose high risk for the thrill and most choose some risk-involving package deals, what is ever wrong with providing people with the opportunity to "buy risk," or to accept it as a free gift? Is that what the owner of a nuclear-power plant or a dangerous coal mine does—namely, give residents and workers the option of accepting a risk, or risk package, or else rejecting that offer?

The morality we have inherited puts considerable weight on the difference between self-imposed harm or danger and danger we have not chosen to face. We are on the watch for paternalism—for those who would deprive us of the right to injure or risk injuring ourselves. Does this respect for individual choice and the right to self-injury require us to tolerate or even encourage the provision of opportunities for new forms of risk-taking, even perhaps to welcome a widening of the range of available risks to life that individuals may decide to bear?

We must make some distinctions to help us think about this hard topic. The first is the distinction between *creating* an opportunity for risking life and exploiting an opportunity already there. Nature and normal life provide us with plenty of opportunities to indulge any taste we have for life-risking thrills. The person who runs a ski resort gets her profits not from enabling persons to take the risks that only such as she make available, but from making the skiing, which could go on without the likes of her, more attractive by amenities of various sorts, including perhaps safety measures and rescue services. It would be a bad joke to see nuclear plants as making it more convenient for people to take radiation risks for whatever reasons they may have to take them. The coal-mine owner and the nuclear-plant owner create the dangers they "offer" others; they do not merely facilitate or enhance dangerous activities that are already available. Other things being equal, creating new dangers is worse than enticing persons to take naturally available risks.

The second distinction is between dangers incurred in work, and travel to work, and dangers incurred in leisure activities. What known dangers people incur in their leisure activities are chosen in a stronger sense than are those they incur in the workplace. As Aristotle would put it, the coal miner may take that job "out of compulsion," even when he is not, like a member of a chain gang, literally coerced into working there. Few go down into coal mines for fun. What we do for fun is more freely chosen than what we decide to do to make a living, even when, as always, we have *some* choice in that matter (we can turn to theft if all else fails). Other things being equal, acknowledged risks in the workplace are harder to justify than acknowledged risks in the adult playgrounds.

Third, we need to draw a distinction not merely between human-created and naturally available risks, but between degrees of human contrivance in gearing that risk (natural or humanly created) to a particular activity that there is frequent reason (other than desire for risk) for people to perform. The risk of death incurred by skiing in avalanche conditions or on very steep slopes is intrinsic to the activity; it is not engineered by anyone. Anyone who decides that she must bear that risk, to get quickly in some emergency from or to some inaccessible place, faces a risk that skiing carries. Anyone who decides to undergo frequent diagnostic X-rays faces the risk that carries. But those who decide to face risk in coal mines decide to take a risk that someone has first contrived and then decided not to remove. Those who decide to remain residents of an area where a nuclear plant has been built decide to take a risk someone else has decided to attach to residence there. Other things being equal, enabling persons to weigh the risks against the benefits of some activity and choose for themselves is suspect when one has contrived the risks, *made* the beneficial activity a risky one.

Fourth, and relatively uncontroversially, we should distinguish those new risks attached to some activity that are accompanied by some newly attached benefit from those newly attached risks that are not accompanied by any attached compensation. Problems arise, however, both about how much and what sort of benefit is a fair return for added risk to life and also in distinguishing added benefit from what it is added to. The worker offered a certain package of wages plus fringe benefits by an employer for dangerous work may be told that some of the money, or some of the rest of the package, is compensation for the risk to life the job carries, and that this would not be offered if the job did not carry this risk to life. How can the potential employee test this claim? If there are other employees in the same plant doing the "same" work but without the danger and who are being paid less, she can verify the claim that *some* return is made for willingness to bear risk. But if *all* the work in that plant—say, a nuclear plant—is unsafe, what does the claim come to? And even if, in other fields such as coal mining, we can compare wages in relatively safe and relatively unsafe mines and can confirm the claim of those running the unsafe mines that they are offering more—so are offering compensation for added risk—we cannot tell if they are offering *enough*. They may be offering enough to attract workers, but that may be because of monopoly, or because unemployment is high and times are hard, and a worker must take what she can get. If times are hard enough, workers will accept the deal at the unsafe mine even if no more is paid there than at the safe mine. It might be stipulated that fair compensation is whatever difference there would be, in perfect market conditions, between what is offered at the less safe and the safer mine if both are to get workers; but how, in imperfect market conditions, can one tell what that is? This distinction between added risk with and without adequate compensation may be as unusable as it is uncontroversial.

Fifth, we need to distinguish those risk-plus-benefit "offers" that can improve the choice situation of some without worsening the situation of others from those where what to one person is a welcome offer is to others a threat. When a community has a nuclear plant built close to it and at the same time gets some community benefits, perhaps parks and concert halls as well as new job openings, some may welcome it and be pleased to have the choice of leaving the area or staying to enjoy the benefits and bear the risks. Others may interpret that offer as a threat: "Leave, or else put up with this." One cannot determine from the actual choice made by persons in this situation whether or not having that choice improved their lot. Some who are threatened may stay; some who welcomed the choice may in the end decide not to accept the "offer." Since the importance people put on risk to life varies, there will probably be both sorts of persons in any place where such plants are built.

By contrast, some risk-benefit offers can be directed only at those who will not find them to be threats. A Russian roulette parlor, unless it is the only employer in town, can restrict the main effects of its offer to interested parties. But in a case where what is "offered" is a risk to life through dangerous air, water, soil, or street violence, combined with some benefits (perhaps lowered taxes and rates), we cannot prevent the welcome opportunity for some being also the unwelcome change of opportunity for others. Should we count heads, or should we adopt a Pareto principle here: not improving anyone's choice situation unless we do not thereby worsen another's? Such veto power by affected individuals over any enterprise that reduces overall security of life, or increases its cost, would surely be unworkable, unless we could agree on some level of overall risk to life above which this power of veto is to come into force. But our moral tradition places a strong onus of justification on those who increase public insecurity of life. We do not vote on whether or not to repeal the law prohibiting assault and violence or that making old-style poisoning illegal. We invest in such criminal laws, however many people might welcome the option of being free of both the prohibitions and the protection they provide, and only anarchists are worried by the paternalism we thereby show to such people. So counting heads isn't appropriate. Some form of enforced safety standards seems more in the spirit of the tradition I am trying to update.

None of these morally relevant differences between sorts of risk-increasings decide the hard questions for us.[19] But the deliberation that leads up to the decisions on those hard cases should not ignore those distinctions. Not merely are there different kinds of costs and different kinds of benefits, but there are different ways in which the costs and the benefits get combined with one another, and different ways to decide who should do such combining as gets done by human decision.

Partitioning, Coordinating, and Conjoining

In the first two sections I have looked at categories already implicit in our present moral beliefs that might help us develop beliefs about what to do about the new dangers to life that face us. Now I want to turn to the question of where responsibility lies for such responses.

Traditionally, both at the community and national level, we have divided the responsibility: The criminal courts and police look after certain threats to security of life; the Coast Guard and firefighters and ambulance services look after other threats; regulatory agencies look after still others. The agencies are not normally individuated by what interests or rights are threatened, but are individuated instead by the nature of a *source* of threat to many interests, many rights. For instance, the criminal courts protect not merely security of life, but security of property and security of personal liberty, and other courts protect security of contract, against threats by individual offenders. The defense department looks after threats from a different sort of source—foreign powers—threats both to the security climate of life and to less easily specifiable public interests, often including the climate of trade. Even agencies with specific names like "environmental protection" are not looking at *all* threats to the human environment, but at those that come from thoughtless or ruthless human policies. Acid rain is in their bailiwick, but not the threat of an ice age, or a meteor strike, or a volcano eruption. Such a division of labor—whereby different public authorities look after different sources of threat and take on different public "enemies," each of which may threaten several vital interests—may mean that no one is thinking about *all* the threats to security of life or coordinating all measures to protect it. Someone, of course, determines the budget of each arm of the public, but there will be no security-of-life budget, no security-of-liberty budget, no security-of-possession budget.

Is this a bad thing? Speaking of public policies to save lives, Zeckhauser and Shepard say that "full efficiency would require that we are able to allocate funds across areas."[20] Would such greater lifesaving efficiency be a good thing? Only if we are quite sure that it is not even *more* "efficient" to be able to allocate funds across all the vital interests, but only in one "area," where an area is individuated by the source of a many-faceted threat. To try to deal in one budget (the total lifesaving budget) with the threat to human life posed by a rise in terrorism, and to deal with the threat terrorism poses to liberty in a different budget (the total liberty-saving budget), would lead to less, not greater, coordination. Doubtless there are better ways to partition our public labor than we have yet devised, but it may be no bad thing to have different "areas" recognized, as well as different public interests that need protection in each area. "Rationalizing," if that amounts to identifying some abstract common goal in several areas and then adopting an efficient total plan to reach it, aiming at consistency in all the areas affected, may be one of those rational strategies that it is even more rational to restrict.[21] The best coordination does not always come from abstraction of a goal and generalization of a method.

When I began to consider these issues, I consulted a systems-analyst friend. His advice was that the important thing is not to go in for "special coddling," reducing risks in one area, such as in nuclear plants, more than we are willing to reduce them in others, such as in coal mines. I asked him just how far such area-uniformity of policy was to go. Was it to be restricted to energy-production industries or extended to cotton mills and steel mills? He was uncertain but was inclined to be in favor of a consistent across-the-board job-safety policy, with some exceptions such as employment in the military. When I raised the question of risk not merely to employees but to the general public, he began to get impatient, and when I asked if the policy of uniform treatment of persons as regards security of life was to apply also to programs concerned with reducing infant mortality, or care for the elderly, or support of the police courts and prison system, he wrote me off as a typical overgeneralizing philosopher. But, of course, the move to generalization was not mine, but his, and is a proper move within certain limits. It is probably best if the only ones who *do* consider what we are doing for security of life across areas are the philosophers and intellectuals, not those in a position to redesign the budget partitions. The dangers that would be involved if we gave the rationalizers a free hand are all too easy to see.[22]

The complex and perhaps inefficient group of methods we have for protecting all our vital interests divides the labor according to the location of multifaceted threats, which give us the "areas"; but within some areas, such as the law (and also in morality, which is not an area but affects and sometimes criticizes what goes on in all areas), we divide the danger according to *what* it threatens, and so have lists of vital interests and rights. Different divisions again give us, within "the" right to life, different prohibitions and requirements that must be obeyed if that right is to be respected—duties of child care as much as murder-avoidance. The divisions of public responsibility, rights, vital interests, and moral duties cut along different lines. This may give inefficiency, but it may also give insurance against perverse versions of efficiency and of rationality. The very multiform nature of our public protection of our vital interests is itself a protection.

The Complexity of the Good

This negative defense of traditional partitions and restrictions of power—namely, that they give protection against total lifesaving take-overs—could be strengthened if a more positive foundation could be given for dividing public power and responsibility more by source of threat than by what is threatened. If the various goods that are protected by different agencies against different sources of threat are intercon-nected, it will be no accident that what threatens one of them often threatens others also. Here I must tread carefully to avoid that abstract variety-denying generalization of which I have accused others. I do not mean that we can abstract some one thing that is what we *really* care about, lying behind life, liberty, property, and that it is *its* enemies we should guard against. On the contrary, I want to emphasize the special-ness and individual importance of each of these goods recognized by our traditional lists of rights and their background practices. But these different goods are not a mere collection of things all of which human beings happen to want to safeguard. They are also mutually supportive goods. I shall call on both Hume and Mill to help me express this claim, which, if fully worked out, might give a theoretical basis for the largely conservative intuitions I have expressed. Talk of mutually supportive goods, or parts of the good, has an idealist ring and sounds more like Bradley and Bosanquet than Hume or Mill, but it is to the latter two that I turn, or return, for that hint of a moral theory with which I shall end this largely antitheoretical paper (no antitheorist is a consistent anti-theorist, for only theorists give first priority to consistency). Hume and Mill helped me at the beginning, and I shall also let them have the near-to-last word.

Mill, although he is in theory reducing the goods of security of life, liberty, and any other goods to the pursuit of happiness, is no suitable father figure for those who would equate practical reason with the use of any sort of calculus whereby we strive to maximize some abstract quantity or utility. He says of his comprehensive and dominant good, happiness, that it "is not an abstract idea but a concrete whole." Its ingredients, he says, "are very various, and each of them is desirable in itself, not merely when swelling an aggregate."[23] Music, he says, is one of those ingredients that is desirable in itself and not replaceable by other pleasure-bringers. Mill does not develop these suggestions about concrete wholes with independently desirable, irreplaceable, and mutu-ally supportive parts, nor shall I here attempt to do that. Whatever the truth of this claim about the good, it cannot and need not be used to deny that sometimes we have to choose which "part" of the good to lose or fail to get, however indispensable that part is for happiness.

This doctrine of the complex unity of the human good may seem like unfounded optimism or displaced theology, and if it is to have a bearing on the fit or misfit between the various ways in which in the real world we pursue the good, or at least the better, and flee from the worse, it needs to be translated into less utopian terms.[24] It is because Hume, who shares with Mill a complex account of human well-being, also has a complex account of the different ways in which we try to improve our situation that his social philosophy seems to be especially valuable.[25] He has an account both of mutually cohering social artifices and of the mutually cohering formal goods they provide—the goods of increased force, increased ability, increased security. These provide examples at least of goods not as "concrete" as music or as abstract as utility, and the way they cohere may be suggestive. They are each "irreplaceable" in the contribution they make to improvement in the situation of a person. One can have great power and much ability, yet be ruined by insecurity. One can have security and power, but no ability to use them to any purpose, or have ability and security, but a crippling lack of power. Separately important though they are, they mutually enhance each other's value when all are present to significant degrees. Each of the artifices Hume describes can be seen to advance all of them, and to do so by all the general means he had specified: conjunction of forces, partition of employments, mutual succor. Mutually supportive means advance mutually enhancing goods, since new levels of power, ability, and security are made possible by the artifices that Hume thought merited moral approval. This is not the place to spell out the details of that Humean scheme of mutually complementary artifices that by complex means advance a complex good. It would provide us with an instructive example of the sort of nonabstract coherence possible in social policy, when the complexity of the good aimed at requires a coordinated family of measures. It would also show how the very measures that cope with some dangers create new dangers.[26] Hume claimed that the scheme of artifices he described gave us "infinite advantages," but some of that endless supply of advantages are the advantages of control over the infinitely proliferating dangers that our own previously advantageous inventions, technological and social, supply. As with individual health and quality of life, so with security of life and the measures needed to protect that, we may have to keep running to stay where we were.

Notes

1. David Hume, *An Enquiry Concerning Human Nature*, Selby Bigge, ed., p. 229n.
2. Allan Gibbard discusses this move, and the motivation for it, in "Risk and Value," this volume, Chapter 5.
3. Douglas MacLean discusses the appropriate form of expression for different sorts of values in "Social Values and the Distribution of Risk," this volume, Chapter 4.
4. Hume, *Treatise*, p. 485.
5. Amartya Sen defends a complex moral theory in which rights are important but can be overridden by what are not rights in Chapter 8 in this volume, "The Right to Take Personal Risks."
6. John Stuart Mill, *Utilitarianism*, chap. 5.
7. Thomas Hobbes, *Leviathan*, chap. 13.
8. Mill, *Utilitarianism*, chap. 5.
9. See Henry Shue, *Basic Rights: Subsistence, Affluence, and U.S. Foreign Policy* (Princeton:

Princeton University Press, 1980), for a vigorous attack on the view that all the basic rights are "negative," and for a discussion of ways of selecting which rights *are* basic. Shue draws attention to the "positive" enforcement costs of so-called negative rights, but he does not attend to the training costs all these rights and duties involve.

10. Mill, *Utilitarianism*, chap. 5.

11. Jonathan Bennett, in "Morality and Consequences," in *Tanner Lectures*, vol. 11 (Salt Lake City: University of Utah Press, and Cambridge: Cambridge University Press, 1981), pp. 45–116), replaces the surface distinction with what he argues at careful length is a real and also a morally neutral distinction between positive and negative instrumentality. He then considers whether causing death by positive instrumentality is worse than doing so by negative instrumentality; he concludes that it is not. To tell whether a person brought about some effect by "what he did" rather than by "what he didn't do," we are to consider, for the agent at the time, all the ways of moving or holding still. When the way the agent actually moves (or is still) is one of a small *minority* of those ways that would have produced the given effect, the instrumentality is positive. When it is one of a large *majority* of ways, all of which would have produced the same effect, the instrumentality is negative. I confess to finding it difficult to count the ways of moving and to compare the number of such ways that would with those that would not be followed by a given effect. To the extent that I can ever draw Bennett's distinction, I find it to be a culturally relative one. For an Eskimo the number of ways of moving that will lead to the hunted seal's death will be much greater than the number of deadly movements I can envisage as possible. So whether a given action turns out to display positive or negative instrumentality will depend on one's culturally acquired ability to see ways of moving and their consequences in a given situation. This may not introduce any *moral* prejudgment of issues into the drawing of the distinction, but it does seem to introduce cultural bias.

12. Although the possibility of killing depends upon no social artifice, the fact that we have action verbs such as "kill," "hit," and "poison" shows something about our culture, about which intentions are readily recognizable, and about which intentional actions are recognizable as such. The list of action verbs of a language gives information about familiar activities. The list of prohibitions of a group and the verbs occurring in it may give indirect information about special duties as well as prohibitions. It is when killing people is the duty of some that others need to have it made clear that it is the monopoly of those whose duty it is. It is when drinking human blood, with or without transubstantiation, is the duty of a priest caste that the general prohibition of cannibalism gets its point. Mary Douglas, in *Purity and Danger* (London: Routledge and Kegan Paul, 1978) shows very clearly how one man's (or occasion's) moral poison is usually another man's (or occasion's) moral meat. So my earlier general formula for moral rules should be revised to: "You, but not you others, may, perhaps must, kill these but not those, now but not on other occasions."

13. Christopher McMahon, in "Morality and the Invisible Hand," *Philosophy & Public Affairs* 10, no. 3 (Summer 1981): 247–77, shows how the liberal's short list fits a market economy.

14. Any short list of don'ts, such as the liberal's, is historically a remnant from a much longer list of rules regulating all aspects of life, from birth to burial, and grave "security." That middle-sized list, the Ten Commandments, is a selection from the full version of the Mosaic law in which it is embedded.

15. Robert Nozick, in *Anarchy, State, and Utopia* (New York: Basic Books, 1974), p. 57, says: "A line, or hyper-plane, circumscribes an area in moral space around an individual," and any unconsented crossings of that boundary will count as "losses" to the violated individual, prima facie grounds for compensation. This inviolable moral space, the invasion of which harms a person, is supposed to arise out of "the fact of our separate existences" (p. 33). This fairly clearly takes interaction to be *either* by consent, for presumed benefit, or to be a harmful "boundary crossing," with no interaction at all between the separate existents being the benchmark. In David Gauthier's unpublished manuscript *Morals by Agreement* (forthcoming Oxford University Press) the espousal of a no-interaction benchmark is very definite. See also his "Rational Cooperation," *Nous* 8, no. 1 (March 1975): 53–65.

16. I use the term *liberal* for those who espouse a minimal morality that protects the

powers exercised in a commercial capitalist society of individualists. But *liberal* is a slippery term and connotes also the espousing of the cause of individual adult liberty and the placing of onus of justification on those who would limit it. Against liberalism in that sense I have little quarrel, but its defenders, Mill included, underestimate the extent to which the liberty of some adults, usually males, has a cost in coercion of other adults, usually females, to prepare new adults for such liberty.

17. Nancy Chodorow, *The Reproduction of Mothering* (Berkeley, Calif.: University of California Press, 1978).

18. Robert Nozick, in *Anarchy, State, and Utopia*, chap. 4, raises the question of when we should prohibit an action as distinct from requiring the agent to fully compensate the victim of that action. Since his discussion takes individual rights as somehow there prior to any social recognition of them, providing proper side constraints on any state requirement of compensation or of anything else, and since I reject that dogmatic conception of rights, I cannot use his ingenious reasoning here to any good purpose. I am assuming that the question of what rights to recognize is as social a decision, indeed the same decision, as that of whether to prohibit an action (and so regard it as a violation of a right) or merely to compensate any victims of that action for the harm done to them—for what Nozick calls a "boundary crossing"—perhaps making the inflicter of the harm pay those compensation costs.

19. There are of course other important distinctions, including that between fair and unfair distribution of imposed risk; between risk of catastrophe (many lives lost from one event, along with loss of cultural and social "capital") and risk of equally many deaths not amounting to one catastrophe; and between that danger where we know the frequency with which the evil falls and that danger where we are ignorant of frequencies.

20. Richard Zeckhauser and Donald Shepard, "Where Now for Saving Lives?" *Law and Contemporary Problems* 40, no. 4 (Autumn 1976): 32. Zeckhauser and Shepard speak approvingly of "a rationalized policy choice process" (p. 6) and see the "accurate" version of the question such a policy answers as "where should we spend whose money to undertake what programs to save whose lives with what probability?"

21. For an illuminating discussion of the rationality of restricting our use of rational methods, see Jon Elster, *Ulysses and the Sirens—Studies in Rationality and Irrationality* (Cambridge: Cambridge University Press, 1979).

22. One is tempted here to present a new "modest proposal," one on how best to use a given amount of the public's resources for lifesaving purposes. The first move will be one in which we determine to use those resources to save the greatest number of lives, weighted perhaps so that the lives of the young and healthy count for more than those of older people, whose prospects are worse. We will ignore the difference of "feel" between saving the lives of identified persons, perhaps under our gaze, and saving "statistical" lives. So if ten people are clinging to a semisubmerged oil rig and we have seen their plight on the evening news, we will, before sending the helicopters, ask ourselves: "Could we save more lives, possibly less visible lives, some other way?" Almost always the answer will be yes: An inoculation program to save children from some disease will save more lives for the same expenditure. So let those clinging to the oil rig drown. We have more efficient uses for our money.

The next move is to consider whether we should spend on the inoculation program or invest to spend more effectively later. Medical methods and technology can be expected to advance, so we will save more children from an untimely death by investing our funds in research than by inoculating them now. So let the present children at risk remain at risk. We have more efficient uses for our lifesaving money.

At the next step we query whether investing in medical research is the best investment we can make. Medical research has progressed nicely without great subsidy from public funds, so perhaps our best bet for eventually saving more lives is to invest elsewhere, wherever the economic returns look best. That way we will have more funds to use eventually on putting to use the then latest medical knowledge to save lives. So let us invest, say, in oil rigs or atomic plants.

Once this decision is taken, we, both as public servants and as shareholders, will have to have a view on what safety measures should be observed in our oil rigs and atomic plants.

We will, to protect our investment and so eventually save more lives, perhaps sacrifice a few workers' lives to keep profits up and return on our investment high. We have more efficient ways to save lives than to waste potential lifesaving earnings in measures to save workers' lives.

The next move comes later, when we face the decision of whether to reinvest or spend our earnings on actual lifesaving. So long as there are still more lives at risk than we can save with our increased funds, and so long as oil or other energy profits are still high and medical knowhow still increasing without our subsidy, we will of course reinvest whenever we face this choice. We still have better things to do with our lifesaving resources than to save lives.

With luck, our very investments and the hazard they produce may kill off enough people so that a time will come when it will no longer make good economic sense to go on increasing our lifesaving funds. We will then disburse our funds to save whoever is left at risk, perhaps the entire now-much-reduced population. We will then congratulate ourselves on our rational use of our opportunities. From a position where, had we spent, we would have saved only a fraction of those whose lives were at risk, we have, by our clearheaded, efficient investment policy, made it possible for us eventually to save all the lives remaining at risk. What more rational course of action for the public good could possibly be dreamed up?

23. Mill, *Utilitarianism*, chap. 4.

24. Ronald de Sousa, in "The Good and the True" (*Mind* 83, no. 332 [October 1974]: 531–51), has claimed that there is no reason to expect different real goods to be jointly realizable. Ruth Barcan Marcus, in "Moral Dilemmas and Consistency" (*Journal of Philosophy* 77, no. 3 [March 1980]: 121–36), has argued on the contrary that the need to choose between evils, or choose which or whose good to sacrifice, should always be taken as a sign that collectively we have reprehensibly failed to create the conditions in which goods are jointly realizable.

25. Hume believed that there were basic needs—"the desire of punishment of our enemies, and of happiness to our friends, hunger, lust and a few other bodily appetites" (*Treatise*, 439)—as well as more general desires for whatever brings pleasure, esteem, and power. His account of the best social means to satisfy these involves a complex interplay among nature, culture, and artifice. In a future work I hope to complete the unraveling of that complexity, which I began in "Hume on Heaps and Bundles," *American Philosophical Quarterly* 16, no. 6 (October 1979): 285–95.

26. Although Hume claims that the social artifices he analyzes bring "infinite advantages," each new artifice he describes remedies an "inconvenience" created by the previous one. The invention of property "fixes" possession, but it is a "grand inconvenience" (*Treatise*, 514) that persons and possessions are then often "very ill adjusted," so transfer by consent is invited to remedy that. Again, after promise and contract have made accumulation possible, thieves and frauds can escape their fellows' detection, and so magistrates become necessary, and they themselves bring dangers of tyranny against which the institution of a free press partially protects us. At the end of his life Hume seemed to see a need for another artifice to correct the excesses of a free press.

4

Social Values and the Distribution of Risk

Douglas MacLean

Risk analysis is the scientific part of hazard management. It consists of a number of different methods for collecting and analyzing information and presenting that information in ways that are useful for making decisions, often about matters of great social concern and importance. Just what role a risk analysis ought to play in determining our social choices about risks and the technologies and policies that cause and control risks is a controversial issue. Its resolution depends on what information is analyzed, how reliable we think these analyses are or could ever be, and the importance and relevance of this information in our decisions.

I shall discuss some of the values that are at the heart of this controversy. The issue is whether analytic techniques that are used to estimate risks and the costs of controlling risks can also be used to measure the benefits of controlling risks, in the broadest sense, so that a wide range of comparisons can be made which would make these techniques strongly prescriptive; or whether these benefits (and some costs) cannot be measured, which would constrain the prescriptive force of these techniques in setting policies. I shall try to explain why the case for the greater prescriptive force of risk analysis is a difficult one to make. I am arguing for a more limited use.

In some ways, my argument would be simpler to make if we were talking about decision analysis and values generally, rather than about risk analysis, social values, and public policies. For some limits of decision analysis are clearer when we consider personal decisions and personal values, instead of social decisions and social values. As individuals, we face decisions that are no less troubling and complex than those a policymaker confronts. In these personal situations we surely want to have good information and to think clearly about options, risks, and likely outcomes. Nevertheless, our values place some clear limits on how we think about our options and the personal decisions we make. If

For helpful comments and suggestions, I am indebted to Ian Hacking, Ralph Keeney, Claudia Mills, Ferdinand Schoeman, and Susan Wolf.

our action is likely to harm another individual in certain ways, or if it would violate someone's basic rights, then it may be that estimating and calculating the benefits and risks involved, and comparing the importance of the harm or the rights violation against other expected values, is simply inappropriate. Likewise, where the decision involves deep personal bonds and commitments, we strictly limit the calculation of the benefits, risks, and costs of our actions. Although we expect our most valued personal relationships to be healthy and mutually beneficial, we cannot aim at maximizing the expected benefits.

In situations of personal choice it is also frequently more important for a decision to be one's own than for it to be, in every other respect and on balance, the choice that produces the best expected result for that person. Unless a more personal commitment connects one to the reasons for choice, an analytic weighing of considerations may require a detachment that would be bad or even self-defeating to adopt. Suppose someone is in a dilemma about whether to declare a religious faith and join a church. The risk analysis for this decision problem was done long ago, by Pascal. His celebrated argument prompted William James to comment: "We feel that a faith in masses and holy water adopted wilfully after such a mechanical calculation would lack the inner soul of faith's reality; and if we were ourselves in the place of the Deity, we should probably take particular pleasure in cutting off believers of this pattern from their infinite reward."[1]

Or imagine someone in a quandary about whether to marry or to have a child. Analytic techniques have been developed to help people with these choices—elaborate, carefully designed questionnaires, run through a computer to generate recommendations, based, of course, on good statistical evidence about how others similarly situated have fared. Even though we might believe that the analysis structures the decision problem more completely and objectively than the subject could, we would not recommend that he follow the results of such an analysis for this kind of decision, unless the results influenced his own perception of the problem or unless he could come to identify with this process of decision-making and regard its conclusion as his own.

But these issues of autonomy and personal integrity do not arise in situations involving public policy choices. We might criticize individuals for being too calculating, analytical, computational, maximizing, or whatever in reasoning through their personal decisions. In public decisions the demands are much greater simply to make the choice that has the best overall consequences and to aim explicitly at designing policies to realize these consequences.

I shall concentrate, therefore, on social values and how they guide our judgments about what, on balance, is the best thing to do in setting public policies about risk and safety. To put that discussion in its proper context, I shall begin with some remarks about the nature and use of risk analysis.

Modest and Ambitious Risk Analysis

Social choices about acceptable risk rarely confront us simply as decisions about whether some level or kind of risk is acceptable. Health risks usually come inextricably bound to other benefits and costs. Our technologies impose risks, which we can reduce only by giving up the technology and its benefits or else by diverting other resources to make it safer; and nature's nasty surprises are controllable, if at all, only at some cost, and usually at marginally increasing costs for extra safety. Some hazards can be controlled more cheaply than others, so different allocations of resources will save different numbers of lives or lives we care more about saving. Risk analyses give us the information we need, in a form in which we can use it, to confront these kinds of trade-offs. Theoretically, more and better information will improve our situation for making these choices. (I am omitting, of course, the cost of getting information, which is itself one important part of risk analysis.) Why, then, should risk analysis be controversial at all?

Decisions about risk and safety are normally divided into two components: an estimation of the possible outcomes under alternative choices, along with their likelihood, and an evaluation of these outcomes and risks which often involves comparing them to other outcomes, risks, and decision problems. We can characterize risk analyses as modest or ambitious according to whether they measure only the risks and the monetary effects of reducing or increasing them, or whether they aim for greater generality and comparability by also evaluating outcomes as a set of costs and benefits. The distinction between estimating and evaluating is not always clear, especially where a range of different consequences is measured and compared, just as the distinction between fact and value is not always clear.

Some defenders of risk analysis are explicit about the prescriptive nature of their methods. They claim that analytic approaches to decision-making, such as decision analysis or risk-benefit analysis, can encompass all important considerations of value while remaining neutral to their claims.[2] These advocates see values as individual concerns that, at the level of social choice, can be regarded comprehensively and scientifically. They would like to develop a satisfactory method for measuring and comparing values.

Other defenders of risk analysis adopt a more modest stance about their enterprise. Their claim is simply that they present relevant information in useful ways, without offering any recommendations. This is sometimes true, but often is misleading. It is a little like describing an action as murder or lying but denying that one is evaluating it. The more relevant information that is brought into risk analysis, the more one leaves only formal considerations, like consistency and transitivity of preferences, standing between the estimation and a decision. If someone says he is only showing you what it would be rational to do, but not prescribing a choice, then he is disingenuous in claiming that his analysis is a modest one.

Even explicitly modest risk analysis can have important prescriptive force and can generate normative controversies. Yet one could not object in principle to modest risk analysis unless it is bad simply to have or know certain facts. The issue with ambitious risk analysis is whether the information in the analysis represents all the relevant facts and represents them accurately enough to yield reasonable prescriptions. Whether ambitious risk analyses are appropriate will depend in the end on the nature of social values. Let us consider, then, some of the controversies surrounding ambitious risk analysis.

The Distribution of Risk

To simplify matters, I shall discuss only the risk of death, thus ignoring some of the other important consequences of hazards, such as injury, illness, anxiety, and property loss. Unlike death, these other consequences come in different qualities and degrees, and so they are more difficult than death to measure and evaluate. I ignore them here because I hope to show that the distributional complexities of even the most unrealistically simple examples threaten to overwhelm our analytic abilities.

Risk analyses need numbers, and there are two common ways to measure the magnitude of risk to a population. The first is to estimate the expected number of deaths in the population and to assign some value to these "statistical lives." The other method is to estimate the incremental risk of death to an average individual in the population and attach some value to that risk. Either measure generates an expected value, which we can compare against other costs and benefits. We might, for example, decide it is worth two million dollars to society to save a statistical life; or we might decide that it is worth two dollars to an individual to accept a one in a million increased risk of death (within some normal range of risk—it would not be worth two million dollars to most individuals to accept certain death.) If we ignore distributional considerations, we can easily translate either of these measures into the other.

Risk analysts have tended to focus only on the magnitude of risk, however distributed. This tendency is perhaps most apparent in the frequent comparing of different hazards, as when a nuclear-reactor safety study compared an individual's risk of being killed by a reactor accident to his risk of being struck by a meteorite.[3] The estimated magnitude of the nuclear-power risk in this study has been challenged, but it is also dubious to compare a potential catastrophe to a large population to a risk that individuals face independently. The risk of a thousand people in one community dying from a nuclear-power accident is surely much higher than the risk that a thousand people will be simultaneously struck by meteorites from a meteor shower. We might speculate that some intuitive sensitivity to distributional issues helps to explain why most hazard comparisons have so little impact on public opinion and concern. Our intuitions about how risks are distributed are nevertheless difficult to make systematic. Risk distribution is complex.

Suppose we were estimating the risk to the surrounding population of radiation-related deaths from a core melt at a large nuclear reactor. Both the amount and kinds of radioactive material that are likely to affect an area change as we move farther from the reactor. Releases that would cause "prompt fatalities" affect those living nearest the plant, while the much lower risk of delayed cancer fatalities extends much farther and typically affects many more people (including, in some cases, the populations of large cities). If we want a single measure of magnitude, what population should we select as the population at risk? If we choose a hundred-mile radius, we will include the potentially large population exposed to the lower level of risk, but the average individual risk will seriously misrepresent the danger to those living closest to the plant. If we select a ten-mile radius, the average individual risk will increase significantly, but the risks to a much larger population will be ignored. Risks can be spatially distributed in ways that do not allow any single measure of magnitude to give an accurate or fair picture. This is a problem of equity for risk analysis.

Similar problems arise when we attempt to translate expected deaths in a population to average risk per individual. Consider an estimate of one expected death in a population of one million people. If the risk is spread equally across the entire population, then each individual faces a one in a million (10^{-6}) increment. But it might be the case instead that ten people face a 10^{-1} chance of being killed, or even that one poor victim has been selected to die for sure, while the rest of the population faces no risk at all. These are morally relevant differences in distribution, for it is important that we distribute risks of death equally or in proportion to the distribution of expected benefits.

Different problems arise when we attempt to translate in the other direction. Suppose that each individual in the population of one million is exposed to a 10^{-6} risk of death per year (from some specific cause). These individual risks may be dependent or independent, and the deaths may be temporally concentrated or spread out, all in ways that are consistent with an expectation of one death per year to the population.

If exactly one person will die each year, the 10^{-6} magnitude indicates our ignorance in advance about who it will be. This is a dependent risk situation, because when it is determined who will die we also learn that the others will survive. If instead each individual faces an independent 10^{-6} risk of death per year, then perhaps nobody will die in a given year, but perhaps also two people, twenty people, or more will die, with vanishingly small probabilities as the number of possible deaths increases. Like the dependent risk situation, the expected number of deaths in the population is one each year, but the independence of the risks allows for greater variation in the number of actual deaths in any year. We might regard this uncertainty or variation as morally better or worse, depending on the particular situation.

Individual risks can be interdependent in another way as well. At the extremes, the outcome for the group may range from exactly one death per year to a small chance (10^{-6} in our example) of destroying the entire population. This is the problem of catastrophe, which is a temporal concentration of effects. Risk analysts debate whether we should treat these different situations equivalently or whether we should be especially conservative with low-probability–high-consequence hazards. Again, it seems that intuitions are very much influenced by the particular example and the perspective taken on it. Risks to entire communities or populations seem to arouse special concerns. On the other hand, if the probability of catastrophe from, say, some high-technology chemical plant is low enough, the plant might operate for thirty years with a good chance that nothing bad will happen, while a risk involving a certain number of annual deaths accumulates over thirty years and might seem, from that perspective, to be a much more serious problem.

An example—rather farfetched, to be sure—may help to illustrate some of these distributional complexities. In this example, both the individual risks and the expected deaths to the population are kept constant and equivalent throughout. I want to show the extent to which a situation can be normatively underdetermined even after the magnitude of risk is established. Let us imagine that a decision-maker must subject six of her fellows to play Russian roulette. We might suppose that she commands a unit that has been captured but cannot convince her captors that she does not have the information they seek. The captors impose the game and set the rules, but they will let her decide how to distribute the risk.

Instead of playing Russian roulette with a six-shooter and one bullet, this game will use six six-shooters and six bullets. (The probabilities are unaffected.) Our decision-maker must make two choices. First, she must distribute the bullets however she wants among the pistols. Then she must decide either that one pistol will be selected randomly and fired once at each of her fellows, or else that all six pistols will be distributed, one to each person, and they will each spin the chamber and fire once.

As the game is constructed, the prior or *ex ante* risk to each person is one in six (or .166) that he will die, and the expected number of lives lost in the population at risk is one. Depending on how one counts, there are nearly 3.9 million variations on this game, but they all have these expected values. What should our decision-maker choose to do?

We can represent different versions of the game with decision trees:

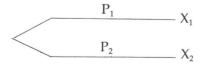

X_n will be the actual number of deaths to the population, and P_n will be the probability of X_n. We can see immediately that some versions are equivalent according to this way of representing the game. The simple decision tree *A*, for example, represents the outcomes of the dependent

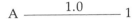

A ———— 1.0 ———— 1

risk games where our decision-maker either puts one bullet in each pistol and chooses one pistol to be fired at each player in turn or puts six bullets in one pistol and distributes the six pistols among the players. Should she be indifferent between these two games? Perhaps it matters that the one-pistol version could be played sequentially, while the six-pistol version could be played either sequentially or simultaneously. This could be an important difference that the decision tree fails to represent. We may want an elaboration of the rules about exactly how the pistols will be fired.

A is the maximally risk-averse strategy for the group, since the magnitude of the outcome is fixed with certainty. Exactly one person will die. Perhaps, then, it would be better to choose a version where the individual risks are independent and where there is some chance that nobody will die. Our decision-maker could realize this possibility by putting one bullet in each pistol and distributing the pistols. The possible outcomes for this version of the game are represented in *B*.

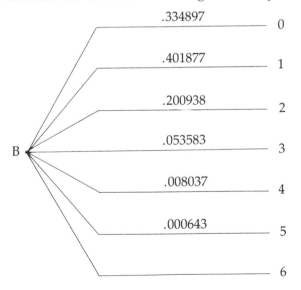

B gives our decision-maker a good shot—better than one in three—that everyone will survive, but she also takes a pretty high risk, roughly 20 percent, that two will die, and she introduces the possibility that larger numbers of her troops will be killed. The worst possible catastrophe—all six dead—has, on this version, a probability of about one in 50,000 of occurring.

B is defined as the maximally risk-prone decision, since it contains the greatest spread of possible outcomes. If we think our decision-maker ought to be attracted to *B* because she ought to make a choice that can spare the lives of all her troops, then perhaps she would prefer choice *C* to *B*. *C* represents a version of the game in which all the bullets are put in

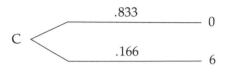

one pistol, and then a pistol is chosen. *C* maximizes the all-survive probability, but it maximizes the worst-catastrophe probability as well. Nevertheless, there is something attractive about the catastrophe-prone choice *C*. By some ways of measuring, *C* is the most equitable version of the game, because not only are the *ex ante* individual risks equal, so too are the final individual outcomes. Everyone ends up the same, dead or alive. We might thus regard *C* as the solidarity choice.

How should our decision-maker balance solidarity against the risk of catastrophe? Clearly we need more detailed information about the situation before we can answer this question. We would need to know, for example, what kinds of bonds exist between the members of this unit, or how important at least one person's survival is, either to pass on important information or merely to bear witness to this torturous punishment. In any case, we need a fuller story than I have given in this highly schematic example.

We have identified a number of different distributive goals, and we have seen how a few versions of the Russian roulette game further some while sacrificing others. We have looked so far only at strategies that pursue different goals to their maximum extent. Perhaps the most reasonable strategy is mixed, or less extreme. There are many more mixed than extreme strategies. We shall consider just two examples. Suppose our decision-maker chose to put two bullets in each of three pistols. If she then chose a pistol, realizing *D*, she would be giving

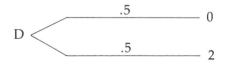

significant, but less than maximum, weight to the all-survive goal. In contrast to *C*, *D* would also make it impossible that more than two people would die, thus limiting the catastrophe potential. Assuming the same distribution of bullets, suppose instead that our decision-maker chose to distribute the pistols, as in *E*. She would then end up imposing independent risks on half the population while guaranteeing the sur-

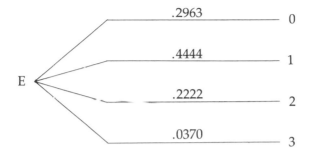

vival of the other half. *Ex ante*, each person has a .5 chance of drawing an empty pistol and a .5 chance of drawing a pistol that has a one in three chance of firing. *E* may not be ideal in terms of equity after the pistols are distributed, but it has some other advantages. It bulges the probabilities around the outcome of one death, though not to the extent of *A*, but it also leaves a reasonable chance that everyone will survive.

I have assumed in this example that the magnitude of risk or the expected number of deaths is constant for all choices. Actual risk management choices are more difficult, because the amount and kind of risk must also be determined. These aspects of the problem may be every bit as complex as the distributional issues. I have argued that even in this simple example we cannot prescribe a way of balancing distributive considerations without having more detailed information. It is fair to assume that real risk management choices will depend on even greater knowledge of the details of specific situations and contexts.

It is often said that the central issue for risk analysis is to determine how safe is safe enough. Critics of this view have claimed that the ideal overall risk-benefit ratio has to be balanced against considerations of equity in public risk decisions. I have been arguing so far that the situation is even more complicated than these critics suggest. Equity is not a simple concept, and it is only part of what matters about how risks are distributed.

A closely related distributive issue, which deserves a fuller and more technical discussion than I shall give here, raises some deeper problems for decision theory and public risk decisions. In terms of fairness, every version of the Russian roulette game is better than having our decision-maker simply select one of her troops in some non-random fashion to be killed. This is true, even though selecting one person non-randomly has the identical outcome as the games described as *A* and can be represented by the same decision tree. The reason, of course, is that every version of the game distributes the one expected death by a procedure that imposes an equal *ex ante* risk of dying to each member of the population. If we assume that all six lives have equal value, this procedure is fair, whereas a non-random selection of one individual is not fair.

This fact cannot be expressed by standard utility theory, as first developed by von Neumann and Morgenstern, which is the foundation for most methods of risk analysis.[4] To put the matter very simply, this is because the independence axiom or the sure thing principle of utility theory requires that things of equal value can be substituted for each other anywhere in the utility equations. Thus, the sum of utilities of each person's dying, discounted by a one in six probability, can be shown by substitution to be equal to the utility of the certain death of any one of them. Utility theory shows that we should be indifferent between these alternatives, although this conclusion is clearly unacceptable.

A proposed solution to this problem is to modify utility theory to allow it to make further discriminations among alternative choices.[5] For example, we value some procedures for making choices, even though the outcomes from using these procedures are no different in value from outcomes determined in some other way. So we can identify the procedure for choosing as one attribute of the alternative choice, and the expected outcome as another, separate attribute. We then assign utilities to each of the attributes we have identified and develop a method for weighing and aggregating them. Thus, we can in principle treat every morally relevant feature of a problem as a separate attribute, which a risk analysis can measure.

In the Russian roulette example we could evaluate each variation of the game in terms of both *ex ante* equity of risk and *ex post* equity of outcomes; we could treat the distributive properties that express solidarity or promote a sense of community as separate attributes to be measured; we could raise the number of individual deaths in each possible outcome by some power α, $\alpha>1$, as a way of measuring our society's aversion to catastrophes; and so on. By carefully defining the decision problem, multi-attribute utility theory can meet most of the technical objections to standard utility theory relating to the moral significance of different distributions of risk.

This will not do, however, as an argument that analytic methods should replace our traditional and largely intuitively based ways of making risk management decisions. It is neither surprising nor very useful to learn that with enough sophistication we can develop an analytic technique that represents our preferences and makes them consistent over a range of cases. What we need in addition is some general way of defining the relevant attributes in our risk management problems and assigning them comparative weights.

The Russian roulette example shows why we should be pessimistic about finding such a general method. Even in that unrealistically simple example, we could see how much judgments about the relative importance of different distributive goals depend on particular knowledge of the situation or context. Why should we think we would be better off allowing our judgments and intuitions to be corrected by some general analytic method?

The Value of Life

Another controversial issue, which concerns the magnitude of risk, is the concept of the social value of human life. Ambitious risk analysts would like to determine a working notion of the value of life by looking at consumer choices that reveal preferences for safety, as opposed to other goods, and at social decisions to accept some level of risk when the cost of reducing it further would be too great. This measure can then be used as a norm for establishing acceptable levels of risk. It is not meant to establish a market for buying and selling human lives; it applies only to statistical lives within a normal range of risk. The point of establishing a social value of life is to become more systematic and more consistent in our risk policies.

A justification for being explicit and analytic about what we are willing to spend to save lives is that in this way we could allocate our risk budget more efficiently, which ideally would reduce everyone's risk of early death. Equally important, according to ambitious risk analysts, we can make better comparisons between improving life's quality and increasing its longevity. Living longer, after all, is a poor substitute for living well.

Yet the establishment of a social value of life remains a subject of persistent controversy. Why is this? Perhaps some critics of "putting a price on life" simply fail to understand what it means. A more charitable explanation might assign political motives to the critics, who see it as a way of perpetuating an unacceptably unsafe status quo.

But the issue is almost always put in moral terms. Critics compare the practice of pricing life to the Pentagon's too thoroughly economic approach to America's involvement in the Vietnam War or to the infamous alleged corporate decision that it was more efficient to pay court damages for deaths and injuries than to redesign the dangerous gas tanks on Ford Pintos. As one philosopher, Stuart Hampshire, puts the issue: "[To some], it seems now obvious that the large-scale computations in modern politics and social planning bring with them a coarseness and grossness of moral feeling, a blunting of sensibility, and a suppression of individual discrimination and gentleness, which is a price that they will not pay for the benefits of clear calculation."[6] Is this a fair charge, or is it more accurate to say, as the economist Robert Solow has written, that "It may well be socially destructive to admit the routine exchangeability of certain things. We would prefer to maintain that they are beyond price (although this sometimes means only that we would prefer not to know what this price really is)"?[7]

The debate over the value of human life usually focuses on whether life is sacred or priceless. I want to defend the idea that human life is a sacred or priceless value, and to discuss the implications of this value for setting acceptable levels of risk. I must begin by discussing what it means to call a value sacred or priceless, because, unfortunately, this concept usually ends up being interpreted in a way that no sane or sober person would defend the sacredness of human life.

A typical discussion goes like this.

> What do we mean when we say things are "not for sale"? This may mean that the implicit price is either zero or infinite. Consider things that have an "infinite price" or are "priceless." This is no doubt a useful rhetorical device. But that does not make it any more helpful as a guide to real decision making. We are not confronted with a referendum or a bill in the Congress that requires an infinite appropriation. Rather, we are asked whether we want to spend an extra $10 billion for this program; whether we want to cut or expand that program. In this context the ambitious risk analyst may be seen as a humble dustman, scurrying around after the famous, trying to clean up the tangle of rhetorical flourishes littering the ceremonial field.[8]

The interpretation of pricelessness as "having an infinite price" is silly. Many of the things we regard as priceless may nevertheless have perfectly well-determined market values. To say of something that it is priceless may be only to say that it is not for sale, not that no one could afford it. At any rate, the idea that human life is sacred or priceless deserves a better interpretation than that. It is one of a handful of moral intuitions, like beliefs that murder is wrong, that promises should be kept, or like taboos on incest, which are deeply rooted and more or less universal. We ought to examine these beliefs carefully before dismissing them as rhetorical flourishes.

For a better understanding of sacred values, we might look to the sciences that study culture. There we find that the analysis of sacred values focuses not on the perceived properties of special objects or on their extraordinary exchange value, but on what we might call the manner of valuing or the expression of values, the activities and rituals associated with them.

Rituals have been characterized as irrational or non-rational behavior, actions in which the relationship between means and ends is non-intrinsic or inefficient. This aspect of rituals indicates their symbolic meaning and draws the attention of the community to objects, relationships, or roles that have a special place in the life of the group. Sacred values can only be observed in public rituals. They are necessarily social, not individual, values.[9]

The primary context for rituals and sacred values, of course, is in religious life, but anthropologists and sociologists have also studied rituals in social and political life. They see them as necessary in all communities, even secular ones. Thus, far example, Robert Bellah analyzed President Kennedy's Inaugural Address as a ritual in what he calls the American civil religion. It indicated "deep-seated values and commitments that are not made explicit in the course of everyday life."[10]

And Steven Kelman calls attention to the same speech, in which the president proclaimed the "pricelessness" or "infinite selling price" of certain valued commodities. "The word 'priceless' is pregnant with meaning. . . . [Kennedy] proclaimed that the nation was ready to 'pay any price [and] bear any burden . . . to assure the survival and success of liberty.' Had he said instead that we were willing to 'pay a high price' or 'bear a large burden' for liberty, the statement would have rung hollow."[11]

This understanding of sacred values owes much to Durkheim's study of the "elementary" forms of religious life. Writing at a time when it had become clear that religion was losing its cognitive role to science, Durkheim discussed the continuing strength of religion as a function of the role of ritual in strengthening social integration. He regarded these elementary forms of religion as universal and indispensable prerequisites of all societies. "There can be no society," he wrote, "which does not feel the need of upholding and reaffirming at regular intervals the collective sentiments and the collective ideas which make its unity and its personality."[12]

I am not suggesting that we should accept all the implications of this neo-Durkheimian analysis. Its adherents presuppose an unrealistically high degree of consensus in American political life. We should also bear in mind that rituals can be used as a socially regressive force to legitimize and perpetuate existing power relationships. Nevertheless, some values, even in a secular culture, seem to be sacred in this sense, and these would surely apply to the taking of human life and the setting of policies that permit taking lives, even if only statistical lives. This, apparently, is Hampshire's primary concern, for he criticizes what he calls the computational moralities underlying ambitious risk analysis for carrying "the deritualization of transactions between men to a point at which men not only can, but ought to, use and exploit each other as they use and exploit any other natural object."[13]

Because health and safety decisions virtually always have economic consequences, we need to guard against treating human life as exchangeable for other commodities. Inefficient or even merely symbolic actions are one such guard. In appropriate contexts, they may be necessary to express the special value of human life in our culture. This is the sense in which human life is sacred or priceless.

Startling examples of ritualized behavior are common in our dealings with hazards and risks. We need only to consider our willingness to engage in rescue missions when identified individuals are involved: saving crash victims, fliers lost at sea, or an astronaut; retrieving the wounded or dead in battle; diverting resources from making mines safer in order to mount rescue missions for trapped miners; or even supporting individual medical treatment rather than more public health research. These actions and policies defy economic or even risk-minimizing sense.

This argument does not deny the value of being efficient and saving more lives. Nor does it deny that once we have made our decisions we can always calculate the costs and figure out what we have decided to spend to save lives. The argument is against determining a value of human life to be used prescriptively to make trade-offs in ambitious risk analyses in order to be more efficient in reducing overall risks and to save more lives.

Thus, we must acknowledge that the value of life is complex. It has at least two aspects, which can conflict with each other. First, human life has intrinsic value: saving lives or preventing early deaths is good, and the more lives saved the better. Risk analyses are an important tool for furthering this value, and if we were confident that we could empirically determine the social value of human life and that the concept would not be abused, it would be an important part of these techniques. Second, human life is a sacred value, which must be expressed through rituals and other special actions. Setting acceptable levels of risk must be guided by both aspects of this value, even though, like distributive goals, they may have to be balanced and traded off against each other.

Just as certain rescue missions are rich in their potential for expressing the special value of human life, so some risk policies might be more important in this regard than others. In these situations we might reasonably choose to accept certain inefficiencies—to save fewer lives than we might otherwise save—in order to maintain the sacredness of human life. Risk analysts insist that we are willing to accept some risks as a trade-off to improve life's quality; why should we not also accept some risks, some localized inefficiencies, in order to maintain the integrity of the value of human life?

I am suggesting that there will be a tension between our rationalistic and revisionist sentiments, on the one hand, and our conservative, ritualistic sentiments on the other. Sacred values are very fragile indeed, and there is bound to be considerable disagreement about just how rich in symbolic content a situation is. Saving more lives, on the other hand, is clearly a value of great importance, and so is allocating our resources to improve life's quality in other respects. Just how we weigh these elements is a difficult issue which requires judgment and sensitivity. We must decide to what degree our analytic techniques can help us make these decisions, and the extent to which this tension determines the limits of the usefulness of risk analysis.

Social Values and Risk Analysis

In the preceding sections I have discussed two of the normative issues most frequently raised in controversies over the use of risk analysis: the distribution of risks, costs, and benefits, and the value of human life. Both are examples of social values: how different individuals are treated with respect to each other; how society is to be structured in terms of the risks its members will jointly face; how public policies contribute to the sense of solidarity and fellowship its members feel toward each other and the group; or how these policies foster the shared values that give the society its identity. In both examples we found a complex of values, which can conflict with each other, as well as with other values, and whose proper balancing seems to resist an abstract or general treatment but depends instead on the details of particular situations. The values involved in different distributions of risk may not be reflected by any single measure of expected outcomes to a group or risk to an individual, for we saw how distributions can change in important ways while both of these measures remain constant. The value of human life is expressed by policies that reduce risk, but it may also demand actions that increase levels of risk, for reasons that are not connected to the gains in welfare that also lead us to accept increments of risk to life and health. The arguments I have given suggest that important social values may not easily be regimented or made systematic, but might instead demand a more complicated set of responses, the details of which must be determined by the particular circumstances. Measuring these values constitutes a challenge for risk analysis.

Even if we acknowledge these difficulties, however, the fact remains that decisions and trade-offs must be made. We might yet ask how an ideally rational decision-maker would balance all these considerations and design a risk analysis that models what such an individual would decide, all things considered, under fair conditions.

We shall have to appeal to an ideal of rational choice. Following a suggestion by Allan Gibbard, we will characterize this ideal by an *ex ante* Pareto principle.[14] The *ex ante* part will have to establish conditions that are fair for considering each person's prospects under different alternatives. We could describe something like a Rawlsian veil of ignorance. The Pareto part says that we should prefer a policy if someone's prospects are better and nobody's prospects are worse from the *ex ante* position. If we filled in the details, we might have a model of choice to which rational individuals would give their consent.

Now suppose we were considering different health risk policies. We might thus argue that, *ex ante*, a person would pay to avoid certain risks and insure himself against others, but that he would choose to accept other low-probability risks that are expensive to reduce. We might argue that rational individuals would choose a policy that gives them greater protection against diseases that are likely to afflict them at any age, rather than against diseases that attack only the elderly. In such a manner, we could determine our public risk policies.

In the preceding sections I argued that the policy it would be rational for individuals to choose under these conditions may turn out to have some uncomfortable social consequences. For instance, it may turn out to neglect the elderly, and in the context in which these policies are announced and enacted, this may seem to express an unacceptable lack of concern for human life, just as a refusal to rescue, which might be rational *ex ante*, could save more lives while undermining society's ability to express concern for the value of human life. Keeping in mind that trade-offs must be made, the crucial question now is this: can we import these considerations into the *ex ante* situation? Some people think we can, and they reason in the following way.

> It may be irrational to lock the barn door after the horse has been stolen, but we feel better doing it, and the feeling itself, however irrational its basis, may justify the action. Perhaps the knowledge that we shall care for each other in calamity, even if the cost is great, stengthens our feelings of social fellowship, and it is in our feelings toward each other, not only in the direct benefits to our health, that we may find ethical justification. Narrow economic loss—loss, that is, reckoned only in terms of effects on the life of the person whose treatment is in question—may be made up for in emotional gain. Whether we should all indulge our illusion that we regard life as priceless may depend on the economic cost of the illusion. I am suggesting, then, that whereas cheap violations of the narrow economic rationality of straightforward applications of the *ex ante* Pareto principle may well be worth in sentiment what they cost in more straightforward economic terms, as violations become costly, we should refine the sentiments involved.[15]

This suggests a way of reducing social values to individual sentiments or feelings of fellowship and incorporating them into ambitious risk analyses. This "feeling factor" could be included as an attribute in the *ex ante* deliberations. Of course it is possible to be so carried away by the expressive force of some policy that we pay an unjustifiably high price in lives and money. Here, as elsewhere, we must strike a balance. But we have reasons to doubt whether we can reduce social values to individual feelings in order to incorporate them into rationalistic decision procedures.

First, we cannot alter the importance of social values as we might be able to manipulate some individual feelings, nor can we control which situations are rich in expressive or symbolic importance. It would make the case for risk analysis easier if, for instance, we could legislate that we express the special value of human life by single-mindedly pursuing efficiency in risk analysis, by treating all risk contexts similarly, and treating human lives as exchangeable for other lives or other valued commodities. But it is obvious that we cannot change ourselves in this way. It is not easy to "refine" or engineer the social bases for expressing the culture's sacred values, such as sentiments about the value of human life or its sense of the importance of fairness and solidarity, without destroying the integrity of these values in the attempt. Perhaps, over time, we can refine our collective sentiments to some degree, especially as we become more accustomed to thinking in terms of risks and the costs of controlling them. But our feelings could never be made compatible with our rationalistic methods without destroying the possibility of keeping some values sacred.

The deeper questions, however, are whether social values can be reduced to individual feelings, and if not, whether we might measure certain feelings as a surrogate for them in risk analyses (as we might double the value of some consequence as a surrogate for some other consequence that we cannot measure). The first question is easier to answer.

We can characterize social values as the importance to members of the group of experiencing their public lives and social interactions in certain ways. In some instances it will be important to an individual's experience of her public life that society actually have certain characteristics. Some feelings have value, that is, only to the extent that they are real or authentic, although nothing in the nature of the felt experience marks it as genuine. The source of some feelings is as important as their nature for determining their value, so values cannot all be analyzed without reference to something external to feelings or experiences. This is one reason why values, including social values, cannot be reduced to individual feelings.

The quality of experiences, moreover, is not the only thing that matters to people. We all know the many ways we defeat ourselves by aiming directly to enhance our own experiences. A biologist or a teacher derives satisfaction from his career only through commitment to the science or the society he serves. In the best personal relationships, likewise, our commitments are not to our experience of the relationship but to the other people involved. The quality of life is improved by our ability to identify and contribute to something beyond our own experiences. In precisely these ways, people can identify, if more abstractly, with aspects of their culture and society. They are proud to be members of a certain kind of society, and they can feel shame for its wrongful acts. People identify themselves as Catholics or New Yorkers or midwesterners or Americans; they know that they embody some of the culture's traits. So it matters that society be certain ways, for we know that our own experiences are not independent of how our society is structured.

Finally, if the values expressed by different distributions of risk could be reduced to individual feelings, then it would be deeply puzzling that we are not indifferent to which version of Russian roulette was chosen in the example I described above. Each of the six captives involved experiences the same *ex ante* risk, and each one is being treated fairly. The aversion to catastrophe would be even more difficult to understand, because none of their experiences are affected by the fact that everyone else dies if one of them dies. When we explored the reasons for altering the probability that everyone would die—lowering it to avert catastrophe or raising it to express solidarity—we were appealing to values about how the society's risks are structured and distributed, which are social values, not individual feelings.

To answer the second question—whether feelings might stand as surrogates for social values—I must appeal to what I have referred to as the appropriate expression of values. Just as we cannot analyze values entirely in terms of our feelings or experiences, neither can we fully understand them by reference to the objects of value; for valuing also implies certain kinds of behavior or an appropriate set of responses.

These responses do not merely acknowledge a value but, we might say, also express its nature.

The obligations and duties that are derived from some moral values are a familiar example of how values carry implications for behavior. Acts of charity, which go beyond these duties, are a different way of expressing values. To understand the meaning of charitable acts, we need considerable knowledge about their circumstances or social context. These will also determine the appropriateness of an act of giving, when it expresses concern and when it is an insult.

Rituals and ceremonies are another way of expressing values. They too are made appropriate by their social context, and they gain their meaning and expressive power by social conventions. We need only to think of the very different ways in which different cultures and subcultures celebrate births and marriages, or mourn and bury their dead.

Risk analysis has developed primarily as a tool for government agencies charged with determining safety and health policies. Idealistic laws created many of these regulatory agencies, like the Environmental Protection Agency and the Occupational Safety and Health Administration. They are not invisible bureaucracies which were established to duplicate the work of the Office of Management and Budget and bring efficiency and coherence to regulatory policies. They are, rather, very public institutions, which the public expects in part to give voice to the ideals of a society that cares deeply about the lives and health of its citizens.

We now realize how important it is to the nation and its economy for these agencies to be cost conscious, and we now understand, as perhaps very few people did when they were established, that we can neither rid ourselves of risk nor afford to control it to the limits of our technological ability. Nevertheless, when the Administrator of EPA appears at a press conference to announce a regulatory decision, often about some hazard that has generated widespread public anxiety, people are not concerned primarily with knowing that he or she has found the ideal cost-benefit ratio. People want to know that the things they value deeply—our health, the environment, and our natural resources—are being guarded and protected by the agency we have created to be the trustee of these values. Whether we like it or not, the actions of such agencies have symbolic and expressive significance.

This might help us to understand the rituals that have been forced on some of these agencies, like the taboos against looking at cost-benefit analyses or establishing a social value of human life. I do not mean to defend these particular rituals but only to explain why expressing sacred values is very much a function of some regulatory agencies.

Our policies for reducing risks must remain sensitive to our social values. These values can determine that the principles that ought to guide policies in one risk context may be inappropriate for guiding policies to control other risks. Whether some form of ambitious risk analysis is justified remains an open question—an important question as well, for policies must be set and trade-offs made, to protect human lives and health and to affirm their special character in our social life.

Notes

1. William James, *The Will to Believe and Other Essays in Popular Philosophy* (New York: Dover, 1956), p. 6.

2. Some carefully qualified versions of this position are represented in the chapters by Herman Leonard and Richard Zeckhauser and by Allan Gibbard.

3. Norman Rasmussen et al., *Reactor Safety Study* (Nuclear Regulatory Commission WASH-1400, Washington, D. C., 1975).

4. This problem was first pointed out by Peter Diamond, "Cardinal Welfare, Individualistic Ethics and Interpersonal Comparisons of Utility: Comment," *Journal of Political Economy* 75 (1967): 765–66. It has recently been the subject of renewed interest, especially for its implications for public risk decisions. See Ralph Keeney, "Equity and Public Risk," *Operations Research* 28 (1980): 527–34; and John Broome, "Equity in Risk Bearing," *Operations Research* 30 (1982): 412–14.

5. Ralph Keeney and Robert Winkler, "Evaluating Decision Strategies for Equity of Public Risks," *Operations Research* (forthcoming).

6. Stuart Hampshire, "Morality and Pessimism," in *Morality and Conflict* (Cambridge, Mass.: Harvard University Press, 1983), p. 86.

7. Robert Solow, "Defending Cost-Benefit Analysis: Replies to Steven Kelman," *Regulation* 5 (March/April 1981): 40.

8. This is edited from Clifford Russell, "The Morality of Cost-Benefit," *Regulation* 5 (May/June 1981): 2.

9. See Steven Lukes, "Political Ritual and Social Integration," *Sociology* 9 (1975): 289–308.

10. Robert Bellah, "Civil Religion in America," in *Religion in America*, edited by William McLoughlin and Robert Bellah (Boston: Houghton Mifflin, 1968), p. 4.

11. Steven Kelman, "Cost-Benefit Analysis: An Ethical Critique," *Regulation* 5 (January/February 1981): 38.

12. Emile Durkheim, *The Elementary Forms of Religious Life*, translated by J. W. Swain (London: George Allen and Unwin, 1915), p. 417.

13. Hampshire, "Morality and Pessimism," pp. 96–97.

14. Allan Gibbard, "The Prospective Pareto Principle and Its Application to Questions of Equity in Access to Health Care: A Philosophical Examination," unpublished manuscript.

15. This is edited from Gibbard, "The Prospective Pareto Principle."

5

Risk and Value

Allan Gibbard

Maximization of Expected Total Intrinsic Reward

Risk is pervasive in life, and so one might expect human beings to be well equipped to cope with it. We ought indeed to have a superb repertory of ways of dealing with risks and their costs, both in public and in private decisions. But we don't, or so various strands of evidence indicate. In public expenditures for safety, for example, we refuse some measures that would save lives as too costly and then adopt other measures that are more costly and save many fewer lives. There is often in such cases nothing about the kinds of lives involved that seems to justify the discrepancy.[1] Experimental psychologists have isolated some of the tendencies that underlie such public action. Daniel Kahneman and Amos Tversky found that when they offered their subjects what amounted to the same choice put in different words, their preferences depended on whether an identical outcome was labeled a "gain" or a "loss."[2] They have even found that an implausible story with plausible details is considered more probable than the same story with the plausible details omitted, although the former entails the latter.[3] In their book *Human Inference*, Richard Nisbett and Lee Ross present numerous other ways in which perceptions of probability are systematically distorted.[4] Ordinary ways of coping with risk, it seems, are replete with blatant irrationalities.

Can we, then, find ways of making decisions about risk that make better sense than common sense? That, I take it, is the problem that formal "risk-cost-benefit analysis" addresses. What I have done so far is to sketch a principal rationale for wanting something like risk-cost-benefit analysis: for seeking a way to regiment our judgments about risk, and so to avoid the blatant irrationalities of unaided common sense.

What would it be for our dispositions for choice not to involve "irrationalities"? That, in effect, was the question Frank Plumpton Ramsey asked in his essay "Truth and Probability."[5] He answered with a set of postulates that, he said, explicated "consistency" in choice. (In what follows, I shall use the terms "coherent" and "incoherent" in place of Ramsey's "consistent" and "inconsistent," so as to avoid the question of whether the kinds of formal irrationalities Ramsey spoke of are "inconsistencies" in any strict sense.) What Ramsey showed was this: Coherent preferences among gambles at least mimic expected utility maximization. For any subject with coherent preferences, that is, we can assign numbers (called his *utilities*) to possible outcomes, and assign numbers (called his *subjective probabilities*) to the various ways the world might be apart from the choice at hand and its effects, and we can do so in a way that *represents* the subject's preferences in the following sense. By the *expected utility* of an alternative, we shall mean a weighted average of the "utilities" of the various outcomes that the alternative might have. The weight given each outcome is the "probability" that the choice of that alternative would yield that outcome. On this characterization, then, what counts as an alternative's "expected utility" depends on the "utilities" we have assigned to outcomes and the "probabilities" we have assigned to the ways the world might be. Ramsey's theorem is that if a subject's preferences are coherent, we can choose "utilities" and "probabilities" so that, for every pair of alternatives, the one he prefers is the one to which we ascribe the higher resulting "expected utility."

Thus if Ramsey indeed succeeded in formulating the kind of coherence that is required for rational decision, then coherent dispositions are equivalent to standing ready to maximize the expected value of something. But of what? The decisions in question here concern social policy toward risks. One vague principle we might apply to such decisions is that alternatives are to be evaluated on the basis of their prospective benefits to affected invididuals. This vague formulation suggests the *ex ante Pareto principle*.[6] Suppose one must choose between two social policies, A and B. Suppose that for everyone, A is of at least as great prospective benefit as is B, and for some, A is of greater prospective benefit than B. In that case, A is said to be *ex ante Pareto-superior* to B. The *ex ante Pareto principle* is that in questions of social policy, if an alternative A is *ex ante* Pareto-superior to an alternative B, then A is *ex ante* preferable to B.

Together, the Ramsey postulates and the *ex ante* Pareto principle tell us much about preferability of social alternatives. In a classic article John Harsanyi showed the following:[7] Suppose

(i) For each individual *j*, alternatives and lotteries over alternatives can be ranked on the basis of prospective benefit to *j*, in a way that satisfies the Ramsey postulates.

(ii) Preferability satisfies the Ramsey postulates.

(iii) The *ex ante* Pareto principle holds.

Then the *ex ante* preferability of an alternative is a weighted sum of its prospective benefit for each individual.[8]

That leaves the question of what weights to use, but we presumably want an impartial way of assessing social policies, and so if we can make sense of the notion, we shall clearly want equal weight for equal benefits. What can be said of the notion of individual benefit? The argument in the form I have given it depends very little on how "benefit" is understood. All that is required is that for any given person, we can compare two alternatives with respect simply to the ways they bear on the life that person leads, and so we can make sense of the claim that one alternative is *ex ante* preferable to another with respect to his life. In the tradition in which Harsanyi wrote, it was accepted that "preferability considering only how things bear on Smith's life" is given by Smith's preferences. Nothing in the argument, though, requires this, and to take preference as a criterion of benefit strikes me as implausible. Smith may care about things other than his own good.

Here I shall have little to say about individual benefit, but I am inclined to think that we have at least a vague notion of the worth, to a person himself, of leading the life he leads; we might call this the "intrinsic reward" of his life. Talk of intrinsic reward is problematical, but I shall proceed as though it were not.[9] Although others might accept the Harsanyi postulates and fill them in with a notion different from intrinsic reward, I shall assume the *ex ante* Pareto principle put in terms of intrinsic reward. The principle so glossed is this: If everyone's prospective intrinsic reward is at least as great given alternative A as it is given alternative B, then A is *ex ante* preferable to B.

With "benefit" thus read as intrinsic reward, the conclusion of Harsanyi's argument is that the *ex ante* preferability of an alternative is the expected value of the total intrinsic reward of everyone involved. What is the relation of this to risk-cost-benefit analysis, which looks not to intrinsic reward, but to money? The Harsanyi argument in my version, then, endorses risk-cost-benefit analysis only if we can take money as a surrogate for intrinsic reward. Now, indeed for a given person, money may serve reasonably well as such a surrogate: A thousand dollars of intrinsic reward for Smith, we can say, is the amount by which the intrinsic reward of Smith's life would be increased by adding a thousand dollars to his income. When more than one person is involved, however, the dollar will often not serve adequately even as a rough surrogate for intrinsic reward. The difference a marginal thousand dollars can make to the intrinsic reward of the poor, it seems plausible to suppose, is much greater than the difference it makes for the rich. If so, then the same total amount of money will make for greater total intrinsic reward if it is distributed equally than if it is distributed in a grossly unequal way. Considerations of total wealth can thus be offset by distributive considerations.[10]

In brief, if we accept Harsanyi's argument with its postulates glossed in terms of intrinsic reward, then we shall want to evaluate risks and benefits in terms of the expected total intrinsic reward of those whose lives are involved. Standard risk-cost-benefit assessment will help us only insofar as it approximates assessment of expected total intrinsic reward. I shall chiefly discuss risk-cost-benefit analysis so taken—that is, the maximization of expected total intrinsic reward as a governing standard for social policy. Hence for the most part, I shall discuss risk-cost-benefit analysis only insofar as it constitutes a rough surrogate for expected total intrinsic-reward maximization.

Analysis and Considered Moral Belief

I began by saying that our normal ways of coping with risk and the costs of safety involve systematic, blatant irrationalities. I then sketched Ramsey's theory of what it would be to avoid incoherence in these matters and explored the relation of this theory to orthodox risk-cost-benefit analysis. Orthodox risk-cost-benefit analysis, I suggested, can be regarded as a crude approximation to something that does make sense: maximizing expected total intrinsic reward. We may regard risk-cost-benefit analysis as practiced as a rough approximation to such a "purified" risk-cost-benefit analysis, and the sole remaining issue, it may seem, is whether the approximations involved are so gross as to make the approximation a bad one.

Now, even such a "purified" risk-cost-benefit analysis can be expected to yield results that are morally dubious. Consider a few examples; take first safety in manufacturing. Even as measured by a risk-cost-benefit analysis ideally sensitive to all aspects of intrinsic reward, the benefits of certain measures for workplace safety would presumably still turn out not to be worth their cost. This may happen even when the expenditures involved constitute only a small proportion of the total cost of manufacture. Now, in a large industry, safety measures forgone must almost certainly mean some deaths. Thus if some measures are forgone, even if the savings are passed on to the consumer, we will be accepting unnecessary deaths for the sake of saving a few pennies on a dollar. Consider next pollution control: No doubt some measures that would reduce pollution will likewise turn out not to be worth their cost. In the case, say, of a single large coal-burning electric-power plant, it may be expected that numerous deaths will stem from the savings if these pollution control measures are forgone. In that case, it is virtually certain that at least one person will die unnecessarily from the operation of the plant. How, we may ask, does building and operating a plant one knows will kill people—people who would not be killed were the plant built more expensively—differ from murder for hire? Finally, take cases of heroic rescue. The rescue of someone stranded, buried, or the like could turn out to be so expensive as not to be worth its cost. It may turn out that in some cases, for the price of a rescue, one could save a much larger expected number of lives through various safety measures. Does that mean that it is better to take the safety measures and stand idly by while the stranded accident victim perishes than to neglect the safety measures and do one's best to rescue a fellow human being in distress? Is not that, we may ask, to face the extremity of human distress with the mind of an accountant?

These examples follow a pattern. They are cases in which we seem to be able to take in the morally relevant features of a situation at a glance and form a firm moral judgment. Once we see that what we are being asked to do in effect is to kill to save money or neglect a desperate person to save money, we see that it would be wrong to do so. There is nothing about risk-cost-benefit analysis, even in an idealized version, that guarantees the humane result in such cases. On risk-cost-benefit analysis, what course of action is right depends on the details of the situation—on how much money one saves with a single killing. Risk-cost-benefit analysis, then, can be expected to deviate from moral judgments in which we place great confidence.

Can we expect that the results of risk-cost-benefit analysis will differ from our informed moral judgments in a systematic way? The cases I gave were ones in which risk-cost-benefit analysis seems to let us off the hook too easily in providing for safety. Is the problem, then, that the precepts of risk-cost-benefit analysis must always undervalue safety? I think not. Consider one kind of example. I argued that risk-cost-benefit analysis will in some cases prescribe "killing to save money" and that that is wrong. "Killing to save money," though, is a tendentious way of describing the operation of a power plant with substantial pollution controls, and in fact we have no clear, shared conviction about which kinds of pollution-control devices power plants must have. The phrase "killing to save money" invites us to see a complicated situation in a simple way that will bring with it an automatic moral judgment. The phrase would allow us to dismiss a thousand man-years of sweat and toil as mere "money" while underlining diffuse effects on health as "killing."

In general, we can say this. There are simple ways of seeing complicated situations, and these simple pictures can bring with them simple, clear moral judgments. A refined risk-cost-benefit analysis, because it is sensitive to details of the situation in a way that no person's intuitive picture of the situation could be, cannot be expected to match a person's clear moral judgments in every case, and anyone who looks long enough should be able to find cases in which risk-cost-benefit analysis fails the test of intuitive moral conviction. The test, though, is not a fair one. For any two people, one could likewise test the moral deliverances of one by the intuitive moral convictions of the other, and there would be frequent failures. It is when human beings can talk that they can come to see things in the same way and so reach a moral consensus. We trust human beings more than impersonal methodologies because we can talk to a person and get him to see things our way, or come to see things his way. Risk-cost-benefit analysis in effect "sees" a situation as no human being could and will not see things our way.

This discussion should leave us skeptical of our capacity to make adequate intuitive moral judgments of complex situations. That in itself, of course, is not to say that risk-cost-benefit analysis improves on common sense. Whatever support the method draws from my discussion must rest not only on skepticism of intuitive moral judgments, but on the general rationale that I offered earlier: on the arguments of Ramsey and Harsanyi. That rationale still needs to be examined. Each of us should be confident that risk-cost-benefit analysis will deliver some prescriptions that he finds clearly wrong—but that in itself is not adequate grounds for rejecting the method. It remains to be asked whether there are other cogent grounds for rejecting it or for restricting its claims.

Technocratic Moral Reform and the Choice of Ultimate Ends

The preceding discussion suggests that a rationally grounded morality will be reformist—perhaps shockingly so. It will not appeal primarily to our capacities to be aroused, as traditional moral reform movements have done, but to ways of regimenting the considerations involved to produce rational, coherent judgments. There is a contrast to be drawn here between the spirit of these reforms and the spirit of many other movements for moral reform with which we are familiar. Many reform movements are evangelical in spirit: They appeal to deep moral emotions and depend on the moral fervor of the righteous to wash away obstacles to reform. The kind of moral reform the things I have been saying suggest is instead technocratic in spirit: We need, it seems, to train people in rational methods of risk assessment and so organize society that those methods really do determine policy with regard to risk.

Is this a chilling prospect? Many, perhaps most of us, will find it so, and we need to ask what stands behind this response. The discussion thus far suggests one kind of answer: that technocratic judgments will contradict many of our cherished, mutually incoherent moral judgments, so that a hostile reaction to technocracy is simply irrational. What I want to ask is whether something more rational stands behind suspicion of decisions made on the basis of risk-cost-benefit analysis.

Part of the chill must surely stem from potentialities for abuse. Technocrats are human, and however well trained they may be in rational methods, they will respond as human beings and fudge the results accordingly. That leaves us with a dilemma: Esoteric methods are subject to abuse; the alternatives work poorly. Now, considerations of technocratic abuse are vital and raise fundamental questions of constitutional design, but I cannot hope to tackle these questions here. The issue I shall examine is whether enlightened risk-cost-benefit analysis, if it could be practiced without distortions, could be a reliable guide to policy concerning risk.

There are reasons for thinking it could not. One such reason we might label the *paradox of approximation*. Suppose we have a method of solving a kind of problem, and, by certain standards, that method is correct in principle. Even then, the paradox is: Our best attempts to approximate the method may not come nearly as close to giving results that are right, according to those very standards, as does some other way of proceeding. Some of the values an ideal decision analysis must countenance are not amenable to practical quantification. A central danger in any method of risk-cost-benefit analysis that can actually be carried out is that only those determinants of intrinsic reward that are easiest to quantify will be counted.

I want now to set aside the paradox of approximation to explore a dilemma that threatens even ideal expected intrinsic reward maximization. The roots of the dilemma are psychological. The urgency we attribute to various kinds of efforts to prevent loss of lives, injury, and illness seems to depend little on the extent of the risk—at least if magnitude of risk is taken to be anything like expected loss in intrinsic reward to the direct victims of calamities and their intimates. Think, for example, of questions of disaster prevention as opposed to rescue, or of weighing air safety against car safety. It may well be that if the views of the world that most gripped us were the ones best supported by the evidence, and if our psychological makeup were such as to yield coherent preferences, we would rank the importance of these matters quite differently from the ways we do.

It does not follow, though, that rational policy consists in ignoring our actual feelings of urgency. Even if a pattern of felt urgency is tied to incoherent tendencies in the ways we see the world and form our preferences, the pattern matters if it is ours. It is our actual feelings of urgency that determine much in the ways we experience our lives and the ways we experience each other—in many of the things that make our lives intrinsically rewarding or unrewarding. Reasonable ways of arranging our lives and our societies will take account of us as we actually are and as we actually might be.

I take all this so far to be almost truistic. The serious question and the one I want to take up is not whether our feelings of urgency should be taken into account at all, but in what ways. Two ways suggest themselves. Perhaps, on the one hand, we should steadfastly maximize expected total intrinsic reward and take our feelings of urgency into account only as contributory factors—factors that enhance or detract from total intrinsic reward or that render some schemes feasible and others infeasible. Alternatively, we could treat these psychological tendencies as guides to what ultimately we should be trying to achieve. The first way, in other words, is to leave our choice of ultimate ends unaffected by actual feelings of urgency, but to take account of these feelings in our choices of means. Even if what maximizes expected total intrinsic reward is not what we find most urgent, intrinsic reward, on this line, is what public policy should aim to promote. Felt urgency is a factor to be considered, but it is in no way an ultimate guide. The second way is to alter our choice of ultimate ends to cohere with what we feel most urgent, even if that means recognizing things other than intrinsic reward as having ultimate worth. On this line, it is felt urgency, suitably examined, that tells us what ultimately to pursue in public policy.

What must be said about risk-cost-benefit analysis, then, depends on the central problem of ethical theory: how questions of ultimate ends are to be addressed. The rest of my discussion will proceed in two parts. I shall first ask what follows if we accept maximization of total expected intrinsic reward as our sole ultimate end. When we take into account the discrepancy between cost-effectiveness and our perceptions of urgency, does that discredit direct applications of risk-cost-benefit analysis? Then I shall take up the alternative thesis: that if caring about something gives significance to our lives, then that thing is good intrinsically, and not merely good as a means of enhancing intrinsic reward. I shall discuss some of the puzzles such a view raises for public policy with regard to risk.

Sophisticated Intrinsic Reward Maximization

Throughout this section, I accept, at least for the sake of argument, that the intrinsic reward of lives is what is ultimately valuable. The best policies, then, are the ones that most enhance total intrinsic reward, and in prospect those policies are best that most enhance the expected value of total intrinsic reward. I shall ask whether we can reasonably conclude from these assumptions that policies should be judged by the kind of "purified" risk-cost-benefit analysis that I have sketched.

It seems clear that we can. If properly conducted, risk-cost-benefit analysis takes account of all costs and all benefits, where costs and benefits are reckoned in terms of prospective total intrinsic reward. By its very nature, then, the method must properly take account of us as we are, with all our incoherences. It must take account of our actual feelings of urgency and do so to the optimal degree and in the optimal way. To be sure, our preferences and emotional tendencies are incoherent, and that fact must figure in our reckonings, but a "purified" risk-cost-benefit analysis takes these things into account.

How do incoherent tendencies and actual feelings of urgency bear on intrinsic reward? In the first place, our incoherent tendencies will figure in predictions about what people will do in response to social decisions, and hence of what kinds of policy outcomes are attainable. The effects of a highway policy, for instance, will depend in part on how people will drive if the policy is implemented. More to the point here, our preferences and our emotional and moral responses figure in how we experience our lives. Suppose, for example, that given any budget for safety in mining, fewest lives will be lost if the entire budget is spent on prevention of accidents and on easy rescues, and no heroic or extraordinarily expensive rescues are attempted in case of disaster. It may nevertheless be dehumanizing to stand idly by when strenuous, expensive effort has a substantial chance of saving lives. It may be dehumanizing even to stand ready to do so. The term "dehumanizing" here can be interpreted in a way that bears directly on intrinsic reward: A stance is dehumanizing if it interferes with the direct psychological rewards of human fellowship. Standing by when there is a crying need for help may make it hard to face oneself, or to face anyone else with feelings of trust. Doing so may so go against normal, sympathetic impulses that it fetters their free expression. Perhaps even to be the kind of person who stands ready to act in this way is to some degree to remove oneself from the normal rewards of human fellowship. That may particularly be so if the disposition is not a matter of weakness in the face of danger, but of conscious policy.

Now, I find it quite unclear to what degree these claims could be made out—particularly if we imagine a society with considerable consciousness of why we have adopted the policies we have. If these effects of "dehumanization" really are significant, though, what follows is simply that a risk-cost-benefit analysis that takes into account all contributions to expected total intrinsic reward must count things other than lives saved, injuries and illnesses avoided, and resources diverted to do these things. It must count effects on the ways people who stand ready to carry out a policy experience their lives. When we calculate expected total intrinsic reward, we may need to take into account deep psychological effects of policies. This raises no difficulty in principle for risk-cost-benefit analysis as I have sketched it, but it suggests that the questions involved cannot be reduced to an automatic calculus.

There remains, however, a more profound charge to be leveled: that the very process of making certain decisions by calculation detracts from intrinsic reward. The very process may be dehumanizing for those who make the decisions. The process itself may break bonds of trust between those who decide and the rest of us whose spontaneous sense of relative urgency is violated. To be governed by standards with little natural appeal may break bonds of trust in each other. Making decisions by risk-cost-benefit analysis, in short, may profane things that must be held sacred—things that, because of who we are, we must hold sacred if our lives are to be deeply rewarding.

The problem here is a general one for any teleological view of ethics— for any view, that is, that starts with an account of what ultimately is of value and then prescribes acting in the rational pursuit of that ultimate value. Suppose, for instance, there is something sacred, and hence immensely valuable, about deciding matters in a certain way. One will not be able to achieve that value by including it in a mathematical function that gives the values of various possible outcomes and then calculating how best to maximize the expected value of that function. To achieve proper detachment, let us make the example highly artificial— let it involve something few of us would regard as a value at all, much less a sacred value. Suppose there is sacred value in faith in decisions based on augury—that is, priests' examinations of the entrails of sacrificial animals. Clearly, that way of deciding will exact a substantial cost in terms of various profane values, such as staying alive and achieving success in our ventures. Sacred entrails, after all, are poor predictors. It will exact a cost as well in terms of whatever sacred values success in our mundane ventures allows us to foster. It seems rational, then, in making decisions, to compare the sacred value that inheres in our faith in augury with the expected value of consequent losses. So to do, however, would be to foreclose achieving the sacred value of augury. For suppose we make our important decisions rationally: by first calculating whether the sacred value of faith in augury is worth its instrumental cost, and then employing augury if indeed it is worth its cost. This is not to act from faith in augury; it is explicitly to repudiate taking the value of augury on faith. The sacred value of augury might on the whole be worth its instrumental cost, but no one who worked out in a rational way whether it was could achieve the sacred value involved. Some sources of intrinsic reward may be available only to the irrational.

We might call this the *paradox of teleology.*[11] By *teleology* I mean the practice of deciding what to do on the basis of the expected value of the consequences of the available alternatives. Whether a decision procedure is teleological on this characterization is not a matter of the nature of the values involved. These values might be entirely hedonic, or at least entirely inherent in the intrinsic qualities of our lives as we experience them. They might, on the other hand, include features of the world that are not simply features of conscious experience, such as true friendship, genuine knowledge, appreciation of true beauty, and the like. They might, then, include sacred values that are not simply values of conscious experience. The paradox is this: What values are achieved may depend on the very ways in which we make decisions, or on the very ways in which we stand ready to make decisions. That may be because certain aspects of ways of making decisions have intrinsic value, or it may be because these aspects have instrumental value. In either case, rationally pursuing maximum value may not maximize value.

Does the paradox of teleology, as illustrated, say, by the augury example, give us reason to question risk-cost-benefit analysis as a guide to policy? The case for doubt could be put as follows. Suppose, in our thinking about public policies, we are guided only by considerations of expected intrinsic reward. We then risk making some intrinsically rewarding aspects of life inaccessible. The intrinsically rewarding life must be a life of intrinsic commitment to values other than intrinsic reward in life. A person capable of leading an intrinsically rewarding life must, for example, stand ready to come to the aid of those in distress, and to do so even at a cost that would be prohibitive if paid whenever equal chances of saving equally valuable lives could be had at an equal or lesser price. To drive carefully, use seat belts, put childproof caps on bottles, and treat water with charcoal filters all contribute to intrinsic reward instrumentally, by preventing disease and accidental injury and poisoning. The same goes for increases in productivity: They contribute to intrinsic reward by allowing people to buy more of the things they want or reducing the time they must spend in drudgery. Not so with heroic lifesaving and visible achievements in areas of current public concern, like pollution control and preservation of nature. These contribute to intrinsic reward not only instrumentally, but in ways that are not instrumental. The life of a person who stands ready to engage in heroic lifesaving measures or pursue the enhancement of beauty without counting the cost is more intrinsically rewarding than the life of someone who is not, and life in a community where these values prevail is more intrinsically rewarding than life in a community where they do not.

What are we to say to this argument? It is important first to distinguish between what might be called "detached" and "engaged" aspirations. The goals and passions that give meaning to our lives as we live them need not be for those things we would find of value in a detached "cool hour." This point is discussed by Sidgwick, who mentions engagement in pastimes.[12] If playing tennis enhances the intrinsic reward of one's life, it may be good to have a passion for the game, and to care intrinsically about winning and about achieving and exercising skill in the game. We do not suppose, however, that to reap the rewards of a passion for tennis one must be unwilling to assess it. One need not refuse ever to look at one's passion from a perspective that does not count skill and winning as goods in themselves. It makes sense to ask from time to time whether the passion has become an obsession that detracts from the intrinsic reward of one's life, or whether at least the passion enhances intrinsic reward less than would a more relaxed attitude toward the game.

The same contrast can be drawn from any goal that is sufficiently encompassing. A person who wanted above all to achieve success upon the stage would be ill advised to calculate his every gesture to that end. Rather, he should try to cultivate an intrinsic concern for good acting and with aspects of the play in which he is performing. It would still make sense, though, for him to take a detached perspective from time to time, and to ask which of the dispositions he is cultivating contribute to his long-term goal. In these cases, in short, we can distinguish *engaged* values from *ultimate* values. *Engaged values* are the things it makes sense to be concerned with, in some cases deeply or passionately, as we live our lives; *ultimate values* are those things it makes sense to be concerned with from a more detached perspective.

In the cases I have discussed, then, the paradox of teleology is defused by noting that the engagements and passions that give our lives much of their value can be assessed from time to time from a detached perspective. From this detached perspective, the objects of our engagements and passions are not seen as having all the value that we feel them to have when in the heat of engagement. It is from this perspective that we can see these engagements and passions as enhancing the value of the lives we experience. Taking this perspective does not render values unattainable; it lets us pursue them if, on reflection, they seem worthy of pursuit.

These reflections support a life of qualified teleology, the kind of teleology involved in the long-term pursuit of any broad goal, such as success upon the stage. Such a qualified teleology, its proponents may say, is immune to the paradox of teleology; only an absurd version of teleology falls prey to the paradox.

What, then, of "sacred" values and personal commitments that give meaning to our lives? Can they be treated as I have been treating the enthusiasm for a pastime? Can they, although unquestioned from the engaged standpoint, be treated from a detached standpoint as valuable only for the ways that holding them enhances the intrinsic reward of human lives? Or must a person who so regards them find that his sacred values and personal commitments no longer give his life a sense of significance, so that his life loses much of its intrinsic reward? The question is, of course, one for empirical psychology, and I cannot establish an answer. It does seem to me, though, that the kind of refined teleology I have been discussing is part of a worthy human ideal: the life that is engaged and committed, but is also reflective. In a cool hour, we should be willing to reflect on what we regard with reverence in normal life. I do not see why such reflection should loosen those of a person's attachments he finds most productive of intrinsic reward.

Ultimate Ends Other Than Intrinsic Reward

In the preceding section I assumed that ultimate value lies only in intrinsic reward. Should we genuinely accept this? Suppose that part of what gives meaning to our lives is a perception of our species as one among a rich variety of species in nature. Why is it not, then, of ultimate value to preserve in nature a rich variety of species? Suppose that part of what gives significance to our lives is the natural link between sexual intercourse and procreation. Why should the maintenance of that link not then be an ultimate value? Can we reduce the "sacred value" of these things to the value of feelings, or even to the value of a sense of meaning and significance in life?

The issue can be formulated in economists' terms. An "objective function" tells us what is to be maximized. This is not to say that there is a single "thing" that it makes sense to maximize. The point, rather, is this: Suppose we have finally decided what it makes sense, ultimately, to want, and what trade-offs it would make sense to accept if we were forced to choose among various competing goods. Then our contingency plans, if they are coherent, can be expressed as plans to maximize some particular function of features of the world. Now what I have been saying so far is that feelings stemming from incoherent dispositions toward preferences may be of intrinsic value. Those feelings, then, it follows, must be counted in the objective function. I am now considering a stronger claim: that the values involved cannot be reduced to the values of feelings, or to the value of a sense of significance in our lives. In a case of heroic rescue, for example, what is valuable is not just the feelings of social fellowship that stem from being ready to rescue each other at extraordinary cost. Additional value lies in being the kinds of people who will go to heroic lengths to rescue others, and in our community's being the kind of community in which we stand ready to go to heroic lengths to rescue each other. That amounts, in economists' language, to saying that we must include the very value of being such people and having such a community in our objective function.

Three sorts of claims must be distinguished here. One is that not all values can be reduced to narrowly hedonic values—to the goodness of enjoyment and the badness of suffering. A sense of the significance of one's life and of what one is doing is a crucial part of the good of human life. This claim I have already granted. Ruth Benedict tells of a Digger Indian chief who told her, "In the beginning, God gave to every people a cup, a cup of clay, and from this cup they drank their life. They all dipped in the water, but their cups were different. Our cup is broken now. It has passed away."[13] The "cup" here is no mere matter of enjoyment in any ordinary sense, and I mean the term *intrinsic reward* to encompass the value of the unbroken cup. The view that intrinsic reward, so broadly conceived, gives the ultimate standard for assessing moral claims might be called *eudaimonism* (after the Greek term *eudaimonia*, which is standardly translated as "happiness," but which broadly connotes being truly fortunate).

A second possible claim is that if we value something intrinsically, and our so valuing it is part of what gives our lives a sense of significance, then our valuing it gives it worth. To value something *intrinsically* is to tend to value it for its own sake, independently of what it can be expected to promote or bring about. Now we value things other than the intrinsic reward of our lives: the respect of others and their concern when we need it, genuine mutuality, a memory that will outlast us. These are things that ordinarily contribute to the intrinsic reward of our lives, but we do not, it would seem, value them solely to the degree that they promise intrinsic reward. Thinking falsely that others respect us and care about us, or thinking falsely that we will be remembered after our deaths, might conceivably contribute to the experience of life in just the same way as would believing these things in a world in which they were true. The belief, though, is not enough; we want these things really to be true. The second claim to be distinguished is that because we value things other than the intrinsic reward of our lives, more is of ultimate value than intrinsic reward. We might call this view *pluralistic subjectivism:* "pluralistic" because it ascribes ultimate value to various things besides intrinsic reward, "subjectivism" because it takes a thing's being valued as the source of its value.

A third possible claim is that various things besides intrinsic reward have ultimate value, and that they have it *objectively*—independently, that is, of whether anyone values them. G. E. Moore thought that knowledge and unmistaken apprehension of beauty were objectively of intrinsic worth.[14] We could in effect "see" the value of these things, he maintained, but they had that value independently of whether anyone recognized it. The third claim, then, is that things other than the intrinsic reward of our lives are of ultimate value, and we value them *because* they are good. It is not our valuing them that makes them good.

The noun *value* can be used to equivocate in a way that insinuates that whatever is valued is of worth. *Value* as a noun has two distinctive meanings. First, it can be used by a person who, like G. E. Moore, thinks that there are such properties as objective goodness or badness, to mean simply a degree of such objective goodness or badness. Such an objectivist can use the term to deride those who know "the price of everything and the value of nothing"; *value* in this sense means much the same as *worth*. Second, the term can be used in a way that is "value-free" in the sense that it does not involve the speaker's ascribing or denying worth to anything. Now by equivocating on these two distinct uses, one can insinuate the view that I call subjectivism: that things have ultimate worth to the degree that they are intrinsically valued. One can establish what values people have in the psychological, value-free sense by establishing what they regard as of worth. One can then speak as if the things that are "values" in the sense of being valued are "values" in the sense of having worth. This equivocation is one to avoid if we want to think clearly.

This equivocation aside, what can we say to the claim of subjectivism—to the claim that something's being intrinsically valued makes it of ultimate worth? Suppose the critic of eudaimonism is right in his psychological claims: Part of what gives our lives significance is that we hold certain things sacred or to be matters of supreme worth. It is reverence or respect for these things that gives our lives a sense of dignity and purpose, although these things themselves are not simply matters of intrinsic reward. Granting all this, we can still ask a normative question: Are these things really of ultimate value simply because we value them intrinsically and our so valuing them helps to give our lives a sense of significance?

I have been speaking as if things simply were or were not "of value," as if being "of value" were simply a property things may have or lack, a property we understand. If we understand the term *of value* in this way, then there is considerable strain in supposing that whatever a person values intrinsically is on that account of ultimate value. We have been given different cups; different things are valued by different people. Some would value that the whole world should be of a particular religion, although different such people adhere to different religions. Some value that their own group preserve the religion that distinguishes them. Are each of these—the preservation of various particularistic religions and the conversion of the whole world by each of the various religions that claim universal validity—of ultimate worth because of this? There is perhaps no logical incoherence in saying so; it may be that we simply have competing ultimate goods, as we do when there is not enough ice cream for all who would enjoy it. The incompatibility in this case is logical, and the values involved are of deeper significance, but the cases may alike be ones of genuine goods not jointly attainable.

Pluralistic subjectivism is consistent; the problem is that once its implications are spelled out, it seems hard to take its claims seriously.

Suppose one thing that gave significance to the lives of our forebears was the hope that we would remain true to their ways, but that those ways are not now part of what gives anyone a sense of the significance of his life. Suppose our dead grandparents hoped that their granddaughters would defer to their husbands and obey them in all things. Is it then *pro tanto* a bad thing if the granddaughters do not do so, although what the grandparents cherished now leaves everyone cold? If not, why not? If we accept that whatever a person values apart from the intrinsic reward of his life is of worth because he values it, that presumably goes for those who died long ago: Their death simply makes it quite clear that we are talking of things that cannot contribute to the intrinsic reward of their lives.[15]

The problem here may lie in hypostatizing value: in treating the question whether something is of worth as a simple question of fact, a question of whether that thing has or lacks a particular property "worth." Perhaps what we should ask is not what sorts of things are "of worth" in any literal sense, but what it is reasonable for us to value. It may be reasonable, after all, for different people to value different things. It may be reasonable for the grandparents to value "womanly virtue" as they conceive it, and thus to value it in their granddaughters, but be unreasonable for the granddaughters to do so. Put this way, the question of what has ultimate value becomes this: Is it reasonable, in a cool hour of reflection, to value a thing intrinsically whenever valuing that thing in day-to-day life is part of what gives our lives a sense of significance? Is it reasonable to do so even if that thing does not itself constitute part of the intrinsic reward of one's life? Or is the reasonable course rather to treat these things as being of value in daily life as we engage in it, but to recognize in our more detached moments that it would not make sense to do so if doing so did not promise to contribute to the intrinsic reward of our lives?

With the alternatives posed in this way, at least two sorts of arguments seem to speak against confining ultimate value to intrinsic reward and in favor of ultimately valuing, even from our most detached perspectives, the things we should hold sacred in the press of life. First, it may be that we cannot fail to value those things ultimately without undermining the grip they have on us in the heat of engagement. If so, then it detracts from the intrinsic reward of our lives if we fail to ascribe ultimate worth to things other than intrinsic reward. Would it be reasonable to accept the thesis that only intrinsic reward is of ultimate worth, if doing so seriously diminished the intrinsic reward of one's life? The claim that it is seems paradoxical.

This is again to raise the paradox of teleology. The paradox, it may be claimed, vitiates not only a moment-to-moment exclusive concern with intrinsic reward, but even the acceptance of intrinsic reward as the sole ultimate value from the most detached perspective it makes sense to take. The paradox of teleology might conceivably apply to any system of values, and so the claim cannot be that the mere possibility of a paradox of teleology discredits a system of values. Perhaps the claim is that the actuality of such a paradox would matter: that reason requires us to adopt ultimate values we could in fact hold, at least as detached values, without impairing the intrinsic reward of our lives.

This claim seems hard to reject, but the price of accepting it is high. A chief attraction of eudaimonism is that it involves a search for what, from a detached standpoint, it is reasonable for anyone to want for himself. Once we realize that we have been given "different cups"—that the things that give a sense of significance to my life are not the things that give it to yours—we can find common ground for our ethical judgments, eudaimonists think, in the reflection that some things that leave me cold give a sense of significance to your life, and some things that leave you cold give a sense of significance to mine. We can then agree ultimately to treat the importance of a sense of significance in life as the common denominator that allows us to resolve conflicts of values. We agree to live our lives engaged by different values, but to recognize constraints on the pursuit of those values—constraints that are justified ultimately by considerations of intrinsic reward.

Instead it seems that we are each to be told something like this: "Stick to your guns. Regard whatever values engage you in the daily course of life as the things it is reasonable to value. Do not let your convictions be undermined by a search for a common basis of value. Whatever values most engage you are those you should use for the kind of thinking that underlies the choice of ultimate moral principles." Such advice should give us pause. Does it allow ethics to be anything more than a search for a *modus vivendi* that each of us would violate for the sake of his own values if he thought he could get away with it? The content of a modus vivendi will depend only on threat advantage and considerations of stability. A modus vivendi is clearly better in most cases than a state of war, but the hope morality holds out is that we can do better.

Still, we can ask what methods of dealing with risk are to be recommended in a modus vivendi. On this I have little to say. It should be recognized, though, that in a modus vivendi there might be much to recommend the *ex ante* Pareto principle. For purposes of a modus vivendi, "benefits" should be reckoned in terms of preferences—including preferences grounded in deeply held values. For if one possible modus vivendi is *ex ante* Pareto-superior to another, and if they are equally accessible from the point of view of salience and stability, that gives everyone a reason to prefer the alternative that is *ex ante* Pareto-superior. Whether that recommends risk-cost-benefit analysis will be a matter of what the values are that are compromised in the modus vivendi.

It would of course be unjust to talk as if the only alternatives were eudaimonism and the search for a modus vivendi. In the first place, a group that must live together may share common values and so may form a community of shared values. Those in a community may act in pursuit of these shared values, and those values may indeed rule out certain direct applications of risk-cost-benefit analysis. In the second place, much recent work on justice draws on the idea of a *fair bargain* or a *fair social contract* as providing a way in which people of deeply divergent values can live together on a basis of mutual respect. The theory of John Rawls is a prime example.[16] A social contract differs from a modus vivendi in that each party intrinsically values the standards of fairness it exemplifies. Thus, because each regards the social contract as fair and wants a fair accommodation of the pursuit of his ideals and interests with others' pursuit of their ideals and interests, each intrinsically values adherence to the social contract.

Whether a theory of this kind can be worked out so as to provide a genuine alternative to eudaimonism is a difficult question. Can we say anything, though, about the kinds of standards for risk assessment a social-contract theory might recommend? Some of the relevant considerations will be similar to those that apply to a modus vivendi: The *ex ante* Pareto principle will have some claim, but it will compete with considerations of salience and stability. Part of what must be required of a social contract will be some standard or procedure for deciding on matters of risk. Much of recent "pluralistic" democratic theory has embraced a procedural standard: Let groups with competing values compete in the political arena. In the past two decades, however, it has become increasingly clear that it is hard or impossible to design a political system with the peculiar virtue that naked competition among competing interests within that system will yield results that it would be rational to want. The more concentrated interest tends to prevail on each issue, leaving a pattern of decisions that is far from Pareto-efficient *in toto*.[17] Perhaps, then, our sense of fairness needs to be enhanced with standards for deciding issues of competing values, and a social contract should require that everyone will work to maintain those standards. It will help if the standards have a fairly automatic quality, so that the struggle of competing interests does not simply emerge in full force, disguised as a struggle over which interpretation of the agreed standards shall prevail.

From this standpoint, a fairly crude version of risk-cost-benefit analysis may have great advantages, especially when there is no agreement on the values involved in a dispute over risks and costs. Perhaps the fair solution to problems of competing values is to ascertain what each person would be willing to pay for the realization of his values and to maximize value realization by this crude standard. In specific areas of life, to be sure, there may be consensus on values, and these standards may be incompatible with crude risk-cost-benefit analysis. In other cases, there may be standards outstanding for their salience and stability that can be applied to conflicts of value involving risk. It remains to be seen whether contractarian theories will ever be put in a plausible form that yields more informative answers to the question: what are fair standards to apply to questions involving risks of death, injury, or illness? Antecedently it seems that such a theory might well endorse, within certain limits, kinds of risk-cost-benefit analysis that are never good approximations to maximization of expected total intrinsic reward. A good social arbiter should be fairly automatic, and that in itself may recommend risk-cost-benefit analysis as a social arbiter.

I began by offering a prima facie rationale for risk-cost-benefit analysis: Ordinary ways of coping with risk are replete with blatant irrationalities. Ramsey formulated what it would be for preferences involving risk to be coherent, and from Ramsey's postulates and the *ex ante* Pareto principle we can derive risk-cost-benefit analysis, or something closely akin. Our perceptions of relative urgency, though, seem grossly at odds with the prescriptions of risk-cost-benefit analysis, and we must ask how we should cope with this fact. Two chief ways seem possible. First, we can adopt intrinsic reward maximization as the goal of public policy and treat our feelings of urgency simply as elements of the situation we face as we devise strategies for promoting intrinsic reward. So to do threatens to detach us from our feelings and thus to undermine significant bases of intrinsic reward in life. This is the threatened paradox of teleology. I argued with Sidgwick, however, that although such detachment would be a bad thing in the course of everyday life, we should from time to time contemplate our engagements and passions from a detached standpoint, and that from a detached standpoint the goal of intrinsic reward has much in its favor. In any case, there is little reason to believe that if from that standpoint we judge policies by their contribution to intrinsic reward, we thereby sabotage intrinsic reward. The capacity for detachment is as much part of our humanity as is the capacity for engagement, and there is little reason to think that if in our detached moments we treat intrinsic reward as our sole value, we thereby frustrate our ability to achieve intrinic reward.

The alternative suggested by the paradox of teleology is to take our feelings of relative urgency not as factors with which we must cope, but as guides to what is ultimately worth wanting in life—and to do this even from the standpoint of detached evaluation. That raises serious questions for ethics: With such a move it becomes unclear how a system of ethics that is to reconcile diverging values is to find its fundamental rationale. One possibility is to consider ethics as the search for a basis of fair agreement among people holding diverse ultimate values. Whether anything like risk-cost-benefit analysis would form part of a fair social contract is not apparent on the basis of anything I have said, but it does have two important advantages as a social arbiter: It is responsive to the interests of all, and it is fairly automatic.

Notes

1. See, for example, John Graham and James Vaupel, "The Value of a Life: What Difference Does it Make?" *Risk Analysis* 1 (1981): 89–95; Chauncy Starr, *Science* 165 (1969): 1232–38; Baruch Fischhoff et al., "How Safe Is Safe Enough? A Psychometric Study of Attitudes Towards Technological Risks and Benefits," *Policy Sciences* 9 (1978): 127–52.

2. Daniel Kahneman and Amos Tversky, "Prospect Theory: Analysis of Decision under Risk," *Econometrica* 47 (1979): 263–91.

3. Daniel Kahneman and Amos Tversky (forthcoming).

4. Richard Nisbett and Lee Ross, *Human Inference: Strategies and Shortcomings of Social Judgment* (Englewood Cliffs, N.J.: Prentice-Hall, 1980).

5. Frank Plumpton Ramsey, "Truth and Probability," in *The Foundations of Mathematics and Other Logical Essays* (London: Routledge and Kegan Paul, 1931).

6. This principle may first have been explored by Kenneth Arrow in "Le Role des Valeurs Boursières pour la repatition la Meilleure des Risques," *Econometrie: Colloques Internationaux du Centre National de la recherche scientifique* 2 (1953): 41–47. I discuss it in "The Prospective Pareto Principle and Equity in Access to Health Care," *Milbank Memorial Fund Quarterly/Health and Society* 60 (1982): 399–428.

7. John Harsanyi, "Cardinal Welfare, Individualistic Ethics, and Interpersonal Comparisons of Utility," *Journal of Political Economy* 63 (1955): 309–21. The theorem as stated here is a variant of the one Harsanyi proved.

8. Harsanyi's argument has been controversial. See, for instance, David Gauthier, "On The Refutation of Utilitarianism," *The Limits of Utilitarianism*, Harlan B. Miller and William H. Williams, eds. (Minneapolis: University of Minnesota Press, 1982).

9. I discuss the notion of intrinsic reward and its difficulties in *The Foundations of Social Choice Theory*, Jon Elster and Aanund Hylland, eds. (Cambridge: Cambridge University Press, 1983).

10. For a presentation of the standard utilitarian arguments on this score, see Richard B. Brandt, *Ethical Theory* (Englewood Cliffs, N.J.: Prentice-Hall, 1958), chap. 16.

11. I discuss the paradox of teleology in "Utilitarianism and Human Rights," *Social Philosophy and Policy* (forthcoming).

12. Henry Sidgwick, *The Methods of Ethics*, 7th ed., (London: Macmillan, 1907), book II, chap. III, sec. 2, pp. 135–38.

13. Ruth Benedict, *Patterns of Culture* (Boston: Houghton Mifflin, 1934), pp. 21–22.

14. G. E. Moore, *Principia Ethica* (Cambridge: Cambridge University Press, 1903), especially chap. 1.

15. Sidgwick discusses intrinsic value and hedonism in *The Methods of Ethics*, book III, chap. XIV, pp. 391–407.

16. John Rawls, *A Theory of Justice* (Cambridge, Mass.: Harvard University Press, 1971).

17. See, for example, Mancur Olsen, *The Logic of Collective Action* (Cambridge, Mass.: Harvard University Press, 1977).

6

To Hell with the Turkeys!
A Diatribe Directed at the Pernicious
Trepidity of the Current Intellectual
Debate on Risk

Michael Thompson

Recently, California and the United Kingdom have approved sites for Liquefied Energy Gas (LEG) terminals. In this, and perhaps this alone, they are the same. After a long, drawn-out process in which it proved impossible to approve any of the proposed sites, California, with the help of a new statute passed expressly for the purpose, was finally able to give approval for an LEG facility at the remotest of all the sites on the list of possibles: Point Conception.[1] California State Statute 1081 requires that within one mile of the perimeter of the site the population should not exceed ten persons to the square mile, and that within four miles of the site the density should not exceed sixty persons to the square mile. Moreover, these stipulations also apply to the tankers laden with liquefied gas, which may be conceived of as mobile sites carrying their zones with them as they make their approach to the terminal or shelter off-shore, waiting for calmer weather before docking.[2]

Scotland has a longer coastline than California, and most of the country is sparsely populated (fewer than 25 persons to the square mile), and yet the approved site, at Mossmorran and Braefoot Bay on the Firth of Forth, lies within the most densely populated part of the entire country (with a population density of between 250 and 500 persons per square mile). Moreover, laden tankers will pass within a mile or so of Burntisland (an industrial town) and sometimes within four miles of Edinburgh, the capital city of Scotland. If the California siting criteria (explicit in Statute 1081) were to be applied to the Scottish case, it would be quite impossible to approve the Mossmorran/Braefoot Bay site, and if the United Kingdom criteria (implicit in the Mossmorran/Braefoot Bay approval) were to be applied to the California case, any of the suggested sites could be approved, which means that the terminal would go to the first site to be suggested: Los Angeles harbor.

What does this little comparison tell us? It tells us hardly anything about what the risks associated with LEG really are, but it tells us quite a lot about British and American society. But we need not be dismayed by this. Quite the reverse: It is the social, not the physical, understanding that is likely to lead us to more effective ways of handling technological risk, especially in those instances where, try as we may, we simply cannot gain the physical understanding we desire.

Three Differences Between British and American Society

1. The British approach to occupational risk is set out in the Health and Safety at Work Act. Here it is explicitly stated that absolute safety is unattainable and that, inevitably, increases in safety will take place against a background of trade-offs between risks and benefits. In the text of the act the phrase "reasonably practicable," although never defined, occurs six times. By contrast, the United States Occupational Safety and Health Administration (OSHA) is charged with the responsibility for ensuring "a safe workplace." Implicit in such a term of reference is the goal of zero risk. These differences in approach to risk highlight a polarity between compromise and negotiation, on the one hand, and intransigence and steadfastness, on the other—a contrast that is sometimes given expression in terms of a gross cultural difference between Britain and the United States: *consensus culture versus adversary culture.*

2. Both Britain and the United States have specialized agencies charged with responsibility for the safe operation of nuclear-power plants. Their very names—the Nuclear Installations Inspectorate (NII) in Britain and the Nuclear Regulatory Commission (NRC) in the United States—hint at a stylistic difference in the handling of the risks in high technology. In the United States the NRC looks to see what might go wrong, looks to see what should be done (in engineering terms) to prevent that from going wrong, and then tries to write a regulation (in legalistic language) that will prevent it from going wrong. In the comparable NII the British inspectors go around the plants (and before that the designs for the plants) and look to see what might go wrong. They then talk (in engineering language) with the resident engineers (and before that with the designers of the plants) and work out with them what needs to be done to prevent it from going wrong.

Much of this process is "off the record" and no statutory regulations are drafted. So in Britain the process remains pretty inaccessible to anyone who does not speak the engineering language. In the United States the process is accessible to anyone (or at least to anyone with the requisite time, financial resources, and education), and almost every regulation gets challenged in the courts. The consensus culture is prepared to tolerate some closure, while the adversary culture demands openness, and this polarity, by the different weights it gives to inspection and regulation, results in two very different styles of risk-handling: *the consultative style versus the statutory style.*[3]

3. The political regime[4]—the relationship between leader and led— also varies as we go from Britain to the United States and is reflected in the rather different ways that the British and Americans extend credibility to their experts. When, after due deliberation, that august body, the Royal College of Physicians, announced that smoking was harmful to health, the British populace by and large believed them. This is not to say that they gave up smoking; only that they trusted the experts. But when the medical profession in the United States made the same announcement, the reaction of many a citizen was that the doctors had discovered yet another way of screwing more money out of them.

America, it would seem, goes in for "bottom up" leadership, in which a truculent populace is forever blowing the whistle on its government. Britain (and many other countries in Western Europe) goes in for "top down" leadership, in which a deferential populace allows government to blow the whistle on groups or individuals who are seen as getting out of democratic line. This culturally induced difference in consent—strong linkage in Britain and weak linkage in the United States—places very different limits on where leader and led can go and still remain linked to one another, and it results in a contrast between two distinctive styles of democracy: *top down versus bottom up.*

These three examples take us all the way from culture or, rather, cultural biases (the patterns in which shared values are arranged), through institutionalized styles of risk-handling (the way people come to act consistently in accordance with those patterns), to political regime (the sort of relationship between government and governed that tends to sustain those institutions that are consistent with the cultural biases of the governed and tends to let drop those that are not). Now for the $64,000 question: *Why* is British culture consensual and American culture adversarial? *Why* do the British favor a consultative style for risk-handling and the Americans a statutory one? *Why* is democracy top down on one side of the Atlantic and bottom up on the other (see Figure 6.1).

	U.K.	U.S.A.
Cultural bias	Consensus	Adversary
Risk-handling style	Consultative	Statutory
Political regime	Top down	Bottom up

Figure 6.1. Some contrasts between British and American society.

Usually when people stumble inadvertently upon momentous questions such as these, they throw up their arms in horror and scurry off to see what Durkheim, or Marx, or Freud, or Adam Smith has to say on the subject. My own preferred intellectual refuge when I find myself in this sort of situation is the great landscape gardener Lancelot ("Capability") Brown. "Confront the object," he said, "and draw nigh obliquely." As you turn in through the gates of a park that has been landscaped by "Capability" Brown, there, confronting you in the distance, is the stately home that is the object of your journey. But then the carriageway veers away and, losing all sight of your objective, you are carried off through glades and valleys, past lakes and over bridges, until all of a sudden you pop up over some artful undulation and there it is right beside you. So having confronted my object—the sorts of differences that exist between advanced industrialized societies—let me draw nigh by way of a detour so oblique as to take in the simple and largely pastoral peoples who long ago established themselves in the remote Himalayan valleys of Nepal.

The Oblique Approach

The Sherpas of Khumbu, the high valley below Mount Everest, have long engaged in the risky business of Himalayan trade, and indeed they actually moved into this previously uninhabited region in order to take advantage of the trading possibilities that it offered. They have carried on this business in an adventurous and individualistic way, and in recent years they have extended these same social techniques to the opportunities offered by the development of mountaineering and tourism.

Himalayan trade and mountaineering are of interest to the student of risk for three reasons. First, there is the cheerful acceptance of appalling risk. The chances of being killed in high standard Himalayan mountaineering are currently around one in six per year, which is nine times more dangerous, according to the tables so assiduously compiled by occidental students of the subject, than being president of the United States. Second, risk-accepting communities—the "adventurous traders" as they have been called—live right next door to risk-averse communities, the "cautious cultivators."[5] In consequence, the Nepal Himalaya provides a ready-made laboratory for the study of risk, risk-handling, and risk-perception. Third, the eager acceptance of risks that could easily be avoided suggests that, for the Sherpas, risk is opportunity. Risk, contrary to the assumptions that are built into many a current approach, is not always nasty.

Since it turns out that the adventurous traders are all Buddhists and the cautious cultivators are all Hindus, the conventional anthropological explanation that individuals are guided in their choice between risk-accepting and risk-avoiding strategies by their shared values and beliefs—their culture—copes very nicely with the problem of Himalayan trade. Or, rather, it looks as though it does. Once you start asking questions about change—about *becoming* rather than just *being*—then the cracks begin to appear. Do people become adventurous traders or cautious cultivators according to whether they are Buddhists or Hindus, or do they become Buddhists or Hindus according to whether they are adventurous traders or cautious cultivators? When Himalayan trade itself undergoes change and evolves to include Himalayan mountaineering as well, the cracks get even worse. The European mountaineers accept exactly the same risks as do the Sherpas, and their style—their way of handling those risks—is also the same, yet they are neither Buddhists nor Hindus. And since not all Europeans go in for Himalayan mountaineering, it is quite easy to find the stay-at-home counterparts to the cautious cultivators, and they too are neither Buddhists nor Hindus. Culture, far from giving an explanation, becomes a way of ducking out of giving an explanation.

Try, instead, the idea that both an individual's risk-handling style and his culture are a function of something else—his social context. The Sherpa lives in an atomized social world in which the nuclear family is the economic unit and in which all sorts of institutions militate against the formation of coercive social relationships. The equal property rights of men and women, for instance, result in even the ribbons that tie the nuclear family together being very loosely knotted. His Hindu neighbor, by contrast, is a member of a joint family that is intricately bound together by all kinds of tightly knotted rights and obligations, and his most important resource of all—land—remains firmly in the control of the elderly head of that family. In such a situation there is little incentive, or even opportunity, for personal risk-taking. Even if he was able to siphon off some capital from the commonweal, the risk-accepting individual would be severely censured should his risk-taking prove unsuccessful and he lose what was rightfully the group's money; nor, if he was successful, would he finish up much better off once all his risk-avoiding fellows had claimed their share of his reward. In such a tightly bound setting the sensible way to handle risks is to avoid all those that can be avoided and to share those that cannot.

For the Buddhist, things, though less cozy, are much simpler. Since, given his individualized context, there is no one around for him to share his risks with, he cannot go in for risk-sharing, and since this also means that there is no one to insist on sharing his rewards, he might as well go in for risk-taking should any potentially rewarding opportunities present themselves. Hinduism, by the emphasis it places on the maintenance of boundaries and on the necessity of sacrifice, dovetails neatly with the group strategy of closing ranks against those external risks that can be avoided and of internalizing those that cannot. Buddhism, on the other hand, in dissolving boundaries and in preaching personal salvation, smoothes the way for that particular variety of economic individualism in which there are no economies of scale, and thereby it encourages personal risk-acceptance while at the same time discouraging any displacement of those risks from one individual onto another.[6]

If we visualize a *group* dimension running from the highly individualized context of the Sherpa to the highly collectivized context of his Hindu neighbor, then we can distinguish between the cultural biases (such as those that distinguish Buddhists and Hindus, or European mountaineers and their stay-at-home compatriots) and the different styles of risk-handling that accompany those biases. This approach by way of social context accounts, moreover, not only for how the adventurous trader and the cautious cultivator *are*, but it also tells us something about the sorts of disengagements and reorientations that would be entailed in the conversion processes—Sanskritization and Sherpaization[7]—by which each can *become* the other, as shown in Figure 6.2.

But this is far from being the whole story. While this diagram may help to clarify many of the interesting things that go on in the mysterious East, it does not cope at all well with some prominent features of the familiar West. For instance, the Buddhist's style of risk-taking without risk-displacement does not line up too well with the sort of risk-shedding that the classic entrepreneur can achieve through his relentless exploitation of any opportunities he can find for economies of scale. Nor would it be safe to assume that all bounded social groups act so as to internalize those risks that cannot be avoided. In other words, although this group dimension copes well with risk-acceptance and risk-avoidance, I still have to provide some way of accounting for the alternative modes—displacement and sharing—that are available for handling those risks that happen to be both unattractive and unavoidable. With this in mind, let us now leave the Himalayas and, drawing a little more nigh to our object, look instead at the antismoking movement in Britain and in the United States.

Both Britain and the United States have active antismoking movements, but the forms they take in the two countries are very different. Since antismoking movements are made up of antismoking groups, this difference cannot be accounted for in terms of the individualized/collectivized dimension that serves to separate the Buddhists from the Hindus, and this suggests that perhaps there is another social-context dimension at right angles, as it were, to this group dimension.

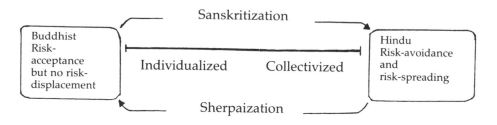

Figure 6.2. The *group* dimension of social context.

In Britain we could find only three or four antismoking groups; in the United States we found forty-one (not counting the ninety-one independent chapters of GASP—Group Against Smokers' Pollution).[8] This imbalance reflects not a difference in the level of concern between the two countries (if anything, the concern is greater in Britain), but, rather, the distinction between "top down" and "bottom up" governance. British ASH (Action on Smoking and Health) is the joint creation of the Royal College of Physicians and the Health Education Council (itself an offshoot of the Department of Health and Social Security). United States ASH (whose similarity to British ASH ends with the acronym) is the creation of one forceful individual, John Banzaf III, a law professor at George Washington University.

British ASH, much concerned with its respectability, is careful to put a little distance between itself and the National Society of Non-Smokers (NSNS), with its rather populist approach and its lineup of nonconformist churchmen and aging showbiz personalities. United States ASH, on the other hand, is not overconcerned about its reputation within the government-sponsored National Interagency Council on Smoking and Health (NICSH), and it maintains amicable and informal links with the charismatic (and smoke-allergic) Clara Gouin, founder of GASP, and all her far-flung chapters, from Anchorage GASP in the north to Albuquerque GASP in the south, and from Rhode Island's Clear Air Now (CAN) in the east to the Fresno Non-Smokers' Liberation Front in the west. British ASH sees its task as but one facet of preventive medicine (the "health wellness concept" as it is called in the United States); American ASH focuses on the single issue of nonsmokers' rights: "Sue the Bastards" reads the sign on John Banzaf III's desk.[9]

Although the smoking that the antismokers are anti remains much the same wherever you are, the antismoking movement does not. Smoke gets in your eyes wherever there is smoke, but this uniformity of nuisance is not reflected in the efforts that are directed at doing something about it. British antismoking is essentially dull, a sober-sided and carefully worded affair; American antismoking is fun, all ad hoc exuberance and righteous razzmatazz. Or to put it at its most offensive, antismoking in Britain is biased toward saving the lives of the poor unfortunate smokers; antismoking in America is biased toward putting those filthy, despicable people in their place (and serve them right if they get cancer!). In Britain antismoking is handed down from on high; in America it sprouts up from the grassroots.

How does all this fit with the idea of a second dimension to social context? The answer, I would argue, is that, even if an individual's social context is strongly grouped, the relationships that his group involvement provides him with can still vary; they can be *hierarchical* or they can be *egalitarian*. But, and this is the crucial part of the argument, they cannot be a mixture of the two.[10] This is because the dynamics of group formation and stabilization are such that only those incipient groupings that arrange things so that their members' relationships are consistent—

either all hierarchical or all egalitarian—stand much chance of cohering and surviving through time. To understand the successes of the groups that actually make it, we have to consider the failures—those countless transient and only partly formed eddies in the stream of social life that disappear before we are even aware of their appearance.

From all this, it looks as though the processes of group formation and group decay are crucial to any global understanding of antismoking movements. But what if we were to reverse this logic and try instead to use antismoking movements as just a means to a much more exciting end: an understanding of the birth and death of groups? If we do this, we move from something of passing concern to something of lasting importance, from a relevant question to an interesting question, from a low intellectual risk to a high intellectual risk. In other words, this investigation has reached a decision point. How, as the saying goes, can you soar with the eagles when you walk with the turkeys? To hell with the turkeys!

A Hypothesis

Only those groups that organize themselves, or are themselves organized, so that the relationships of their members are largely consistent—either quite strongly biased toward equality or else quite strongly biased toward hierarchy—are likely to be viable.

A corollary is that the distribution along the equality/hierarchy dimension of those individuals who share a strongly positive group context will in the general case be bimodal. This is because most of those inconsistent (and therefore unviable) groups that, if they were there, would make the distribution unimodal cannot, thanks to their very short life expectancies, be there. Rather, in the way that political parties are able to form around the modes in the voter distribution that, paradoxically, they themselves create, so two fundamentally different kinds of groups condense around these peaks—*sects* around the equality peak and *castes* around the hierarchy peak (Figure 6.3).[11]

The essential organizational differences between sects and castes is that in the sect the overriding goal of equality precludes any internal differentiation, while in the caste the premise of inequality ensures a high level of internal differentiation.[12] The sect's structure, therefore, has to be concentrated at its boundary—at the edge of the group—and the result is the setting up of a "wall of virtue" that can be seen as protecting the soft, vulnerable "us" on the inside from the nasty, predatory "them" on the outside. In contrast to this sharp cutoff—this uncompromising rejection of the outside world—the caste is able smoothly to transfer the same clearly defined patterns of rankings and interrelationships that characterize its internal organization across its boundary and onto the wider society of which it is a part. The members of a caste, therefore, do not reject the outside world; they take up a clearly specified and carefully negotiated position within it. In conse-

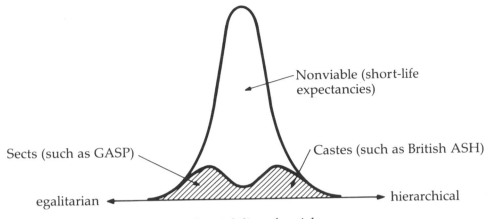

Figure 6.3. Bimodality and the viability of social groups.

quence, truculence—distrust of anything outside, lack of compromise, and resistance to negotiation—is built into the sect, while deference— the subordination of the parts to the whole, the respect for proper channels and correct procedures, and negotiation aimed at clarifying rank and position—is part and parcel of the processes that maintain caste.

The evidence from the antismoking movements suggests that in the United States the distribution along the equality/hierarchy dimension is strongly skewed in the egalitarian direction, and that in Britain it is strongly skewed in the hierarchical direction. Here, in the divergent forms taken by a movement that is only a few years old, we see the imprint of more than two centuries of history. Having thrown off the hierarchical colonial yoke, the youthful American Republic saw to it that sectism was built into its Constitution. And since that Constitution was built to last, this sectist bias in American life remains as strong (some would say stronger) today as it was then. As Hunter S. Thompson has nicely put it: Those who believe that George III is still alive and living somewhere in South America are always with us![13]

If the process of social life, whether it is American social life or British social life, is continually throwing up both sects and castes, then the persistence of the American regime—the robustness of constitution and constituency—has to be seen as something quite remarkable. And the same applies to the British regime that has similarly persisted around its hierarchical skewing. How, in the midst of so much movement, have they managed to stay in roughly the same places? How are incipient sects nipped in the bud in Britain, and how are emergent castes knocked on the head in the United States? And how is it that as this happens over and over again there are not ever-growing masses of disaffected citizens resentful of being either nipped in the bud or knocked on the head and anxious to withdraw their consent from the regimes that did this to them? How, in other words, is the switch from sect to caste rewarded under the one regime and penalized under the other? And how might subtle changes in these patterns of reward and penalty lead to the transformation of one regime *into* the other?

Lest all this seems a very far cry from the practical business of risk management, and from such real-world problems as LEG terminal sitings, let me now place my cards on the table.

Description, Prescription, and Transplantation

Even a cursory international comparison will reveal that the same risks get handled differently in different countries, that there are different *institutionalized styles of risk-handling*. But institutions are not just *there;* they have to be legitimated. They have to be credible to the populace (or at least to the influential sectors of the populace). This means that institutionalized style can exist (and continue to exist) only if there is some stability, some repeatability, in the relationship between institution and individual. In other words, institutionalized styles presuppose stabilizable social regimes.

When a government department sponsors a research project based upon the comparative method, it has two aims in mind: (1) to discover how things are done in other countries; and (2) to discover whether, in the light of this new understanding, it could perhaps do things better in its own country. That is, first there is *description*; then there is (or, rather, there should be), *prescription*. The point I wish to make is that if you have not got a typology of regimes, you have no basis for comparison, and if you have no way of relating one case study to another, you cannot produce any prescriptions. Or rather (since whoever heard of a research project not giving the client what he asked for), any prescriptions you do come up with will not be worth the paper on which they are written. An adequate theory of risk-handling style—a theory that, when applied, is capable of generating nonarbitrary prescriptions—will have to go below the institutional level and take account of socially induced variations in individual perceptions of risk and in individual strategies toward risk. And if that involves digressions into Himalayan trade and antismoking, too bad.

When we look at what goes on in one country and at what goes on in another country, and we see that each has a rather nice little feature that the other has not, we think to ourselves: "Couldn't we just pick up the *consultative style,* say, from Britain and put it down in the United States?" or "couldn't we take *loser compensation,* say, from the United States and just fit it into Britain?" We are looking for prescriptions—possible ways of making things better—and transplantation is tempting. So the big question is, "Is transplantation possible?" The answer is, "Sometimes it is; sometimes it is not." The problem then becomes to know when it is possible and when it is not possible, and why. Because if we knew when something could be transplanted and when it could not, then and only then could we do something to improve matters.

Institutions of all kinds become effective or become paralyzed according to whether or not they enjoy the credibility of the populace (or at least of the politically effective populace). So transplantation will be effective if the institution or procedure, or whatever it is that you have picked up from one country and want to put down in another country, still continues to enjoy credibility in the social and cultural soil into which you put it. If, for instance, we pick out something from Britain and plant it in the social and cultural soil of the United States (or, conversely, from the United States to Britain), will it take root? Before you can answer that question you will have to have the metaphorical equivalent of soil science, and that, I will argue, is provided by cultural analysis.

Cultural analysis does not try to explain variations between countries in terms of the cultural differences (in the sense of national culture) between them. Its concern is not with those gross cultural differences *between* countries, but more with those differences that are to be found *within* them—within American society, within British society. For, as well as cultural convergence, there is cultural divergence. The former can be captured by the concept of *national culture* and the latter by the less familiar concept of *cultural bias*.[14] One Britisher may bias his national culture in one direction, another in a different direction, and so on, but the directions in which these biases are possible remain the same in any culture, and this means that for comparative purposes we must focus on differences in the strengths of representation of these possible biases as we go from one country to another. For instance, the member of an egalitarian group will tend to bias his national culture in a distinctively sectist direction, while the member of a hierarchical group will tend to bias that same culture in a distinctively casteist direction. (And as we move away from the strongly grouped contexts and toward the more individualized ones, so we will come across another three distinctive biases, making five in all.) So the cultural-bias approach is essentially a comparative method for taking account of differences between nations in terms of their differing patterns of cultural divergence.

Take, for instance, the idea of the consultative style in the management of nuclear-power-plant risk. Could you, if you thought it was a good idea, transplant that to the United States? What conditions would have to be satisfied for that set of procedures—that institution—to flourish once it had been transplanted? Well, there would have to be trust in experts, and the American regime is very much characterized by the distrust of experts. At times it is almost as though being an expert disqualifies you from having a say in anything. By contrast, there is in Western Europe, and in the Soviet Union as well, a general assumption that the experts are the people to handle these things; that you can trust the experts and that you must trust the experts, otherwise where would we be? It is this strong mutual trust, incidentally, coupled with the hierarchical codes of *noblesse oblige* and sacrifice, that renders the reverse transplant—loser compensation from the United States to Britain—very difficult. There would have to be a considerable acceptance of secrecy. The consultative style of risk management is not particularly open, but is conducted between experts and in technical engineering language, and it requires that a lot of talking goes on behind the scenes—a lot of candid interchange that if it were all on the record simply would not happen. It would be difficult to make the consultative style work in the absence of centralized governmental control; it thrives in a climate of clear chains of command and well-defined areas of responsibility.[15] And then again, the consultative style requires the qualitative expert use of quantitative analysis. Quantitative analysis must be taken with a large qualitative pinch of salt, used just as a rough guide to indicate where the weak parts of the system are likely to be. Otherwise there would be no room for the exercise of the mysterious skill *sound engineering judgment*, and the consultative style is all about the exercising of that skill.

This little (and incomplete) catalog of favorable conditions suggests that an institutionalized style of risk-handling is a whole package; that it is not just an agglomeration of elements, but a living organism capable of gathering itself together and of responding to its environment—absorbing into itself new procedures and agencies that are stylistically consistent (or can be subtly persuaded to become stylistically consistent) and vigorously rejecting those that are not. "Style," as Oscar Wilde once remarked, "is the only essential," and the decision-maker might well fare better by listening to him than to the sweet but oh so styleless reasoning of his systems analysts.

Having reached the point where we understand that risks get handled differently in different countries, we need to turn to cultural analysis to tell us why. By providing us with a typology of regimes—of stabilizable relationships between government and governed—cultural analysis gives us *some* prescriptive guidelines. Transplants between like regimes are likely to be successful; transplants between unlike regimes are likely to be unsuccessful.

Nor is that all. To the extent that they are unsuccessful, these cross-regime transplants will be acting so as to alter the subtle patterns of rewards and penalties that stabilize the host regime. In other words, a stylistically inappropriate transplant is not just useless, it will make things worse—unless, of course, your aim is not to uphold the regime, but to transform it. Cultural analysis (unlike systems analysis, with its in-built bias of toadying to power) is, quite properly, silent on whether regimes should be upheld or overthrown. All it does is help us avoid doing the one when we are seeking to do the other.

I have gone on at some length about cultural analysis because of its unfamiliarity and because of the stress it lays upon two key concepts: *style* and *regime*. Within the context of the positivistic, scientific, technical-fixing, objective kind of systems analysis that developed during the 1960s, "style" is a dirty word[16]; and, of course, the last thing the applied systems analyst wants to do is look too closely into the nature of the regime over which his client holds sway. Applied systems analysis has over the years been content to define its client as a person who wields "legitimate authority"; cultural analysis goes beyond this to investigate the dynamic basis for that legitimacy.

So much for the deeper implications of this cultural approach; let me now conclude by outlining the remaining three biases that complete the analytic framework, and by giving an example of the way this framework, when applied, gives us some kind of handle on social regimes.

The Framework

Not for one moment do I wish to suggest that American society is composed almost entirely of sects and British society almost entirely of castes. All I am saying is that *in those reaches of American and British life where bounded social groups predominate*, this contrast is valid. But this still leaves undescribed all those reaches of both American and British life in which groups are not predominant. An adequate comparison will have to take some account of what is simultaneously going on in these reaches as well. So the question we have to ask is: What happens to this bimodal distribution when the strongly grouped condition is progressively relaxed?

Relaxing the strongly grouped condition means being less stringent about the boundedness of the group: moving toward what are called "open-ended groups," for instance, or tolerating some borderline or perhaps part-time members. Such relaxations will immediately result in a decrease in consistency in the kinds of relationships that the group supplies to its members. In other words, the bimodality of the distribution will be eroded, and, as the relaxation proceeds (and assuming no new countervailing forces intervene), so the distribution will gradually fill in toward the middle until finally it becomes unimodal.

But somewhere along this line, other countervailing forces do begin to intervene. As group affiliations decay, so the opportunities for individuals to construct *personal networks* increase. Unlike a bounded social group, whose membership remains the same no matter which individual is chosen as the initial reference point, a personal network is ego-focused. This means that the network of the rather ineffective individual who finds himself indirectly related to some forceful and energetic entrepreneur is not at all the same as that of his successful patron. (Nor is it the same as those of the individuals through whom he establishes his linkage to his patron.) The former is a pathetic little thing, just himself out at one end of a long chain that ends at the patron; the latter is an impressive and balanced affair, with the patron sitting at the center of a whole array of radiating linkages culminating in a dense encircling fringe of ineffectuals. Our particular ineffectual therefore is *peripheral* and *one among many*; his patron is *central* and *unique.*[17]

But this network-building process does not automatically cut in the moment the strongly grouped condition is relaxed. Personal networks can get going only if the forceful individual can obtain some sort of purchase on those whom he wishes to make (in varying degrees) peripheral to him, and such a purchase is possible only when opportunities exist for economies of scale. Once such opportunities exist, however, networks will proliferate throughout the individualized social fabric. The result is a pattern that, although generated entirely from the processes of network-building, has one thing in common with the pattern that is generated by the altogether different processes of group dynamics: It is bimodal.

It is not too easy to see what is going on in all this network proliferation. Unlike groups, which have clear boundaries and remain the same regardless of the individual we happen to choose as our initial point of reference, networks interpenetrate one another in an apparently chaotic way, and to make matters worse, there is a different network for every single individual. The chaos is only apparent, however, and individuals do become sorted out according to whether they enjoy *network centrality* or *network peripherality*. Those inconsistent cases—individuals central to some networks and peripheral to others—that, if present, would make the distribution unimodal are rendered unviable by the requirement that social relationships must always to some extent be transitive. Again, this bimodal distribution (along the central/peripheral dimension, this time) is best advanced as a hypothesis. Although it is possible to provide theoretical arguments to support this hypothesis, empirical ones are simpler and carry more conviction. How, for instance, if this bimodality was absent would we in the West have been able to perceive those recurrent regularities of *the bourgeoisie* and *proletariat*? And how, on the other side of the globe, would the New Guinea Highlanders have been led to denominate two fundamental categories of social beings—*Big Men* and *Rubbish Men?*

But one more step is needed before we can express these consequences of relaxing the strongly grouped condition in terms of a second dimension of social context. At present, although the three different distributions in Figure 6.4 are laid out at right angles to the individualized/group axis, each has its own dimension. At the strongly grouped condition, the bimodality of castes and sects is revealed by the hierarchy/equality dimension; at the strongly individualized condition, the bimodality of ineffectuals and entrepreneurs is revealed by the peripherality/centrality dimension; and at the relaxed condition, the yet-to-be labeled unimodality is revealed by a dimension that is still undefined. All these distributions can be mapped into just one dimension—a dimension that expresses the extent to which an individual has the scope to open up options for himself or, conversely, finds that options are closed off to him.

For instance, at the strongly individualized condition, the ineffectual finds that his scope to form network relationships with other individuals is severely constricted. Wherever he turns, he finds himself hemmed in

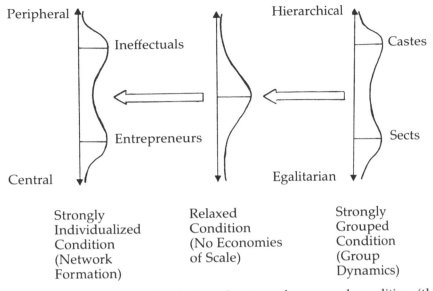

Figure 6.4. Progressively relaxing the strongly grouped condition (the relaxation runs from right to left).

by the ramifying networks of other, more successful individuals. The vast personal networks of the Big Man result in the preemption of most of the relationships that, at first glance, appear available to the Rubbish Man. So it is not simply that the Big Man *finds* his options open and the Rubbish Man *finds* them closed; the Big Man, in his coercive exuberance, is actually opening up options for himself and, in the process, closing them for the Rubbish Man. So we can say that the Rubbish Man is subject to a high level of *prescription* in that his freedom to form network relationships is severely restricted, while the Big Man is not just free from prescriptions, but is actually *prescribing*. If we use *prescription* as the dimension onto which the peripherality/centrality distribution can be mapped, then the ineffectual emerges with a strongly positive score, the entrepreneur with a strongly negative score, and the zero point on the scale (corresponding to the absence of both prescription and prescribing) turns out, not surprisingly in view of all the network-formation that is going on, to be only sparsely and transiently inhabited.

At the strongly grouped condition, the hierarchy/equality distribution similarly maps onto the prescription axis. Within the egalitarian group—the sect—there is no internal differentiation and, in consequence, no obstacle to interpersonal relationships and transactions. But this picture—in which there is no preemption, no closure of options—changes dramatically once the boundary of the group is reached. Here the members of the group act in concert to reject the outside world. Their freely proliferating relationships suddenly stop dead at this line, and all relationships with those beyond the wall of virtue are preempted. So the members of a sect are not just free from prescription; they actually maintain themselves by prescribing. Like the entrepreneur, they score strongly negative on the prescription dimension.

By contrast, the members of a caste voluntarily submit themselves to all manner of prescriptions. Rank, gradation, separation, interrelation, and completeness are the qualities that have to be preserved and sharpened if any hierarchical arrangement of groupings is successfully to perpetuate itself. Whether it be the dietary observances of the Hindu silversmith or the tea-tray niceties of the senior British civil servant, there can be no doubt that it is prescription that maintains the caste member in his appointed station.

One interesting consequence of mapping the results of both group dynamics and network formation onto this single dimension of prescription is that as one goes from right to left—from the strongly grouped condition to the strongly individualized condition—so the power axis is reversed. In great empires it is the hierarchs who wield the power and the poor little sects (like the early Christian church or the Mennonites) that find themselves persecuted. But in those more individualized social reaches that generate the trade that follows the imperial flag, it is the entrepreneur who exercises power over his un-unionized "hands." To avoid the complexities of a third dimension, we can represent this right-to-left reversal of the power gradient by drawing in two diagonals on our picture—a *positive diagonal* that links the centers of power, the castes and the entrepreneurs, and a *negative diagonal* that links the centers of impotence, the sects and the ineffectuals.

At the crossover point these diagonals form a saddle-point—a flattening out at the midway position between power and impotence, between prescription and prescribing, and between the strongly grouped and strongly individualized conditions. And this crossover point, with its zero scores on the power, prescription, and group axes, corresponds to the still unlabeled peak on the remaining—the unimodal—distribution. We can now see that this single peak forms a sort of absolute zero—a stationary point at which both the forces of group dynamics *and* the pressures of network formation are stilled. So this depicts the rather tenuous social equilibrium attained by those truly autonomous individuals—Himalayan hermits, New York taxidrivers, British owner-driver haulage contractors—who successfully resist all coercive social involvement. So with this fifth cultural bias, the *autonomist's,* mapped onto the prescription axis, the analytic framework is now complete (Figure 6.5).[18]

An Application: Two Risk Debates Compared

This analytic framework is a tool for disaggregating individuals and for interpreting a debate in terms of the pattern of disaggregation. Such an interpretation allows us to uncover the social processes that, working sometimes toward stability and sometimes toward instability, cause the

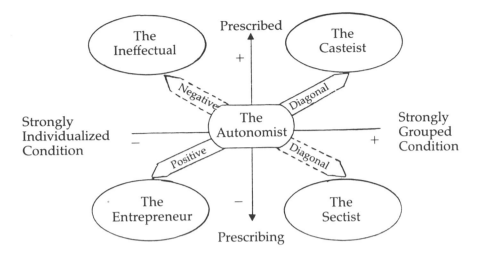

Figure 6.5. The analytic framework.

debate to develop in one way rather than in another. But, although these processes begin and end with individuals, they are also *modified* by public policy. Public policy is something that happens at one remove from the individual: It is the product of social and cultural institutions. More specifically, the social and cultural institutions that we call "government" are the means by which the debate is modified.

Because the debate takes place right there in the midground between populace and government, it provides the key to understanding the relationship between individual and institution. We can identify three clear levels, which, in order of increasing exclusiveness and control, are *populace*, *debate*, and *government*. The question we want to answer is: When it comes to the matter of risk, who gets to talk about it, and, out of those who get to talk about it, who gets to be listened to? According to the democratic (or Benthamite) ideal, all three levels are concentric—each is a miniature version of the one below—and the debate is the mediating mechanism by which government accedes to and implements the wishes of the populace. In practice, government, to a considerable extent, goes its own way: "You can fool all of the people some of the time, some of the people all of the time . . ."[19]

So, in practice, the three levels are not concentric. The composition of each is skewed from that of the one below. The debaters are drawn predominantly from certain social contexts and hardly at all from others. In turn, government, in formulating policy, pays more heed to some of these contradictory counsels than it does to others. The attraction of the cultural-bias approach is that it allows us to steer a precise course between the Scylla of insisting that everyone is the same and the Charybdis of insisting that every individual must be treated as a special case. By enabling us to recognize five distinct kinds of social individual, it provides us with some sort of methodological grip on the skewing of the three levels.[20]

To put it another way, the paradoxes of social choice, by their insistence that these three levels cannot be concentric, suggest that skewing (of one kind or another) is only to be expected in any workable arrangement—in any realizable regime. So this three-tiered system, when mapped out in terms of the five cultural biases, allows us to describe the different workable varieties of Arrow's celebrated "machine," into which citizens feed their preferences at one end and out of which, at the other end, the best social choice is produced.[21] Since Arrow's Theorem proves that it would be impossible for the machine to do this if it swallowed and digested all the individual preferences, there will have to be some fairly well-disguised rejection mechanism: The machine will have to secrete quietly somewhere along the line those preference orderings that it is incapable of processing. The analytic framework in terms of cultural biases enables us to pinpoint these secretions and to identify different social regimes according to the different ways in which those secretions are patterned.

When we look at nuclear-power debates in the United States, we find that three cultural biases are strongly represented. The entrepreneurs (in the shape of the utilities, the manufacturers of the reactors, and their subsystems, and the consultants who pronounce on everything from the economics to the engineering to the safety aspects of it all) are well entrenched. But so too are the castes (among which must be included certain government agencies, the antinuclear Sierra Club, and the pronuclear Scientists and Engineers for Secure Energy) and the sects (the Clamshell Alliance, the Abalone Alliance, and the Friends of the Earth, to mention a few of the antinuclear ones, and, on the other side, the pronuclear Fusion Energy Foundation).[22]

Much the same sort of pattern obtains in the case of the California LEG terminal debate, and, when we look to see who out of these speakers in the debate gets listened to—when we look at the decision (or, as is more often the case, the indecision)—it is fairly obvious that the sectist position carries at least as much weight as do the other two. Government, if it is to preserve an adequate measure of consent, has somehow or other to strike a complicated three-cornered balance between these three strongly represented positions within the debate. That at least some of these positions are themselves divided into pro- and anti- factions only exacerbates an already difficult task.

When we look at similar debates in Britain, the picture is remarkably different. In the debate surrounding the Braefoot Bay/Mossmorran siting decision, the entrepreneurial bias is well represented (for instance, by the initiators Shell/Esso and by the local Chambers of Commerce), and so too is the casteist bias (in the shape of the strongly anti Conservation Society and the Aberdour and Dalgety Bay Joint Action Group and of the cautiously pro Health and Safety Executive). But the sectist bias is conspicuous by its absence. In all this great debate just one voice—that of Mr. Jamieson, a member of the ADBJAG, who also registered as an individual objector at the Public Inquiry—is raised in the name of sectism. With fine and xenophobic frenzy, Mr. Jamieson castigates the proposers and their allies for despoiling "the land that fed a thousand Scots."[23]

When we look at the final decision, we see, first, that there *is* one and, second, that it pays scant heed to poor Mr. Jamieson. In fact, it is a straight trade-off along the positive diagonal—a congenial settlement between the entrepreneurial bias in favor of "wealth creation," "employment opportunities," and that great argument-stopper, "the national interest," and the casteist bias that insists that the decision should be reached in a rational and orderly way and that due consideration must be given to questions of safety (although, here again, weight is given, in the interest of order and rationality, to those parties who have "standing" within the debate). (See Figure 6.6.)

To abstract from these two machines the different patterns in which

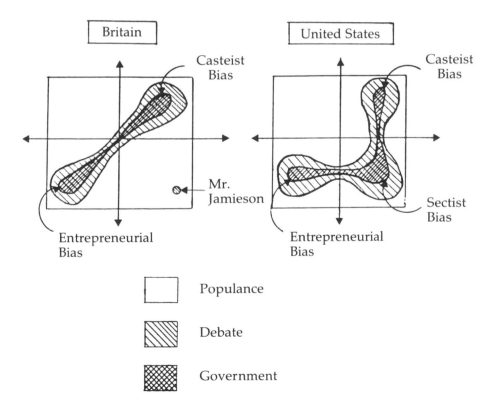

Figure 6.6. The British and American versions of Arrow's machine.

each secretes[24] the individual preferences it cannot digest, we need to look at the mismatch between the top layer (government) and the bottom layer (populace). In the strongly different patterns of balances that each system of government has to strike in order to husband consent—in order to arrive at a social choice that looks (to the more troublesome members of the populace, at least) as if it might be the aggregation of individual values—we can see just what it is that distinguishes the British regime from the American regime. The iron law of consent—that you can't fool all of the people all of the time—holds true for both sides of the Atlantic, but what these pictures reveal is that in Britain you can fool the sects, the ineffectuals, and the autonomists all of the time and get away with it, while in the United States you can fool only the ineffectuals and the autonomists (Figure 6.7).

Finally, it is perhaps worth pointing out that the two familiar notions of rationality, market rationality and bureaucratic rationality, correspond nicely to the entrepreneurial and casteist cultural biases, respectively. In consequence, these two notions of rationality are adequate for describing the British regime (but not for understanding the obstacles that, from time to time, it runs up against). But in the case of the American regime, we need a third kind of rationality, a *rationality of truculence*, which is remarkably different from the two rationalities that lie at opposite ends of the positive diagonal—but no less rational for that.

Notes

1. Subject to clearance on seismic risk, a Californian preoccupation that does not enter into the Scottish debate.

2. Implicit in this is the assumption that residents and their houses are "given"—that you cannot first remove them and then apply the criteria. By contrast, in the Soviet Union relocation of settlements is one of the variables and relocation costs are among the factors that have to be considered in what is seen as essentially an optimization problem. The legislation surrounding compulsory purchase places Britain somewhere between these extremes.

3. See O. H. Critchley, "Aspects of the Historical, Philosophical, and Mathematical Background to the Statutory Management of Nuclear Power Plants in the United Kingdom," *Radiation Protection in Nuclear Power Plants and the Fuel Cycle* (London: The British Nuclear Energy Society, 1978), pp. 11–18.

4. "Regime" (in the sense that it has to do with the relationship between leader and led) is certainly "political," yet at the same time it can also be seen as the arena (in the sense of a particular framework of social arrangements) within which the political action takes place. To emphasize the way in which arena and action are static abstractions from what is a far-from-static system, I will use the terms "political regime" and "social regime" interchangeably.

5. Christoph von Furer-Haimendorf, *Himalayan Traders* (London: Murray, 1975) and *The Sherpas of Nepal* (London: Murray, 1964). Both provide an excellent and readable account of Sherpa society and its changing involvement with the wider world.

6. I refer here specifically to the Nyingmapa (or "Redcap") variety of Lamaist Buddhism practiced by the Sherpas, although what follows may be valid for other varieties of Buddhism as well.

7. "Sanskritization," the process by which people on the fringe of the Hindu world become incorporated into it, has tended to be viewed as a one-way historical trend. But

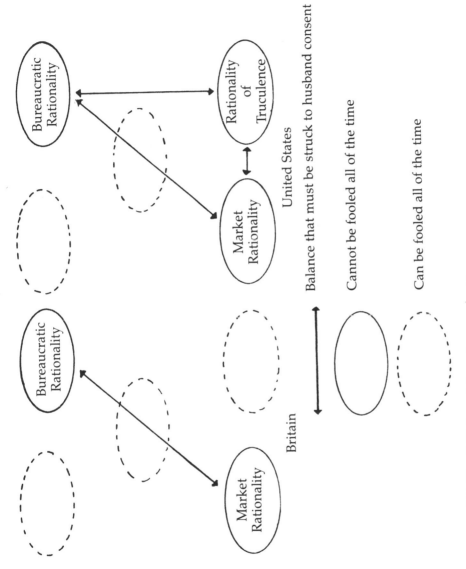

Figure 6.7. The British and American regimes.

transitions in the reverse direction, although less obvious, do occur. Haimendorf, for instance, describes the rather casual way in which all kinds of non-Sherpas become Sherpas, but there seems to be no general description of this sort of process. "Sherpaization" serves as a label for the specific instance, but I am at something of a loss when it comes to labeling the general transition away from the group constraints of Hinduism and toward the individualized yet nonexploitive world of Tibetan Buddhism. "Modernization" would do nicely were it not for the economies of scale that usually accompany it (and the gratuitous insult to Hindus). Perhaps "autonomization" would be best.

8. This was a research project carried out in 1979 by David Vachon, Aaron Wildavsky, and the author as staff members of the Institute for Policy and Management Research.

9. British ASH is prepared to add the issue of nonsmokers' rights to its present range of issues only if there is good evidence in support of the claim that passive smoking (inhaling the smoke produced by others) is injurious to health. This evidence is now emerging, and British ASH is now taking up the issue.

10. I am simplifying the argument a little. It is a balanced (or near-balanced) mixture of the two that is impossible or rather, I should say, uncommon. There will be *some*, but the essential point is that this middle ground is sparsely inhabited.

11. This hypothesis, if valid, will call into question some rather deep-seated assumptions. I use the anthropological terms "sect" and "caste," rather than the perhaps more familiar "voluntary association" and "bureaucracy," for two reasons. First, to establish some psychic distance from organizations that, because of their very familiarity, we have difficulty in discerning. Second, to avoid the confusions that would otherwise ensue once, thanks to this increased discernment, we are confronted, on one hand, by egalitarian groups, who by imposing high exit costs on their members are voluntary only at a price, and, on the other hand, by "bureaucracies without hierarchy" and "hierarchies without bureaucracy."

12. The premise of inequality, although it pervades the entire casteist context, does allow some scope for those who are lower in the hierarchy to pursue latent goals that are to some extent in conflict with the manifest goals that are defined toward the top of the hierarchy. Students of organization are familiar with the different *information cultures* that tend to crystallize out at the lower levels of all but the smallest of organizations. And indologists similarly point to the alternative strategies that can be adopted at different levels of the caste hierarchy without seriously infringing the premise itself—the all-pervasiveness of rank. See Louis Dumont, *Homo Hierarchicus* (London: Paladin, 1972); and McKim Marriot, "Hindu Transactions: Diversity Without Dualism," in *Transaction and Meaning*, Bruce Kapferer, ed. (Philadelphia: Institute for the Study of Human Issues, 1967).

13. Hunter S. Thompson, *Hell's Angels* (Harmondsworth: Penguin, 1967).

14. As defined in Mary Douglas, "Cultural Bias," *Occasional Papers of the Royal Anthropological Institute*, no. 34, 1978.

15. The contrast perhaps is not between "centralized" and "decentralized," but between *sharp hierarchies*—those with clear chains of command and well-defined areas of responsibility—and *fuzzy hierarchies*—those with some ambiguity in delegation and some overlapping of responsibilities. Although all four countries fall within the consensus-culture category, France and Britain would seem to have sharper hierarchies than the Netherlands (with its proportional representation and resultant fluid coalitions) and the Federal Republic of Germany (with its conflicts between Federal and Lander spheres). Crises of rationality might be related to failures in the fuzzy parts of the hierarchy and crises of legitimation to failures in the hierarchy.

16. A point that has been well made in the context of architecture and systems theory. See James Powell and Barry Russell, "Model Blindness," *CUBE Working Paper* (Portsmouth: Center for the Utilization of the Built Environment, Portsmouth Polytechnic School of Architecture, 1982).

17. For a more detailed discussion, see Michael Thompson, "A Three-Dimensional Model," in *Essays in the Sociology of Perception*, Mary Douglas, ed. (London: Routledge and Kegan Paul, 1982).

18. Complete, that is, for present purposes. For a more detailed discussion of how this works out in three dimensions, and for some suggestions about the nature of the possible

transitions between these positions, see Michael Thompson, "A Three-Dimensional Model."

19. Abraham Lincoln, attributed September 8, 1858.

20. A note on relativism and universalism is called for here. Since the cultural-bias approach begins by rejecting the universalist hypothesis, it might appear that this places it firmly in the relativist camp. But this is not so. The relativism of its position is severely constrained, both by nature and by social context. It is not *so* constrained that there is only one mode of being-in-the-world (universalism), nor is it *so* relaxed as to provide an infinitude of such modes (extreme relativism). Rather, it is a position of *constrained relativism* within which the considerable constraints limit us to just a small number (I would suggest five) modes of being-in-the-world, patterns of values, socially induced rationalities, or whatever.

21. Kenneth J. Arrow, *Social Choice and Individual Value* (Chichester, England: Wiley, 1963); 1st ed., 1951.

22. For further elaboration of the bases on which these groups are assigned to caste and sect, see Mary Douglas and Aaron Wildavsky, *Risk and Culture* (Berkeley and Los Angeles: University of California, 1982), and Michael Thompson, "Fission and Fusion in Nuclear Society," *RAIN (Newsletter of the Royal Anthropological Institute)*, no. 41 (December 1980).

23. Recorded in the transcript of the Public Inquiry.

24. If this metaphor appears mixed—after all, it is organisms that secrete, not machines—I apologize. The idea of style does not fit comfortably into mechanistic analogies, and, if the option were open to me, I would prefer to speak of Arrow's *genus* and of the regimes as its *species*.

7

Culpable Ignorance of Interference Effects

Ian Hacking

We are familiar with widespread public hostility to the introduction of new technologies that may have bad or disastrous but largely unknown consequences. The hostility has numerous elements that are seldom clearly distinguished. There is fear of commercial or regulatory negligence, dishonesty, and corruption. Many opponents are skeptical of over-precise calculations of danger. One school of environmentalism believes in the inherent fragility of our ecology. There are straightforward political objections, some concerned with unemployment and others arising from a deeper sort of sectarianism. I will consider one further element that has not yet been made explicit. I in no way urge that this species of doubt about new technology is conclusive. I am trying only to disentangle one of the causes for concern—one that combines some rather old-fashioned moralizing with some new-fangled philosophy of science.

Psychologists tell us that we are too afraid of disasters of a kind that occur very infrequently. That was the very first remark made in quantitative risk analysis. In 1662 the authors of the Port Royal *Logic* observed that fear of death by lightning was far in excess of the actual odds. Risk analysts since then have never ceased to point out this fact of human nature. Hence, it is said, we overract to fears of disasters we label "meltdown," "cancer," and the like.

I have no quarrel with the claim that we overreact to dangerous possibilities of low probability. However, this phenomenon may be confused with others. We are by now familiar with mildly left-wing conservatism about new technologies and old ecologies, warning of untold catastrophes. Innovators and industrialists urge that this fear is wrongly weighted. They say that it is only one more example of our instinct to overreact to scary remote possibilities.

I shall urge that there is something in the conservative position that has not yet been brought to light, and it is different in kind from excessive dread of lightning. Thus I am not concerned with the general issue of low probability of disaster. I am preoccupied by a relatively new phenomenon of novel large-scale technology, which I call "interference effects." I am also concerned with ignorance, and with decisions in which one is simply ignorant of something both relevant and important. I shall consider the extent to which some ignorance falls under an idea that moralists have called culpable ignorance.

Long ago, the economist Frank Knight distinguished decision under risk from decision under uncertainty. In the former case we know the probabilities of various good and bad outcomes. In the latter case we are simply ignorant. Subjective Bayesians suppose that they can assign subjective probabilities to every outcome and then, making none of Knight's distinctions, speak simply of decision under uncertainty. I have particular qualms about possibilities that we have not even thought of. That is the worst kind of ignorance and I question how well probability ideas apply to it. I will deal with such unprobabilistic ignorance in the second section. It is ignorance of a kind specifically connected with new technology, ignorance of interference effects.

Culpable Ignorance

Maybe we do not respect ignorance enough. We think that we can tame it with a calculus of uncertainties. Suppose that we are fearful of some remotely possible consequence of a course of action. We may not even have much idea about how the evil would come about, but the possibility still frightens us. We cordon off the fear in a familiar way: We grant some probability to the bad consequence and multiply that by the immense harm that it would cause if the event occurred. We compute the overall expected utility for acting in the way proposed. We are relieved to find that although the overall expected net benefits are diminished by a factor resulting from the remote possibility, they remain such as to make the action worthwhile.

Any rational person is supposed to see that the ignorance has been sufficiently accommodated and may now be forgotten. That seems to me to be fine for personal fear of death by lightning. But in some other cases nagging doubts remain. Do they involve anything of substance? Perhaps they do when the probabilities are connected with ignorance rather than with the precise knowledge of degrees of risk and uncertainty. Before addressing that familiar distinction, I shall first consider one of the few philosophical concepts that takes ignorance seriously. This is the notion of culpable ignorance. It can be made out in Aristotle and is discussed by Aquinas. It has little or no role in the philosophers who set the stage for industrialism; namely, Bentham and Kant. Although variants of culpable ignorance retain a foothold in common law, the industrial philosophers, whether consequentialists or deontologists, have little to say about it. Only philosophers steeped in the writings of an earlier era, such as Philippa Foot and G. E. M. Anscombe, pay much attention.

Three Roles

The idea of culpable ignorance can be put to at least three uses: (a) "You are to blame for acting in ignorance." (b) "You would be culpable if you acted without finding out more." (c) "Given that you cannot find out any more, you should not pursue this kind of course of action at all." In slightly greater detail:

(a) *Blame.* An agent does something harmful, not knowing that harm would result. But the agent ought to have found out, so the ignorance is culpable. The ignorance is also culpable even if, by luck, no harm does result from an action that might have done substantial damage.

(b) *A prod to inquiry.* An agent may decide to find out more before acting, realizing that acting in the present state of ignorance would be blameworthy.

(c) *A ground for inaction.* An agent may decide to do nothing, being unwilling or unable to find out more about possible bad consequences. To act in such a situation would be a matter of culpable ignorance, even though the ignorance itself may be unavoidable.

In each case, the source of blame is not merely being ignorant, but acting in that state of ignorance. It is easy to give examples of clearly culpable ignorance; it is equally easy to give perplexing borderline cases.

I drive a 1967 Bonneville convertible, still in fair shape thanks to a generous climate. If I do not have the brakes checked every few months, then I am culpably ignorant of the state they are in, for I know that old brake systems fall prey to numerous dangerous defects. If I do not have good reason to think the brakes are safe, I am wrong to drive the car any distance. If I do drive and because of brake failure I hit someone, I am to blame because of my ignorance. Even if I am lucky and nothing happens, my ignorance was still culpable. We can if we like distinguish "culpable ignorance that contributed to real injury" from "fortunately inconsequential culpable ignorance." Naturally, we punish the former more than the latter.

Note that if my brakes have been checked by what I have every reason to believe is a good mechanic, or if I am driving a new car, then even if my brakes fail and cause actual harm, I am not thereby blameworthy. I was ignorant of the fact that my brakes were dangerous, but that was not my fault. My ignorance was innocent, no matter how guilty I feel and no matter how much I am punished for the resultant accident.

A remark of Aristotle's suggests one way to distinguish innocent from culpable ignorance. The culpable concerns the universal rather than the particular. I think that, on this already generous reading, what Aristotle means is this. My repairs may be done by a temporary, unreliable mechanic at a usually reliable shop. He loafed and failed to inspect; I paid for the service in good faith. This is a particular matter of fact that may have disastrous consequences, but I have no duty to determine every particular obscure possibility of this sort. There is no end to such particulars. On the other hand, it is a universal truth that old cars develop all sorts of problems: worn shoes, leaks in the line, and so forth. In the light of this universal and some other universals about cars whose brakes fail, I am culpably ignorant if I do not check the brakes often.

It is not altogether clear how to work the distinction. It aims at sorting things one ought to know from things one could not be expected to know. But surely one ought to know many particulars. Suppose you build a nuclear-power station or a weapons laboratory full of plutonium on top of some geological faults in an area of high seismic activity. Are you not culpable if you are ignorant of the geological pattern? Yet is that pattern not a particular rather than a universal fact? So don't we have to know some particulars? Yes, but we ought to know them because of some universals that we also ought to know: that plutonium is bad for living beings, that earthquakes are bad for buildings, and so forth. We ought to know particulars that can be expected when they are combined with universals that make them harmful. I am not culpable if I ignorantly build a vineyard in an earthquake-prone area. Likewise, I am not culpable if I am ignorant of an entirely fortuitous fact that is not the sort of thing that tends to happen in the circumstances of my choice of action. I am not responsible for knowing the unlucky fact that the new car has bad brakes or that the temporary mechanic was fraudulent.

Probabilities

It may appear that there is nothing special about culpable ignorance, for it can be accommodated in the elementary calculus of probabilities and utilities. The more dangerous the unknown event, the greater the culpability. The less probable the unknown event, the less the culpability. Can we not cast all this into a familiar scheme? I shall urge that we ought not to do so, but first let us see how such a scheme might go. For simplicity, suppose that brakes have only two states, "safe" and "dangerous." We would be concerned with probabilities and utilities like these:

$P(D)$:   The probability that the brakes are dangerous.

$P(D/IR)$:   The probability that the brakes are dangerous after making an inspection and doing the recommended repairs. (This includes many possibilities. The brakes may start out dangerous and inspection may fail to show that. They may start out safe, be wrongly diagnosed, and the resulting "repair" may make them dangerous. They may start out dangerous and undergo sound inspection but receive defective treatment that makes them even less trustworthy. Thus this quantity is a sum of probabilities.)

$U(D)$:   The expected (dis)utility to others of my driving (some set

distance) with dangerous brakes. (There will be disagreement about what to factor into this. We could start with the
insurance-company distinction between liability to others
and insurance for my own losses, but that ignores losses to
my family if I am injured. I intend that $U(D)$ ignores the
benefits or losses to others that result from my driving but
that are unrelated to the brakes. It ignores the utility of my
taking a sick person to the hospital and the disutility of my
using the car in a bank raid. Nor does $U(D)$ include the cost
of investigation and repair.)

Now, I am not culpably ignorant if there is no reasonably effective
method of investigation that can lead to improving the safety of my car.
Hence, we may assume that in an evaluation of culpable ignorance, $P(D)$
exceeds $P(D/IR)$, and a measure of culpable ignorance would appear to
be Q:

$$Q = [P(D) - P(D)/IR] \, U(D)$$

I would be culpably ignorant if I drove without inspection and Q were
negative and "sufficiently large."

Note that an enormous negative Q does not yet determine what I
ought to do. Even if Q were large, investigation might be so costly that I
should decide not to drive this car. That is case (c) above, of inaction.
Conversely, other benefits may make me decide to drive in a state of
culpable ignorance. A theory of duty could teach only that I have a
prima facie duty not to drive if Q is large and negative. This might be
overridden by more compelling duties. I have a duty to drive an injured
person for help. I do so not because my ignorance is less culpable, but
because I decide to swallow that vice to serve a greater virtue (gulpable
ignorance). What of a poor person who has to drive to work every day to
support a family and cannot afford the inspection of the ancient car? At
any rate, a person can have a good excuse for driving in a state of
culpable ignorance and may even be fully justified in doing so.

Universal and Particular

Our formula for Q, or some more sophisticated version, seems nicely
to cordon off even Aristotle's culpable ignorance within a wire net of
probabilities and utilities. For example, can we not now say that the
distinction between culpable and innocent ignorance is a matter of
degree, depending on the size of Q? Indeed, the Aristotelian distinction
between universal and particular seems to become irrelevant. If it is
relevant, the particular seems merely to be the event of low probability,
while the universal is high probability. Moreover, neither universal nor
particular—neither low nor high probability—is itself decisive. Each is
modified by the relevant disutilities.

I cannot agree. The importation of P's and U's masks something of importance. Aristotle's view was that the universal is what we would now call lawlike; the particular is the fortuitous. The universal we may now allow to be probabilistic, a lawlike relative frequency or propensity, but then what is probable must be grounded in nature. Improbable events then contrast with fortuitous events; namely, events that under the description presented to us have no natural frequency at all.

Thus Q does not distinguish culpable from innocent ignorance. When in nature or by the arrangements of human society there are real quantities such as $P(D)$, then we may multiply utilities and determine the degree of culpability. But we cannot determine culpability in this way when we are unable to compute because the events of interest or danger are entirely fortuitous.

Two Models of Probability

A proper vindication of the distinction between the probabilistic and the fortuitous requires too long an excursion into rather sterile debates about probability. Here I can only sketch a standpoint within which to see the distinction. I am entirely eclectic about probability notions. It seems that we have two well-understood models and that very little in real life exactly fits either. Yet many situations in real life correspond roughly to both, so it does not matter much which we use. That is why debates about the relative merits of subjective and objective probability seldom amount to anything. Only when we have a case at some remove from either model should we begin to worry.

In the *objective model* there is a well-defined set of options, in which possible states of the world have well-known objective probabilities. These probabilities are relative frequencies within ideal reference classes, and nothing is known to determine a finer, more relevant set of reference classes. If there are only minor disagreements about utilities of possible outcomes, then we should act so as to maximize expected utility. Naturally, such a computation can be conducted using upper and lower bounds on the probability and upper and lower bounds on the utility.

In the *subjective model* I am considering a course of action that will have no significant effect on others. In the classic example, F. P. Ramsey, who started subjectivism in 1926, is considering which way to get home across the muddy fields of Cambridgeshire. Then I can represent my beliefs about the world by coherent probabilities that feel good to me. Likewise for utilities. When I am comfortable with all that, I can compute the option of greatest expected utility and act accordingly. Bayesians less sensitive than Ramsey assume without argument that their reasoning applies in public domains, but I do not accept that without argument.

Most real-life decision problems are unlike either model. Few decisions are private, yet objective probabilities are seldom available. Hence, we construct a machinery for consensus weighing and comparing of subjective probabilities and attempt a theory of interpersonal utility. But all we are really doing with that machinery is saying that many real-life situations are sufficiently analogous to either model that we can usefully reason as though we were in either sort of situation, hardly bothering to specify which.

I think that Aristotle's notion of a "particular" is an event that has little place in either model. It is an event that does not occur with any definite regularity, and there may be untold masses of particulars about which we have no ideas whatsoever. At one time subjectivist Bayesians used to say we should leave a little probability mass for "the rest"—for all the possibilities that we have not even thought of. That is fine in a genuinely subjective situation. Just possibly it is also fine in public affairs so long as one is concerned only with *particulars* of which one is ignorant (not just uncertain—ignorant). The idea of culpable ignorance could be used to defend this point of view. We are not required to know these particulars, and if we like, we can adopt a fictitious probability for "the rest" to keep our calculations coherent. It is, however, different with unknown universals. This is particularly so if the universals are of the sort I call interference effects, and which are in themselves "fortuitous." Let us then turn to fortuitous universals.

Ignorance of the Universal

One could schematize my by now somewhat imaginary Aristotle as follows. Suppose that one is in state S and contemplates action A. It is a universal that in state S there is some probability that one is also in dangerous state D. Suppose, moreover, that if one is in S and D, doing A has an expectation of harmful results. Then one is culpably ignorant if one does A without seeing whether one is in state D.

Of course, there is a problem about which of the conditions in the antecedent are supposed to be known. What if you don't know you are in state S? What if you do not know the universal? In legal cases one is typically required to know what any reasonable person can be expected to know and to foresee as the consequences of action. That seems to be right for practical affairs.

In the time of Aristotle or Aquinas there was a perfectly good rough classification of the universals that any reasonable person might be expected to know. It was rather clear what those engaged in specialist enterprises ought to know about their crafts—the navigator, the metallurgist, and even the physician or the general. But with the rapid introduction of technologies it is no longer clear what one ought to know. I refer not to the problem of access to present knowledge, which is severe enough, but to the fact that unknown universals are always lurking around the corner. Our discovery of new universal facts about nature proceeds at an amazing rate and still does not keep up with detecting those universals that bear on the introduction of new technologies.

Soon after their discovery, X-rays were used for diagnoses and as such were a boon to patient and physician alike. No one could have known at the beginning that their unguarded use would also cause cancers. The good effects of the early and naive enthusiasm for X-ray machines almost certainly exceeded the harm that was done, but had one known of the harm, most of it could have been avoided.

At this point, traditional notions of culpable ignorance become a little shaky. We are concerned not with ignorance of a particular, but rather with what, relative to knowledge of the day, might be called a fortuitous universal. There is an absolute lawlike regularity about the effects of exposing humans to X-rays, but it was not the kind of regularity that could in 1900 reasonably have been expected to occur in nature. Certainly it would have made no sense at all to assign a probability to this possible effect of X-rays.

It is clear that ignorance of X-ray cancers was not culpable around the turn of the century. It does not follow that the ignorance of unforeseen fortuitous universals is not blameworthy today. For suppose we can make the meta-inference: it is in the nature of rapidly expanding deployment of new technologies to produce such effects by unforeseeable universal facts. Then perhaps culpable ignorance, or some updated form of that old concept, does come into play. That is the topic of the next section, which consists of some reflections on the ways in which experimental phenomena are created, and then on how they are turned into technology.

Interference Effects

The idea of an interference effect is a variation on the idea of a side effect, but it can be located within a setting that is of some philosophical interest. It is best understood in a general conception that I call "the disunity of science." The unity of science has long been a dominant theme in Western conceptions of the growth of scientific knowledge. It has several aspects.

(1) Methodological unity: All sciences should employ the same methods. (This is usually invoked as part of a ploy to make the human sciences as much like the natural sciences as possible.)

(2) Metaphysical unity: There is only one world, and all investigators are trying ultimately to contribute to a single account of this one reality. Any two natural phenomena of any generality may be expected to interact, moreover, and their interaction will itself be governed by higher-level universal laws of nature, which are the deepest, most fundamental of laws. (Typically, such ideas go along with some kind of reductionism, whereby all the sciences gradually reduce to physics.)

(3) A research recommendation: Try to unify your science with some other branch of science. Try to discover interactions between different kinds of phenomena in nature. For example, Faraday spent twenty years trying to discover some interaction between light and electromag-

netism, chiefly because he believed in (2). These different aspects of nature must (he thought) be part of one whole, and he tried to find the connection. He finally found the magneto-optical, or Faraday, effect. A magnetic field can change the plane of polarization of light passing through suitable substances.

(4) Epistemological unity: The laws of nature that we at present have good reason to hold true are consistent, and when several interact in a real-life situation, their upshot is essentially a matter of resolution of forces. In practice, this may be messy and require approximations, but in principle it is unproblematic.

These four theses are logically independent. I have the highest respect for recommendation (3), which has led to profound advances in our knowledge. It may be motivated by the metaphysical doctrine (2), but one need not believe the metaphysics to search, in particular cases, for specific unities. I do not believe in the metaphysical unity of science. Nor do I believe in the methodological unity, but that is just another sign of my permissiveness. Like Paul Feyerabend, I say let there be many methodologies.[1] My attitudes toward (1), (2), and (3) may display a certain cast of mind, but they are logically independent, and they are also independent of what concerns me here: a profound disagreement with the epistemological unity (4).

All science, especially applied science, works in part by making limited models of little bits of manipulable materials, and the models for any one manipulation are inconsistent with, or only very loosely consistent with, models appropriate to another manipulation. That is epistemological disunity. We may have the ability to create two different phenomena in nature and a very good sense of how, under laboratory conditions, each phenomenon works under the conditions that we use to create it. But the phenomena we create seldom exist prior to our creation of them. When we bring them together, moreover, there may be no overarching law that says what will happen when both phenomena are brought into play. Compared to most philosophy of science, such disunification of nature and practice is fairly radical and hence requires detailed argument.[2]

An Example of Interference

Before providing a theoretical ground of disunity, a humdrum example might be useful. I take it from conversations with people at the High-Temperature Gas Laboratory at Stanford. It may be a slight exaggeration of what I have been told, which in turn may be a slight exaggeration of the engineering facts. I am concerned here only with providing a slightly idealized example, which at the same time is located in practical affairs of some consequence.

HTGL has undertaken a project connected with fly ash emitted by coal-fired electric-power stations. Perhaps 20 percent of the cost of both building and maintaining a power station arises from the elimination of fly ash before it pollutes the atmosphere. More efficient antipollution systems using present methods would be disproportionately more costly.

At present, fly ash is eliminated by building a tall chimney with many baffles. The walls and baffles are electrostatically charged, and the fly ash is charged in the opposite direction so that it will stick to the walls and baffles. After a certain amount of ash is collected, the process is stopped and the walls are banged to dislodge the caked ash, which is rather difficult to remove. This is a simplified version of a procedure in use for more than half a century, designed chiefly not by theoreticians, but by sheet-metal fabricators.

Two quite different phenomena are involved in these chimneys. One is the mechanical, aerodynamic turbulence of the particles going up the chimney, a turbulence greatly increased by the presence of the baffles and the velocity with which the hot gases escape. Precise analysis of this turbulence is difficult, but it belongs to a class of problems long investigated and now well understood in essentials, especially now that computer simulation relieves us of the need to solve all the messy equations that arise. We can construct models, susceptible of calculation and analysis, that describe the passage of particles in turbulent fast flow through a baffled chimney. The second phenomenon is the attraction of the charged particles in motion to the walls and baffles. This phenomenon is also well understood.

We may form the picture of the particles being subject to laws of turbulence and behaving accordingly. We may also form the picture of charged particles being subject to laws of electrostatics and behaving accordingly. The trouble is that the fly ash falls under both laws. The practical assumption, perhaps made implicitly, is that the ash will behave as a sort of average effect of both laws: The ash does its best to obey both laws, satisfies neither master, but to some extent goes along with both. Such an assumption, dressed in less metaphorical but no more precise language, has been the basis for building half a century of coal-fired power plants.

According to my sources, the truth is entirely different. The behavior of fly ash under conditions of turbulence and electric charge is altogether unlike what understanding of either or both sets of laws would lead one to believe. At present, we are at the level of terribly empirical research, trying to observe the behavior of millions of tiny, man-made, uniform particles going along tubes of various shapes and charges. Some tentative models have been proposed. It has begun to look as if the standard power-plant chimney is almost the least efficient way to trap fly ash. It might even have been better to have had no baffles (to diminish mechanical turbulence) or to have had no electrostatic charges, for the benefits of each system interfere with the benefits of the other. More important, altogether different designs could prove to be much cheaper to build, much cheaper to operate, and a good deal better at controlling this kind of pollution.

This reminds us of the complete instability of grandiose computations of relative risk: A single low-technology invention of this sort might completely dislodge present cost-benefit ratios for comparing coal and other energy sources. Was failure to investigate this rather evident question of the chimneys a case of culpable ignorance? The answer must be complicated. It was not culpable ignorance on the part of the sheet-metal fabricators. It was culpable of the energy companies not to find out how their chimneys worked. Note that I began by taking culpable ignorance to be a matter of ignorance of bad consequences of action, but we are now reminded of the importance of good consequences that could be achieved by answering some rather obvious questions.

Laws of Nature and the Creation of Phenomena

Realistic philosophy of science tends toward the following picture. Nature has laws. Theoreticians conjecture them and experimenters elicit their behavior. We understand nature better when we see how diverse phenomena fall under a single deep law. The laws are given. The phenomena exist. Trivially they are at least consistent and doubtless all part of some deep unified theory.

My picture of experimentation is different. It is a long story that I can only sketch. It applies chiefly to experimentation in the physical sciences in the past 120 years and to experimentation in the life sciences in the past 20 years. It is a picture that may come to replace older pictures and that is one of the conceptual issues at the heart of present problems about the growth of technology and its associated risks.

Experimenters *create* phenomena that do not exist in nature, at least not in their "pure state" (whatever that might be). This is an easy doctrine to advance in a casual way in some fields. There were (almost) no masers and lasers until a short time ago. I do not just mean there were no such off-the-shelf devices, but that this phenomenon did not occur in the universe, or it occurred only very rarely. (I insert the saving clause because of some conjectures in cosmology, where maser effects would make some sense out of some oddity in space.) Today, there are perhaps 9,000 lasers within 15 miles of my home. Ultrasound machines have become standard for looking at the unborn fetus and much else. Floppy discs pervade my environment, although a generation ago there was not a digital device anywhere in nature. Plutonium has become all too plentiful. When Francis Bacon wrote of "twisting the lion's tail"— the lion being nature—he well foresaw the future. I do not deny that nature herself gradually generates new phenomena, as new species evolve and ice ages take their toll, as supernovae explode and a background temperature of 3°K comes to pervade the universe. Such rare novelties contrast with the unbelievably rapid human creation of phenomena in the past few years. Maybe our phenomena are piddling events when viewed from a stellar distance. Certainly our nuclear power is trifling compared to that generated on the sun. It is, however, the phenomena we create that will affect our destiny, especially if they go wrong.

It is not only sensational and self-evident examples that make me speak of the creation of phenomena. This idea of creation was implicitly recognized over a century ago, when physicists began to introduce the word *effect*, preceded in many cases by a proper name: the Faraday effect, the Zeeman effect, the anomalous Zeeman effect, the Compton effect, the Hall effect, the thermocouple effect, the photoelectric effect. By now, students of the environment are up to the greenhouse effect. Leaving aside the last and most recent example, "effects" are usually phenomena that are created in the laboratory, often before any theory will predict their existence. Yet each effect becomes the instantiation of an at least phenomenological law of nature, and it is typically in these phenomena that we find the foundation for what we call laws of nature. I in no way imply that laws of nature concern only our creations. That would be an absurd reversal of the whole spirit of modern science. Our deepest laws apply, we conjecture, throughout the universe. But when we test them and use them, we commonly can attach them only via approximations and intermediate phenomenological laws to devices where we generate phenomena "in the pure state."

In real life, outside laboratory conditions, these "pure" phenomena are not in general to be witnessed. This is because—to use a picture to which I am in the end somewhat opposed—other laws of nature intervene, and we cannot see the phenomena in their pure state. The skill of the experimenter, not knowing in any detail what laws of nature might intervene, is the curious ability to get nature to behave in a regular way while eliminating all the other "laws" as part of the "noise" that hitherto prevented the eliciting of the pure phenomenon. The experimental skill, on this picture, must be knowing how to eliminate the action of laws of nature so as to get a pure phenomenon, without actually knowing what the relevant laws are. In more mundane language, a gifted experimenter can not only get the experiment to run, but knows, without benefit of analysis, when the experiment is running well. That is typically for a time span of a few hours, but sometimes it may be made to happen for a week, if enough compensation for instrument drift is built into the apparatus. Seldom does anyone literally repeat a good experiment, but many will re-create the phenomena using related ideas.

Technology and the Creation of Phenomena

Experimentation creates new phenomena. One aspect of new technology is that it transforms a one-time display into a phenomenon that can be produced with high reliability. We pass from an experiment that created a phenomenon through a series of prototypes to regular production of that phenomenon, perhaps in combination with others. X-rays become X-ray machines.

But phenomena produced in a laboratory are different from those possibly mass-produced for consumption. The experimentalist tries to produce the phenomenon in as pure a state as possible, deliberately tuning out interference from other aspects of nature. In real life, unforeseen or unforeseeable side effects of the sort I have mentioned may occur. X-rays cause cancer. Supersonic transport can affect the ozone layer. So too, we have learned, can aerosol sprays using inert gases—a side effect we might not have attended to early enough had it not been for the SST scare. These are side effects rather than interference effects because we introduce a piece of technology that interacts with an extant, stable part of our environment and produces something unexpected, unintended, and undesirable.

Interference effects occur when we combine two pieces of technology, perhaps in the same overall plant, and obtain a radically new resultant that is not merely the averaging out of the "pull" from different laws of nature. We have in general been very lucky with interference effects. There have also been costly errors. One of the more sensational is also of a humdrum sort: The use of impure river water as the coolant in the stainless-steel tube system of nuclear-power plants caused the tubes to rot far faster than planned. Given that the tubes are embedded in radiation technology, the already large cost of correcting the problem is then magnified enormously. It will be a matter of negotiation and litigation to determine to what extent this costly and dangerous result was due to ignorance and to what extent it was due to negligence.

The process of turning experimental phenomena into technology has in our day been immensely accelerated, and the sheer volume of such changes grows fast. The theoretical physicist will complain that the process of making applications of genuinely deep, new ideas is not any faster than it was eighty years ago, and perhaps it is slower. Some experimental programs in which vast sums have been invested have almost no known applications: high-energy physics, for example. But in a wide range of other areas we have an almost daily introduction of new technologies hot off the experimenter's table.

I do not imply that as we produce more and more technology we are bound to encounter side effects, some too late. Indeed, it is arguable that the parallel growth of regulatory agencies has been just as fast, forcing at least a great deal of serious thought about possible side effects. My topic is interference effects. At the experimental level, the task is to create a new phenomenon. At the technological level, the task is to remove that phenomenon from the pure state of the laboratory, where all other effects are absent or damped down as far as possible. Now, if we had a genuinely unified or readily unifiable science, whenever we combined a number of phenomena, we would be able to figure out or simulate what would happen. But if we doubt the practical unity of science and suppose that at least sometimes different laws of nature intersect in ways that cannot be foreseen, then we will suppose that interference effects are a genuine threat involving a kind of ignorance that we do not know quite how to handle.

Note that the problem I point to here is different from the familiar environmental or ecological idea that our world lives in a rather delicate balance that has evolved through the interaction of a large number of cycles of life, mountains, atmospheres, and so forth. Indiscriminate introduction of new technologies may "destroy the balance" in unforeseen ways. That is a legitimate worry. It is contested by another ecological point of view, according to which our world is extraordinarily resilient and will match each destabilizing change by new surviving structures, organisms, and societies. My observations are almost entirely independent of that polarizing debate between different visions of ecology. Mine is a claim about the nature of technological innovation. It emphasizes that not only are our instruments introduced piecemeal but also the laws of nature that govern those instruments are piecemeal laws that may act up and interfere in ways that one hardly knows how to contemplate.

Side Effects and Interference Effects

I do not pretend that there is a sharp distinction between side effects and interference effects. A side effect results from transferring one phenomenon from the laboratory to the world. An interference effect is the result of taking two different new phenomena from different realms of experience and putting them together. Both kinds of effect can be harmful or beneficial. In the next section I shall note that in fact we know of a number of beneficial side effects, but of virtually no beneficial interference effects. That is one purely contingent ground for distinguishing between them. Another ground has to do with the possibility of early detection of bad effects.

Our search for side effects has been most assiduous in medicine. We have a certain (ever-expanding) class of dangerous side effects to look for. Each new drug is tested against a range of consequences, and the best testers have hunches about possibilities not on the list: Witness the thalidomide story. Even though such testing is costly and time-consuming, it is feasible. But now consider the problems of testing a drug for its interference with another drug that is just now being tested in another laboratory. It is extremely common for older people to be treated with two or more drugs for two distinct ailments. Cross-testing of all possible pairs of prescriptions is impossible, so interference effects cannot practicably be discovered early. My mother-in-law got one drug for her heart and one for a nervous condition, in consequence of which (her doctor says far too late in the day) her teeth fell out. In technology the problems are far worse, for engineers constantly combine technologies from completely distinct branches of science. My fly-ash example is only a true parable of what is done all the time. Moreover, in engineering one is falsely more confident than in medicine. Seldom do we understand how even one drug works. But we understand perfectly well the phenomenon of turbulence and baffles. We also understand perfectly well the phenomenon of electrostatic attraction. We then think we know what happens when they are combined, when we have not the remotest idea.

Until recently the rate of progress was sufficiently slow that there were hardly any interference effects. New phenomena were turned from experiment into technology one by one. Now a single device will incorporate a hundred new phenomena all together at one go. Interference effects are a new problem to worry about, different from side effects not just in degree, but, by now, in kind.

Need Interference Effects Be Harmful?

There is certainly no a priori argument that all interference effects are contrary to human interests. It might have been the case that combining turbulent flow and electrostatic charges would completely eliminate fly ash and noxious gases as well. Yet such beneficial effects of interference seem virtually never to occur. Two questions are to be asked about this seeming asymmetry: Why should we believe it exists, and, if it does exist, why?

First consider some parallel asymmetries. Side effects of medicines are nearly always, but not universally, harmful. Aspirin is given to people chiefly to relieve headache, although why it relieves headaches is even now not very well understood. It has some bad side effects: some people get indigestion, for example. On the other hand, time and again aspirin proves to have good side effects in connection with complaints as different as arthritis and high blood pressure. Inderal, prescribed for angina, unexpectedly relieved migraine in angina patients with migraine. These are, however, the exceptions. Most side effects are disagreeable and some are awful. When we turn to interference effects in medicine, the record is even more gloomy. When a patient receives two or more medications at once, bad interference effects frequently occur that do not occur when only one of the medicines is taken. I understand that medicines almost never have beneficial interference effects.

For a different sort of example, consider biological mutations. I know of no systematic study to show that mutations induced by radiation, for example, are in general bad for the individual and the species. We could radiate a few million fruit flies and see what proportion of mutations were actually good for survival twenty generations later, but I know of no such investigation. Instead, there is an almost universal prejudice against mutations. On the one hand, we believe that our present species are the consequence of mutation and survival of the fittest. On the other hand, we believe that mutation is especially bloodied. Most mutants almost immediately go under.

A mutation is a fortuitous alteration in a system that interacts with elements of a larger and rather stable system. I use the word *fortuitous* in much the same sense as in the first part of this chapter. It appears that the stability of the larger system is such as to eliminate nearly all fortuitous alterations in subsystems—even though in the long run there will be rare alterations in one species that will change the stable patterns of a larger world.

It is important that interference effects are in the same way fortuitous. We are not, however, concerned with a biosphere, but with, for example, an industrial plant of our manufacture. I suppose it is a general truth that such plants are never as efficient as planned. (No power station of any sort is ever as efficient as its designers hoped.) Fortuitous interference effects within the goals and aims of the plant are not such as to enhance those goals and aims. Those goals are served within the plant in a delicate and highly organized way. Fortuitous unplanned variations almost never do any good, and they can be disastrous.

If we turn to unanticipated goals, we have no better luck. It might have been the case that the chimneys of industry poured forth materials that cleared our lungs and, after settling on the soil, grew better potatoes. In fact, we have smog and acid rain. Is there an analysis, drawing, say, upon catastrophe theory, that would predict this? It hardly matters: we have enough experience to see that it is in general true.

Ignorance of Interference Effects

Ignorance of interference effects is largely inevitable until after something has happened. That is of course an exaggeration: a great deal of interference is detected at the prototype stage. Moreover, we routinely search for certain kinds of effects in just those areas where we have been stung. New drugs are severely studied for certain kinds of side effects. By now, some skeptics fear that all food additives are carcinogenic, and the FDA tries to check this out.

We are cautious about foods and increasingly alert to wastes and pollutions. But even in these much-studied domains, we still tend to think in terms of one treatment and its possible side effects, rather than of several treatments and their interference effects. It is almost impossible to cross-test all medications for interference effects of simultaneous treatments. At the level of engineering, we also construct our prototypes not far from the experimental stage, where interference is artificially minimized. Then we hope nothing very bad happens when the prototype works in the real world. Usually nothing bad does happen, but that is an incalculable risk, as well as one that will escalate with increasing innovation.

I should emphasize here that I do not claim that innovation is the only creator of harms of which we may be ignorant. Many of my forbears worked in printing shops, using traditional methods of casting lead type. So they died rather miserable deaths of lead poisoning. Then there is the interesting case of cows and bracken. It appears that cattle in Wales eat a kind of bracken that puts carcinogens into milk. Similar ferns grow in New Zealand, where it is reported that powerful interests are eager not to find out whether the consequences on milk cows and then on people are similar. Assuredly, that is culpable ignorance! My emphasis on interference effects derives from my announced purpose here: to explore and make explicit a new kind of reason for being leery of new technology. It should not invite complacency about our familiar practices.

When is ignorance of interference effects culpable? Earlier, I stated three applications of the concept of culpable ignorance. The third is a ground for inaction. An agent may decide to do nothing, being unable or unwilling to find out possible bad consequences. We have had one famous case of new investigations being severely curtailed because of ignorance of possible effects. The leading molecular biologists met at Asilomar, California, and in due course the NIH and other national agencies drew up firm limitations on recombinant DNA research. Ironically, or perhaps characteristically, these restrictions are now being relaxed. With hindsight one can now say that in a laboratory that needs to work with only a liter of material there is little ground for being scared of creating a bug that will devastate the world's wheat, or whatever. But now that genetic engineering companies want production that will require something more on the order of a ton than a liter, things are, some say, not so clear. Nor do we now have the remotest idea of how to decide. There are no probabilities to enter into our calculations.

In conversation, the economist Amartya Sen gave a different and more personal case. When he was a teenager, he was treated with radiation for a type of cancer. At the time, no one knew or could readily find out the range of bad effects of radiation. People were fixated on the then-novel radiation sicknesses of Hiroshima. But the treatment saved his life. In my view, would not inaction have been preferable to treatment? As the story is told thus far, this is a dramatic version of my earlier case, in which someone drives an injured person to safety, not knowing whether the brakes are safe. A positive benefit may outweigh culpable ignorance. Sen adds, however, that another fairly well-understood option was available, namely, surgery. The doctors and the patient's family (a family, as it happens, of doctors) decided on radiation. Would I come out *against* that decision, which was, as it turns out, so beneficial not only to the patient, but to a whole generation of contemporary economists? Not at all. But I would deny that there were probabilities with which to compute the unthought-of effects of dramatic radiation treatment. After certain initial and obvious reflections, no cost-benefit analysis was thinkable here.

Interference Effects and Probabilities

It is not that in early radiation therapy or recombinant DNA research there was a "small" probability of creating catastrophic genetic material. There were *no* probabilities there in nature. More generally, interference effects arise from what are presumably Aristotelian "universals," but they are ones we do not know, for they are the unknown interference products of phenomenal laws, products that until known we must regard as fortuitous.

So long as there are objective probabilities and agreed utilities, I am prepared to go some distance down the utilitarian road. I am also prepared to correct intuitions: If we irrationally abhor small-probability, horrible events, then let us at least consider modifying our intuitions. But when there are no probabilities for a certain kind of possibility, I am reluctant to pretend to calculate, and I look with suspicion on others who would calculate on my behalf.

Note that I am not saying that we do not know the probability of this or that interference effect. I am saying there is no sense to the notion of any public usable probability here. If a hermit will produce some new technology in isolation, perhaps he may make a purely subjective calculation that is entirely his business, if that is how he wants to conduct his life. He is thereby comfortably lulled into an imitation of reasoning. Such imitations are not permissible in the public realm.

I have been saying that it is part of the nature of the production of increasingly complex interacting technology to bring in the possibility of more and more interference effects of whose nature we have no inkling. This creates a new question of culpable ignorance. It is not to be cordoned off by the pretended probability calculation of Q above. Q is not the right analysis of culpable ignorance; moreover, the entire calculation of that sort fails when there are in principle no probabilities with which to calculate. I said that ignorance of the carcinogenic effect of X-rays did not seem to me to be culpable ignorance. One could not have expected such an effect. But as we produce more and more technology, and as we recognize the constant generation of all sorts of unexpected effects, we clearly have a duty to guard more and more against what is almost a complete unknown. We have no way of foreseeing those cases in which laws of nature and new phenomena will interact in a single technological achievement in a harmful or even catastrophic way. Are we then culpable if we introduce new technology in this ignorant way? Is our only recourse inaction, or at least severely curtailed endeavor?

Such a conclusion is plainly wrong. On the other hand, I see no cost-benefit or other calculational way out of the impasse. Even were we to find in some groping case-by-case way a mode of reaching at least consensus, I have tried to lay bare an element in the left-wing conservative opposition to certain kinds of large-scale change, combined with opposition to the calculations that are used to justify or rationalize the desire for such changes. Because it employs several abstract and perhaps slightly shaky conceptual formations, put together in a nonstandard way, it is of course not to be found explicit in the conservative position. Other loosely related considerations are more familiar. There is the widespread environmental lobby, founded above all on a doctrine of the ecological fragility of nature. There are those who urge that fear of low-probability horrors is perfectly justified within a social setting and that no general rule of computation is to be followed there. There are those who contend that the danger of new kinds of risk is not to be measured equally against the danger of risks already entrenched within a community. All these are different reflections that may, in political argument, be combined in a sort of popular front, but they are conceptually distinct.

No traditional concept of culpable ignorance will suffice for ignorance of interference effects, partly because these effects are fortuitous universals rather than fortuitous particulars. Yet we do certainly have a notion of ignorance here, rather than calculable risk, and we do have ignorance to which, from time to time, blame may be attached. I believe the resolution of the obscurities I have discussed cannot come from ethics alone. Rather, it requires harder thinking about the nature of phenomena, effects, and technology.

Notes

1. Paul Feyerabend, *Against Method: Outline of an Anarchistic Theory of Knowledge* (New York: Schocken, 1978).

2. Some of the argument about models and approximations may be found in Nancy Cartwright's *How the Laws of Physics Lie* (Oxford: Oxford University Press, 1983), and some of the argument about experiment and the creation of phenomena is in my *Representing and Intervening* (Cambridge: Cambridge University Press, 1983).

The Right to Take Personal Risks

Amartya Sen

The Nature of Rights

Does a person have the right to take personal risks? Is he or she free to drive a car without seat belts, to take a dangerous drug, or to put a hand in a tiger's cage in a zoo? Are others free to stop him or her? The questions can be given a legal interpretation,[1] but I am not directly concerned with that interpretation here. I take the questions as moral ones. If law comes into it, it is because of its relevance to the moral issues. The moral questions have some deep-seated ambiguities. What is a *right*? What counts as a *personal risk*?

Acknowledged rights could of course be purely *instrumental*. They may be rules justified on grounds of their favorable consequences and judged in terms of right-independent goals. The utilitarian case for recognizing certain rights falls in this category. Such rights are not really moral rights at all. They are rules with a moral justification. They may or may not be actual rules backed by laws or by convention, but the moral claim is that such rules would be justified if they were to be in operation. One must distinguish between a *right with moral justification* and *a moral right*. The former does not entail the latter. In the utilitarian view there are no moral rights, which, as Jeremy Bentham put it, are "nonsense on stilts," with doctrines of natural rights being no more than "bawling upon paper."[2] On the other hand, there are many rights that a utilitarian would justify on moral grounds. Bentham did too.

What, then, are moral rights? These are rights that are intrinsically valuable, irrespective of whether they also have instrumental justification. There are at least two different ways of seeing moral rights. The constraint-based deontological way asserts that a person's moral rights

I am grateful for discussion following the presentation of an earlier version of this paper at the meeting of the working group on Risk and Consent, May 31–June 1, 1982, and also for comments and suggestions sent later by Douglas MacLean.

impose constraints on what others may or may not do. If a person has a moral right to take a particular personal risk, then it would be morally wrong for anyone to stop him or her from taking that risk, no matter how good the consequences of stopping might be. "Individuals," as Robert Nozick puts it, "have rights, and there are things no person may do to them (without violating their rights)."[3] Such "deontological rights" directly rule out certain actions, rather than being taken into account in the evaluation of states of affairs and then affecting actions through consequential links. In contrast, in the goal-based consequential view, moral rights *are* reflected in the evaluation of states of affairs—a right-fulfillment being favorable and a right-violation being unfavorable to the value of the state of affairs. Such "goal rights" influence actions through consequence-sensitive assessment.

While "instrumental rights" and "deontological rights" are familiar categories, "goal rights" might appear to be odd and irregular. I have, however, tried to argue elsewhere that not only do goal rights constitute a sensible moral category, but many moral problems involving rights cannot be at all adequately viewed in terms of instrumental rights, or deontological rights, or any combination of the two.[4]

To avoid some possible misunderstandings, some disclaimers are in order. First, while goal rights may or may not be incorporated in a full consequentialist system,[5] even when they are thus incorporated, such a consequentialist, goal-rights system would continue to be fundamentally different from other consequentialist moral systems, such as utilitarianism. In fact, utilitarianism shares with the constraint-based deontological system a refusal to incorporate rights in the evaluation of states of affairs. That is indeed a common feature of moral theories of such diverse philosophers as Bentham and Nozick, and other differences between these theories must not make us overlook this common denominator. In contrast, in a goal-rights system the goodness of the states does depend on the fulfillment and violation of rights.

Second, while goal rights may be incorporated in a *fully* consequentialist system, they need not be. The dividing line is whether consequences are important and not whether they are exclusively important.[6]

Third, a goal right may also have instrumental value in terms of consequences involving other rights or right-independent goals. The ubiquity of instrumental considerations related to rights[7] does not in any way weaken the claim to intrinsic value of some of these rights.

Fourth, goal rights can be characterized in several different ways. One particular view, which I have tried to explore elsewhere,[8] is to see rights as "capabilities"—the capability to *do* this or that, or *be* this or that (such as free from hunger or free to move about). The failure to have such a capability, whether or not this is caused by the interference of others, makes the state of affairs worse, other things given. This fits into the general approach of valuing freedom *positively*. It contrasts with focusing on "negative freedom"—the right not to be prevented by others from doing things one can do. Negative freedom has been traditionally seen as imposing deontological constraints on others (stopping them from interfering), but if negative freedom, in the form of absence of interference, is *valued*, then it is natural to incorporate such freedom in a goal-rights system. This would imply attaching "disvalue" to interferences violating negative freedom. In assessing states of affairs, each agent should then have to consider the negative value of such interferences, and this applies not only to a person who may himself be interfering, but also to others whose actions could possibly prevent, or otherwise affect, such interferences.[9]

Perhaps an example will help to bring out the contrasts involved. Consider the case in which person A bashes up person B. In the *deontological constraint formulation of negative freedom*, person A is asked not to do this, but other people, such as person C, are not asked to do anything at all in this context. In the *goal-rights formulation of negative freedom*, not only should A (the basher) take note of the disvalue of such violation of negative freedom, but so should others, such as C.[10] A's violation of B's negative freedom in this view is a bad thing, and C may be required to consider what he can do to help stop this bad thing.

Note, however, that the thing disvalued in this view is not the bodily harm done to B as such, but the fact that someone else—in this case A— is causing this harm to B. If B should face the possibility of being equally battered through some natural course of events without anyone interfering in B's life (such as B accidentally falling down the staircase), then this negative-freedom-focused system of goal rights would not require C to do anything even if he could easily save B from the fall. In contrast, in the *capability view of goal rights*, B's inability to maintain his bodily integrity is itself a bad thing, and if other such as C can help, they are asked to consider doing so. Both the capability and the negative-freedom views of goal rights require that violation of rights be incorporated in the evaluation of states of affairs, and that these evaluations of states be taken into account in evaluating actions (in contrast with the deontological constraints view of negative freedom), but the rights that are thus taken into account differ in the two views of goal rights. The capability view values the freedom to do this or be that positively, whereas the negative-freedom view disvalues interferences in doing this or being that (or, equivalently, values the absence of such interferences).

Fifth, the distinction between "control" and "power" in the characterization of liberty can also be important. The control approach focuses on whether the person in question himself controls the decisions affecting his life, but not on whether he is getting what he wants. In contrast, the power approach focuses also on whether he is getting what he wants, rather than only on whether he himself controls the decision. It has been argued that John Stuart Mill's view of liberty was concerned exclusively with control, concentrating on "procedures" rather than "outcomes," demanding that "certain issues ought to be delegated to, or reserved for, individual decision-making."[11] I do not accept that the purely procedural requirements incorporated in the control view provide an adequate approach to liberty,[12] nor that they reflect Mill's views on the subject, but I do not wish to deny that control might have importance of its own *in addition to* power.

The focus on control can take either the form of action constraints stopping others from interfering in the person's control, or the form of valuing control and disvaluing interference in evaluating states of affairs. It is the latter case that falls within the sphere of goal rights; the former is essentially just another way of stating the constraint-based deontological view.

The distinctions presented in this brief account are not specifically concerned with rights to take personal risks, but I shall argue that many apparent puzzles in assessing such rights arise from overlooking some of these distinctions. So far as the general approach is concerned, I cannot conceal that my sympathies are basically with the goal-rights approaches.[13] The view of goal rights as capabilities seems to me to be reasonable and cogent.[14] The advantages of that perspective are not inconsiderable even in the context of the right to take personal risks.

Personal Risks and the Effects on Others

What is a personal risk? The pilot of a passenger plane does indeed take a personal risk if he decides to ignore instructions from ground control, but obviously the right to take personal risks cannot give him a free hand in this decision. There is nothing particularly perplexing in this, since personal risk is not the only thing he takes when he decides to disobey instructions from ground control. Personal risks rarely come alone, and that is undoubtedly one source of complication in dealing with the right to take personal risks.

It might be tempting to think that the paradigmatic case of the right to take personal risks must be one in which a person is entirely isolated from others who cannot be affected in any way. Did Robinson Crusoe have the right to go deep into the island jungle without being armed, thus taking a serious personal risk? Pure though this case might be, it is scarcely an engaging one, since the importance of rights rests largely on their implications on the actions of others, and if there is no one else who can act, Crusoe's rights will have little cutting power. Indeed, in the constraint-based deontological view, even the *content* of the right is seen purely in terms of the implications on others, and if there are no others, the content is empty. With the goal-rights approach, the content is not empty even if there is no one else around, and the goal of Crusoe's being able to take this risk may be acknowledged and valued, but its practical implications would be very limited.

So the interesting cases involving the right to take personal risks might appear to be those in which others are present, but not in some sense directly involved. In this way of looking at the dichotomy, it might appear that the *case* for the right depends on others not being directly involved, whereas the relevance of the right (and in one limited view, even its *content*) depends on others being there and being put under obligation to do or not to do certain things. This is a possible way of seeing the issue, but it puts too much weight on the hazy dividing line of "direct" involvement.

In fact, it is possible to take a more "positive" view of something's being "personal": that the ability to do this is of importance to the person's way of life (rather than adopting the "negative" perspective of checking that others are not directly involved). This way of viewing personal liberty and the related rights, including the right to take personal risks, would run immediately into difficulty in the constraint-based deontological view, since the interests of others cannot be irrelevant to imposing constraints on them and thus to defining these rights in the form of constraints. This problem need not arise in the goal-rights view, since the interests of others might also figure in the evaluation of states of affairs *in addition to* the value of the fulfillment of a person's right to do certain personally important things. In short, it is the absence of trade-off in the constraint-based deontological perspective that would force it to consider the involvement and interest of others in the judgment of *whether or not* a right-type consideration applies. The alternative way is to admit the right-type consideration on grounds of the importance of the ability to do the act in question to the personal life of the individual involved, and *then* to weigh the thus-acknowledged moral right against the interests of others, if any.

To illustrate in terms of the rather extreme case of the passenger plane pilot, it may be consistently thought that he does indeed have the right to take personal risks of this kind, if taking such a risk is important for his personal life (perhaps a difficult supposition in this particular case?), but there is no way in which he can take the risk without also putting other people in danger. On this view it would be morally wrong for him to ignore the ground instruction, not because he has no right to take personal risks, but because the actions through which he could take personal risks would also have the effect of endangering others. Others would be free to stop him for the same reason.

It must of course be admitted that even under the capability view in particular and the goal-right approach in general, there does indeed remain the necessity to decide what would count as imporant for personal life, and also to determine what relative weights to attach to the fulfillment of such rights vis-à-vis other goals, including fulfilling other rights and meeting other interests. But the eschewal of the all-or-nothing feature of the constraint-based deontological perspective permits the rejection of a terribly limited format and allows greater sensitivity to different moral claims.

Seat Belts and Other People

Take the issue of seat belts. A person, call him Hero, decides not to wear seat belts when driving and takes the additional risk of injury or death resulting from this courageous act. We have two immediate questions: (1) how important is this freedom for Hero's personal life and way of living? and (2) how are others affected?

On the first question, there is obviously quite a bit of person-to-person variation, but in most cases it probably is neither in itself a central concern nor a part of an important feature of one's life style. There are exceptions (I have heard some people—all Italian males, it so happens—claim that going unbelted is indeed a matter of great personal importance), but they are relatively rare. Certainly, it will be difficult in this respect to compare the taking of risk involved in going unbelted with the taking of risk that a dedicated mountain climber deliberately chooses.

Insofar as most beltless drivers are beltless "simply to avoid bother,"[15] it is not clear that a moral right based on personal liberty is involved. But in refusing to accept the status of something as a moral right for members of a group, it is not enough to be sure that a majority of that group does not see anything of moment involved in the activity in question. The passionate involvement of a minority of the group cannot be ignored just because the majority sees things differently. It is possible that a minority group values a life style that includes going unbelted. In the decisions regarding regulations and rules, the numbers won't be irrelevant, but at this stage let us concede that possibly for a group, perhaps a relatively small group, going unbelted is important as a part of a life style, and that this makes it plausible to consider that a serious moral right might well be involved.

How are others affected? There are at least five different types of effects on others.

(1) *Injury effects:* It has been argued that a driver is in a better position to drive his car safely in case of minor accidents if he is wearing a seat belt, and thus the passengers benefit directly from the belting of the driver. Also, the belted passengers do not land on others, causing them injury. This may not be a common problem, but it obviously is of some relevance.

(2) *Psychological effects:* Other persons may possibly suffer from Hero's demise or injury, and the suffering might arise not only from sympathy for Hero but also from other causes: people might be badly shocked and shaken by seeing a car crash and the resulting gore.

(3) *Opinion-offending effects:* Others, of more sedate temperament might disapprove of Hero's habit of going around without buckling his seat belt, and Hero's actions might well be offensive to them.

(4) *Medical effects:* Hero may need treatment when injured, and others may have to bear a part of the medical costs. Sometimes these might well be enormous.

(5) *Economic and social effects:* Hero's injury may affect his earning power and productivity, and a number of others might well be affected by these changes: members of Hero's family, the business in which Hero works, the public at large through the need to pay Hero Social Security benefits. Similarly, some people may be affected by social rather than

economic links: friends losing someone to talk to, the local community losing a socially active member, children losing a loving parent.

Other possible effects are easy to think of, but let us confine ourselves to these. In this list of five different types of effects, only the third, the "opinion-offending effects," would involve an intrinsic conflict with Hero's moral right to go beltless as a part of his life style, since it is precisely that life style to which the others in question object. This is of course John Stuart Mill country. I have other issues to deal with, and so I choose not to pursue this particular question. I accept instead Mill's argument that the right to lead a particular type of life is not compromised by the existence of others who object to that life. I have pursued this issue elsewhere in essentially Millian lines,[16] and the focus on risk in the pursuit of one's personal life does not alter the argument substantially.

It might be tempting to think that for similar reasons we must also ignore "psychological effects" in evaluating states of affairs. But this analogy does not hold. In asserting that one should ignore adverse opinion about a particular life style (in determining whether leading such a life can be a moral right), it was *not* also asserted that the suffering of those with an adverse opinion is morally irrelevant to the evaluation of states of affairs. It is indeed possible and plausible to take the view that given other things any suffering, no matter how caused, makes a state of affairs worse. The adverse opinion in question is intrinsically in conflict with the assertion of the right to lead such a life, and the Millian argument is primarily concerned with asserting the right despite that conflict. But when it comes to evaluating actions and rules by taking into account consequential links, the issue of whether or not to weigh the sufferings of others remains a separate question, requiring a treatment of its own. If all sufferings are accepted as disvaluable, then even the sufferings of the moral prig will come inter alia into the general evaluation.

This might look like a defeatist concession, through which authoritarianism might deeply compromise the exercise of liberty. In a system with trade-offs that possibility cannot indeed be fully ruled out, but three clarifying remarks are in order here. First, the alleged force of the position of "the guardians of public morality" does not rest on their personal disutilities (indeed, our "guardians" seem often enough to find much pleasure in fighting obscenity and such), but on the claim that the actions in question are intrinsically objectionable, or will in fact offend others "with good reason." The acceptance of the moral disvalue of any suffering thus does not amount at all to a concession to the authoritarian argument.

Second, to accept that any suffering is disvaluable (or that any pleasure is valuable) is not to limit all evaluations to computations of quantities of pleasure and pain. The latter is the prerogative of the utilitarian, and I am happy to leave him as the sole owner of that approach. What relative weights can be attached to suffering (and happiness) vis-à-vis other qualities of states of affairs remains an open question.[17]

Third, even in weighing utilities vis-à-vis one another, one is not obliged to value them according to quantities only, and one can use differential weighting depending on the nonutility features associated with each case. Even Mill's utilitarianism—admittedly of a rather unusual kind—did not stop him from asserting that "there is no parity between the feeling of a person for his own opinion, and the feeling of another who is offended at his holding it."[18]

The psychological effects on others might well be serious, and it would then be absurd to assert that the fulfillment of the moral right of an individual to take personal risks should invariably be judged more important than any suffering it might cause. The shocking experience of those who see someone's arm being chewed up by a tiger as he puts his hand into the cage might well be judged to be of greater disvalue than the violation of the person's right to put his hand in (if that is seen as a right in the first place). In other cases the balance may be seen as going the other way. One would certainly hesitate to give greater importance to the satisfaction of the "Jewish mother" than to the right of the adult son to diet if he so chooses.

The injury effects, the medical effects, and the economic and social effects typically arouse less suspicion than the psychological effects. If my driving without seat belts exposes you to greater danger of injury or death, or reduces your opportunities of getting medical attention, or harms you economically or socially, then it seems natural that these adverse effects must be weighed in the goal-rights system.

The sources of worry lie elsewhere. Three in particular may be taken up here. First, there is the problem of *robustness* of the right to take personal risks. This is a general worry about the nature of goal-rights systems. Since the acceptance of a moral right does not necessarily imply that the person having that right can do the thing he has a right to do, does this not make moral rights terribly flimsy? Do they have any bite at all? What sense does it make to say that we have a moral right to take personal risks, such as not to wear seat belts, and at the same time assert that it is morally appropriate to curb the exercise of that right, such as through seat-belt regulations? Hasn't the baby been thrown away with the bath water?

Second, there is the problem of *interactivity consistency*. If seat-belt wearing is made compulsory because of, say, the medical effects, then does this not threaten the right to undertake such activities as mountaineering? Might it not even compromise the right to drive a car (with or without seat belts), since driving also increases the chances of being injured and being in need of medical services?

Third, there is the problem of *interindividual sensitivity*. While the compulsory wearing of seat belts might be accepted to be more beneficial than harmful in most cases (taking into account all the effects, including the disvalue of violating a person's right to lead the kind of life he would like to lead), this would not be so in some cases, as when someone drives alone, has no dependents, and has private medical attention. Such a person's right might seem to require that he be exempted from the seat-belt regulations. And if no such concession can be made, then should one not see, on grounds of liberty, the seat-belt regulations as unacceptable?

Robustness of the Right to Take Personal Risk

The constraint-based deontological formulation of moral rights has the great merit of simplicity: Either others are prohibited from doing certain things, or they are entirely free to do those things. Those who tend to think of rights in such all-or-nothing terms might feel that the framework of goal-rights does not give the robustness that is expected of rights. One should be able, it might be argued, to insist on one's rights come what may. Indeed, the familiar view of rights seems to demand an overwhelming, possibly irresistible, force, at least in some circumstances.[19] The absence of such force might be seen as undermining the entire goal-rights approach and specifically the application of that approach to the right to take personal risks.

In taking up this question, I begin with a purely formal point. If irresistible force is sought, then that can be provided even *within* the goal-rights system by giving the fulfillment of the rights in question lexicographic priority over other goals. While goal-rights systems allow trade-offs, they also permit evaluations without trade-offs. I do not, however, intend to pursue this line further; one of the chief reasons for adopting the goal-rights approach is precisely the scope that it gives to the possibility of trade-offs.[20]

Is it reasonable to expect that all moral rights must have irresistible force? Such a point of view immediately produces a problem of consistency, since conflicting rights cannot each have irresistible force. Your right not to be forced to wear seat belts might conflict with my right not to have you land on my shoulders at the touch of a brake. The problem is avoided either by formulating rights in such a way that they cannot possibly conflict (such as in terms of abstention from certain conscious actions[21]), or by taking rights in the "everything considered" form, so that a right is not established until it wins, as it were, over all conflicting claims.[22] The former procedure is very restrictive and permits only a narrow class of rights. The latter, if pursued fully, would make rights no more than "outputs" of moral arguments rather than being able to *influence* such arguments. Neither procedure is satisfactory.

Turning to a different issue, suppose a person does have an irresistible right. He is permitted to do something, and others are prevented from stopping him from doing it. It is of course quite possible that the exercise of this right might harm the interests of everyone else. Indeed, in considering a hypothetical example, we can take it to harm those interests as badly as we care to specify, and we can go on to ask: What is the moral status of the right in that case? If the right were really to be irresistible, these consequences on others, no matter how bad, should not make any difference. Even if exercising your right not to wear seat belts wipes out the world, on the irresistible view of moral rights you still have moral freedom to act in that way. While the consistency of such a view is not in doubt, its plausibility is, and even the most demanding systems of moral rights seem to admit some ad hoc trade-offs when faced with such conflicts, such as Nozick's willingness to consider the moral permissibility of violating a right to prevent what he calls "catastrophic moral horrors." Total irresistibility is difficult to defend.[23]

If trade-offs are permitted in rare or unrare circumstances, the issue of robustness of rights cannot really be seen in terms of a yes-no scale. The relevant question is: How strong a moral argument does a moral right provide? Certainly, it should *sometimes* be able (to use Dworkin's term) to "trump" other moral arguments (outweighing the welfare-based consideration, say), but it could be trumped on other occasions by some conflicting claim. Trade-offs do not make moral rights empty, although the extent of robustness of rights does of course depend on how much relative force it exercises in the moral system in question.

To come back to seat belts again, if seat-belt regulations were to be accepted as morally appropriate, this would not indicate that people did not have the right to take personal risks of this kind, but only that this right (if accepted) has been outweighed by some conflicting consideration, such as the importance of medical or economic effects on others. Since the taking of personal risk in this case—as in most cases—comes coupled with effects on others, there is nothing odd in the need to balance the force of the right to take such risk against the weight of other effects.

The point can be brought out with a thought experiment. If the unfavorable effects of not wearing seat belts were taken counterfactually to become smaller and smaller without vanishing, at some stage the case for seat-belt regulations, even if enforceable without administrative costs, would collapse, and the right to take personal risk in the form of not wearing seat belts would then trump the other considerations. Call this the "contingent trump case." The moral right to take such risks can be seen as involving a finite cost of violating that right through seat-belt regulations, rather than involving an infinite cost that could not be outweighed by any conflicting consideration. In the contingent trump case, the balance goes one way, whereas in the case of the moral appropriateness of seat-belt regulations, the balance goes the other way.

In this way of seeing the issue, however, there is a problem of picking up "noise." Something *other than* moral rights, but *correlated with* the exercise of those rights, might be doing the work here, and that possibility would have to be sorted out. I refer in particular to utility. It would be reasonable to assume that stopping someone from doing something that he wants to do would be typically bad for his welfare.

Thus the case against seat-belt regulations might also rest on "welfarist" considerations. This problem of "collinearity" can be dealt with by taking up cases in which the welfare consideration goes *against* the exercise of the freedom of choice. This is not easy to do in the particular framework of behavioral thought—common in much of economics—that identifies utility maximization with choice and sees the highest feasible utility level in whatever the person chooses (no matter why). However, even in this case, valuing the right to choose and valuing utility can be separated out by considering a case in which the person chooses *inconsistently*. This would not permit a rational behavior model to be fitted to his choices and no utility function could be attributed to him (since that presupposes consistency), but his inconsistent choices could still be defended on grounds of rights.

More important, the view of welfare exclusively in terms of consistent choice has to be acknowledged to be a very limited one.[24] It should be possible to consider a case in which the person in question conceded that in terms of his own assessment of his own welfare, wearing seat belts would be better, but he would not in fact choose to wear seat belts given the "carefree" life style to which he is for the moment addicted. Even if stopping him from pursuing that "carefree" life may increase his welfare as seen by others and also by himself, the case for respecting his right to choose remains. The contingent trump case would now need further modification to involve the moral value of that right to outweigh the welfare advantages, *as well as* other benefits from seat-belt regulations. I would be surprised if the set of such contingent trump cases were to be empty.

The case for seat-belt regulations must then rest on the importance of the adverse effects of not wearing seat belts (such as the medical effects) vis-à-vis the badness of violating a person's right to pursue his life style. What makes the case for seat-belt regulations quite strong is not the absence of the right to take personal risk, but, on the one hand, the *seriousness* of the adverse consequences, and on the other, the *triviality* of not wearing seat belts in the typical person's ability to lead the life he or she wants to lead. One would have to have a very "heroic" life style for the taking of this type of risk to be truly important for that life. And one would have to be, I guess, rich, independent, reclusive, for the possible adverse effects on others to be minor. There might of course be such a person; let us call him Mahahero and relegate him to a later section.

Interactivity Consistency

If we restrain the beltless driver, what about the mountaineer? This argument often occurs, since the two issues might appear similar. Indeed, injury effects, psychological effects, opinion-offending effects, medical effects, and economic and social effects can be found also in the case of mountaineering without looking very far. The probabilities of accidents might be much less with mountaineering, according to the usual statistics, but there is also a sharp constrast in the force of the moral right to take risk in the two cases. In terms of the capability perspective of goal rights, the two cases are quite different. The capability to go climbing for those who would like to be mountaineers is clearly much more central to their lives than the capability of the typical anti-belt driver to go unbelted. The adverse effects—medical and others—would have to be a good deal stronger to outweigh violating as important a right as would be involved in stopping a dedicated mountaineer from climbing. This would be so even if the former mountaineer would in fact get just as much utility after settling down to, as it were, "plane" living, so that the utility difference could not be given a central role in that moral judgment. The mountaineering case is *not* similar to the seat-belt case.

What about driving, which is itself risky? Once again, the difference that would be brought about in the lives of people in economically advanced countries by stopping them from driving would be very great indeed—some would say catastrophic. In this case, too, the utility impact might be important. But once again, to see the contrast in terms of rights as such, utility effects can be taken out by assuming—not entirely implausibly—that the inner peace and risk-reduced tranquility found in a nonmotoring society could make the utility levels no lower once people get used to the dramatic change. The definite negative effect in this case comes directly as a result of stopping people from choosing the kind of life they may lead, rather than from any presumption of reduced utility levels. The right violation in banning driving can be seen to be a great deal more important to the life of the people involved than the violation of people's freedom to drive around in beltless ecstasy.

The apparent puzzles involving interactivity consistency in the right to take risks arise from taking a nondiscriminating view of the role of rights in moral arguments. In the goal rights approach, which balances the pros and cons of restricting freedoms of different types, there is no general presumption that all cases with formal similarity would be assessed in the same way, since the assessment must go ultimately into the balancing of the relative weights of conflicting considerations.[25] In terms of what is involved, seat-belt regulations are hardly comparable to prohibiting mountaineering or banning driving.

Interindividual Variations

What about Mahahero, the recluse millionaire whose taking of personal risks in not wearing seat belts would have little adverse effect on others and who, we assume, is bent on pursuing a life style involving beltless travel? Let us concede that to force him to be belted would involve a greater loss than gain from the moral point of view. Not only, like others, does he have the right to take personal risks, but that right in his case, unlike in those of others, is important when applied to beltless driving; and the adverse effects in his case, again unlike in those of others, are relatively tiny. There is a good case, then, for letting him go unbelted, if that can be done without the difference itself causing some adverse effects.

The rub, of course, is precisely there. It might be politically impossible to let our heroic recluse millionaire go unbelted while others are forced to belt up. Even if it is possible, it may be socially costly in terms causing resentment, misunderstanding, and *perceived* discrimination.

Suppose that a separate arrangement for Mahahero is not possible. What should be done then? In a "zero-one" system the barrier of Mahahero's personal right is of course hard to cross. But the goal-rights system permits trade-offs, and it is a question of interindividual balancing. The net disadvantage of violating Mahahero's right—a "winning" right if separate rules *were* costlessly possible—has to be compared with the net advantages, related to others, from enforcing seat-belt regulations.

So it is possible that *general* seat-belt regulations, applicable to all, are judged to be morally appropriate, and at the same time (1) everyone is acknowledged to have the moral right to take risks in these matters, and (2), furthermore, some people, such as Mahahero, have a moral right in this respect that outweighs the adverse effects of their not wearing seat belts. There is no real puzzle in this apparent oddity.

Concluding Remarks

Moral rights must be distinguished from rights with moral justification. If individual moral rights are admitted, it is difficult not to concede that people do have the moral right to take personal risks. The real issue, then, is not whether such rights exist, but how important they are vis-à-vis conflicting objectives.

The constraint-based deontological approach admits only all-conquering rights, although even there ad hoc compromises are made for the sake of plausibility. Such all-conquering rights lead to moral dilemmas that can be resolved only in a consequence-sensitive system with trade-offs.[26] The framework of goal-rights systems can provide systematic accounting of conflicting objectives to arrive at informed moral judgment.

In the goal-rights systems the fulfillment of the right to take personal risks can compete with other goals. Personal risks can rarely be taken without other important consequences. This fact does not in any way "cancel" the right to take personal risks, but it does make that right compete with other objectives. Much of this paper has been concerned with issues involved in the balancing of competing claims. The importance of the right to take risks varies with the nature of the activity involved. It also varies from person to person. Public decisions, such as seat-belt regulations, call for integrated assessment of pros and cons. In this calculus, rights do figure, but they are not irresistible: They win some and they lose some.

There are of course many apparent puzzles in attitudes toward the right to take personal risks, such as those involving interactivity consistency (between, say, beltless travel and mountaineering) or interindividual variation (between different roles of the same activity in the lives of different persons). These puzzles seem to arise from attempts to fit the right to take personal risks into a nondiscriminating framework. More room has to be made for sensitivity to different types of information. The notion of moral rights should help us to conduct informed moral arguments, rather than getting us tied up in knots in moral maneuvers in partial darkness. There is no escape from discriminating consequential calculation in assessing the implications of rights. The right to take personal risks is no exception.

Notes

1. Cf. L. H. Tribe, *American Constitutional Law* (Mineola, N.Y.: The Foundation Press, 1978), sections 12–15, pp. 938–41.
2. Jeremy Bentham, *Anarchical Fallacies*, in *Two Works of Jeremy Bentham*, Bowring, ed. (London, 1843), p. 494.
3. Robert Nozick, *Anarchy, State, and Utopia* (Oxford: Basil Blackwell, 1974), p. ix.
4. Amartya Sen, "Rights and Agency," *Philosophy & Public Affairs* 11 (Winter 1982): 3–15.
5. On the characteristics of consequentialism (and a forceful critique), see Bernard Williams, "A Critique of Utilitarianism," in *Utilitarianism: For and Against*, J. J. C. Smart and B. Williams, eds. (Cambridge: Cambridge University Press, 1973).
6. See "Rights and Agency," pp. 28–32.
7. See Thomas Scanlon, "Rights, Goals and Fairness," in *Public and Private Morality*, Stuart Hampshire, ed. (Cambridge: Cambridge University Press, 1978), and P. Dasgupta, "Decentralization and Rights," *Economica* 47 (1980).
8. In Sen, "Equality of What?" in *The Tanner Lectures on Human Values*, S. McMurrin, ed. (Cambridge: Cambridge University Press, 1980); reprinted in my *Choice, Welfare and Measurement* (Oxford: Blackwell, and Cambridge, Mass.: MIT Press, 1982), and "Rights and Agency," pp. 15–19.
9. See Sen, "A Positive Concept of Negative Freedom," in *Ethics: Foundations, Problems and Applications*, Proceedings of the 5th International Wittgenstein Symposium (Vienna: Holder-Pichler-Tempsky, 1981), and "Rights and Agency," pp. 6–15.
10. It is not required, however, that they should both attach the *same* disvalue to A's bashing of B, and it may be right that A himself should attach a greater disvalue to this event than C. I investigate this type of "evaluator relativity" of the valuation of states of affairs, related to the position of the respective persons involved, in "Rights and Agency," sec. VII, and in "Evaluator Relativity and Consequential Evaluation," *Philosophy & Public Affairs* 12 (Spring 1983).
11. R. Sugden, *The Political Economy of Public Choice* (Oxford: Martin Robertson, 1981), pp. 196–97.
12. See Sen, "Liberty as Control: An Appraisal," *Midwest Studies in Philosophy* 8 (1982), and "Liberty and Social Choice," *Journal of Philosophy* 80 (January 1983).
13. See Sen, "Rights and Agency," and "A Positive Concept of Negative Freedom."
14. I have discussed these issues in "Rights and Capabilities," to be published in a volume of essays in memory of John Mackie, edited by Ted Honderich. This is also published in my *Resources, Values and Development* (Oxford: Blackwell, and Cambridge, Mass.: Harvard University Press, 1984).
15. Tribe, *American Constitutional Law*, p. 939.
16. See Sen, "Personal Utilities and Public Judgments: Or What's Wrong with Welfare Economics?" *Economic Journal* 89 (September 1979): 549–54.
17. It should be obvious that a goal-rights system would typically take a pluralist form. Pluralist moral theories are often viewed with great suspicion and are accused of arbitrari-

ness, or inconsistency. This may not be deserved. On this general question, see Sen and Williams, *Utilitarianism and Beyond* (Cambridge: Cambridge University Press, 1982), pp. 16–20. See also in the same volume the papers by Stuart Hampshire, John Rawls, and Charles Taylor.

18. J. S. Mill, *On Liberty*, 1859. Reprinted in J. S. Mill, *Utilitarianism: On Liberty: Representative Government* (London: Everyman's Library), p. 140.

19. See Ronald Dworkin, *Taking Rights Seriously*, 2d ed. (London: Duckworth, 1978).

20. Sen, "Rights and Agency," pp. 4–20.

21. See Nozick, *Anarchy, State, and Utopia*.

22. See Dworkin, *Taking Rights Seriously*.

23. Except in the case of the "everything considered" view. But then the moral right does not affect any moral argument; it simply reflects the *outcome* of that argument.

24. See Sen, "Rational Fools: A Critique of the Behavioral Foundations of Economic Theory," *Philosophy & Public Affairs* 6 (1977); reprinted in F. Hahn and M. Hollis, eds., *Philosophy and Economic Theory* (Oxford: Oxford University Press, 1979), and in Sen, *Choice, Welfare and Measurement*.

25. It is also important to emphasize here that the weights apply to the *freedoms* of different types (in the context of goal rights) and not just to the *activities* actually performed. Thus a goal-rights system is not in general reducible to a pure system of activity weighting.

26. See Sen, "Rights and Agency," pp. 4–20.

Index

Notes on Contributors

Annette Baier is Professor of Philosophy at the University of Pittsburgh. She has published widely in the areas of ethics, philosophy of mind, and the history of modern philosophy. Some of her essays have recently been collected in *Postures of the Mind: Essays on Mind & Morals*.

Allan Gibbard is Professor of Philosophy at the University of Michigan at Ann Arbor. He has published some influential articles in decision theory and has also written on rationality, ethics, and political philosophy.

Ian Hacking is Professor of Philosophy at the University of Toronto. He has published widely in the areas of the history and philosophy of science, epistemology, and the philosophy of language. He is the author of *The Emergence of Probability, Representing & Intervening,* and several other books.

Herman B. Leonard is Associate Professor of Public Policy at the John F. Kennedy School of Government at Harvard University. He has published in the areas of policy analysis and economics.

Douglas MacLean is Director of the Center for Philosophy and Public Policy. He has published articles on risk and energy policy and has edited several volumes in the Maryland Studies in Public Philosophy, including, most recently, *The Security Gamble: Deterrence Dilemmas in the Nuclear Age*.

Amartya Sen is Drummond Professor of Political Economy at Oxford University and Fellow of All Souls College. His many books include *Choice, Welfare and Measurement, Collective Choice and Social Welfare,* and *Beyond Utilitarianism* (edited with Bernard Williams).

Michael Thompson, a cultural anthropologist, was until recently a Research Associate at the International Institute for Applied Systems Analysis in Laxenburg, Austria. He is currently on the faculty of the Centre for Research in Industry, Business and Administration at the University of Warwick. He has written many articles on the cultural determinants of risk attitudes and has also written on mountain climbing. He is the author of *Rubbish Theory*.

Richard J. Zeckhauser is Professor of Political Economy at the John F. Kennedy School of Government at Harvard University. He is a frequent contributor to professional journals in economics and related disciplines and works actively with many agencies of the federal government. He has published widely on issues in risk analysis and is the coauthor, with Edith Stokey, of *A Primer for Policy Analysis*.